LOST STORYTELLERS

UNIVERSITY PRESS OF FLORIDA

Florida A&M University, Tallahassee
Florida Atlantic University, Boca Raton
Florida Gulf Coast University, Ft. Myers
Florida International University, Miami
Florida State University, Tallahassee
New College of Florida, Sarasota
University of Central Florida, Orlando
University of Florida, Gainesville
University of North Florida, Jacksonville
University of South Florida, Tampa
University of West Florida, Pensacola

LOST STORYTELLERS

The Information Apocalypse in the Modern Newsroom

JOHN PENDYGRAFT

UNIVERSITY PRESS OF FLORIDA

Gainesville · Tallahassee · Tampa · Boca Raton

Pensacola · Orlando · Miami · Jacksonville · Ft. Myers · Sarasota

27 26 25 24 23 22   6 5 4 3 2 1

Library of Congress Cataloging-in-Publication Data
Names: Pendygraft, John, author.
Title: Lost storytellers : the information apocalypse in the modern
  newsroom / John Pendygraft.
Description: 1. | Gainesville : University Press of Florida, 2022. |
  Includes bibliographical references and index. | Summary: "In this
  firsthand look at the landscape of community news today, photojournalist
  John Pendygraft uses his own experiences to show why trusted local
  reporting matters now more than ever, making the case that the decline
  of local journalism threatens the future of democracy"— Provided by
  publisher.
Identifiers: LCCN 2021054549 (print) | LCCN 2021054550 (ebook) | ISBN
  9780813068664 (paperback) | ISBN 9780813070131 (pdf) | ISBN
  9780813072326 (ebook)
Subjects: LCSH: Journalism, Regional—United States. | Local mass
  media—United States. | Community newspapers—United States. | Reporters
  and reporting—United States—History. | Newspaper publishing—United
  States. | BISAC: SOCIAL SCIENCE / Media Studies | SOCIAL SCIENCE /
  Anthropology / Cultural & Social
Classification: LCC PN4784.R29 P46 2022 (print) | LCC PN4784.R29 (ebook)
  | DDC 070.4/33—dc23/eng/20220210
LC record available at https://lccn.loc.gov/2021054549
LC ebook record available at https://lccn.loc.gov/2021054550

The University Press of Florida is the scholarly publishing agency for the State University System
of Florida, comprising Florida A&M University, Florida Atlantic University, Florida Gulf Coast
University, Florida International University, Florida State University, New College of Florida,
University of Central Florida, University of Florida, University of North Florida, University of
South Florida, and University of West Florida.

University Press of Florida
2046 NE Waldo Road
Suite 2100
Gainesville, FL 32609
http://upress.ufl.edu

For my parents, Janet and Joe Pendygraft

Contents

List of Figures   ix

BOOK 1. THE FISH

1. Dangerous Times and Safe Spaces   3
2. 2016   20
3. Storytelling Animals   39
4. The Ghost of the Sacred Trust   61

BOOK 2. THE WATER

5. Brittany's Bowl   85
6. Master Narratives   108
7. Unicorn-Killing Broken Trust   125
8. The Damned-Dirty-Trick Story: An American Master Narrative   137

BOOK 3. HOPE

9. Four Black Holes   161
10. Journalism, Period.   175
11. 2020–2021   191

Acknowledgments   215
Notes   219
Works Cited   233
Index   241

Figures

2.1. Exotic dancer in a Pinellas courtroom 23

5.1. Media bias chart, 2018 89

6.1. Kurt Vonnegut's "Shapes of Stories" graph 1 113

6.2. Kurt Vonnegut's "Shapes of Stories" graph 2 113

6.3. Kurt Vonnegut's "Shapes of Stories" graph 3 113

6.4. Kurt Vonnegut's "Shapes of Stories" graph 4 114

6.5. Kurt Vonnegut's "Shapes of Stories" graph 5 114

6.6. Blake Snyder's beats and Vonnegut's "Shapes of Stories" 117

7.1. Newsroom employment 2008–2019 129

7.2. Employment in selected information industries 129

8.1. *New York Times* headlines 149

8.2. Social media advertisements 150

9.1. Reliability and validity 167

11.1. Pierre Bourdieu's concept of doxa 202

BOOK 1
The Fish

1

Dangerous Times and Safe Spaces

The purpose of anthropology is to make the world safe for human differences.
RUTH BENEDICT

When I joined the photography staff of the *St. Petersburg Times* in 1997, we had forty-nine full-time employees in our department.[1] As I write this, there are eleven of us.

It is Monday, and my boss just let me know there will be one less by Friday.

＊　　＊　　＊

This book begins in 2016, during a historic presidential primary, and ends in 2021. Those years were challenging for me, my family, and my friends. As journalism became more unstable, complicated, and confusing, I started taking anthropology classes at the local university to try to make sense of it all. Those classes led to a master's degree, and now I am a PhD student.

That anthropological journey took me back 40,000 years, to the dawn of human culture and the first emergence of storytelling. I wondered how storytelling may have helped *Homo sapiens* evolve from struggling primates into Earth's apex species.

I learned how the stories people tell are remarkably and mysteriously universal. Unrelated cultures separated by vast oceans of space and time tell amazingly similar stories, for similar purposes. It seemed like human brains were wired for storytelling a long, long time ago, but how is that ancient and powerful wiring working out for us today?

For millennia, communal storytelling built cooperative human cultures by creating the myths we live by. For most of that history, stories were an oral tradition. Storytellers lived among us. Their stories were filled with life lessons that brought small communities together in ways that helped people survive and thrive collectively.

But modern storytelling tools have become so much more powerful. Does the song remain the same? Or has the primal need for stories become weaponized by global interests in the digital age? Why did humans begin telling stories in the first place, and why do people tell them today? What calls storytellers to become storytellers? As the waves of layoffs kept coming, I wondered why we were losing so many local storytellers.

Safe Spaces

Many years ago, when I was an anthropology undergraduate wondering how I might seek my fortune, I read a quote from anthropologist Ruth Benedict that helped solidify my path: "The purpose of anthropology is to make the world safe for human differences."[2]

I believed anthropology and journalism shared that common value and that a career in photojournalism could be a rewarding way to practice that sense of purpose. Both fields felt like a call to public service. But it all feels so much more difficult in today's media world. Over the past fifteen years or so, I watched public belief in those humanizing media spaces slowly die. I wondered why.

So many of my journalist friends' career identities are getting lost in that shrinking space. There are economic explanations, and there are technological explanations. In this book I seek deeper roots. I explore the universality of human stories and the possibility that greedy and power-hungry people are abusing our ancient human need for culture-building storytelling for their own selfish gain. I wonder if attacks, intentional and unintentional, on spaces designed to make the world safe for human differences are the real and most fundamental root of today's media challenges.

I weave my personal newsroom journey into anthropological perspectives on media, power, myth, and magic in troubled times. My training and growth as an anthropologist took place in a local newsroom during an information apocalypse, a pandemic, a racialized cultural-political revolution, the slow bleeding away of a 137-year-old newspaper, and the erosion of my own very cherished career identity.

I cared, very much, every step of the way. I struggled hard to find concrete solutions that might be helpful to a dying industry.

Dark Times

Community journalists are living in dark times. One-fourth of newspapers across the country, more than 2,100 in total, have closed since 2004. More than half of all newspaper journalists have lost their jobs. Many Americans now live in news deserts, communities that are no longer served by a newspaper or other news outlet – and studies show those communities have fewer voters, less informed and more polarized voters, an increase in local corruption, and rising municipal costs.[3] Harsh staffing cuts have created thousands more "ghost papers," newsrooms that have managed to keep the doors open but just can't cover communities like they used to.

The statistics are grim. According to the Pew Research Center, newsroom employment at US newspapers dropped by 57 percent between 2008 and 2020.[4] As I write this, the economic impact of Covid-19 is still being assessed. Kristen Hare, who covers the people and business of local news at the Poynter Institute, struggles to keep up with all the newsroom layoffs. Some of them made the news, and some are underreported. Kristen keeps an exhaustive list of all the layoffs, furloughs, and closures, but she just can't keep up with what she describes as "all the bad news about the news right now." When I asked her for a ballpark figure of job losses in 2020 she shook her head, looked downward, and said "thousands." The pandemic was being described as an extinction event for local media and may well have pushed fragile media companies from hospice care to the grave.

*   *   *

Some people are calling journalists nasty names. You, dear reader, can judge for yourself whether we are "enemies of the state," part of a "deep state," "fake," "socialist," "conspiratorial," and/or "scum." But before you do, come with me and meet some journalists for yourself.

Journalists who shed tears in bathroom stalls after learning a reporting mistake was published. Journalists who walk out of the building chin-up and dry-eyed after being laid off. Journalists who stay in the business despite pay cuts, lack of job security, uncertainty about retirement, growing public backlash from the left and right, and a shrinking belief in the fair, objective reporting ethics that define their waking hours.

I was waiting on the lobby elevator with Bill Varian, who was an assistant metro editor. I noticed he had bags under his eyes as we began wondering how pending layoffs will go. He described how, at 3 o'clock every morning, he bolts awake, heart pounding.

His words startled me. Last night I had the exact same experience. It happens more and more often as layoffs intensify. Somehow, it felt a little better to know I was not the only one.

Of course my colleagues and I worry about ourselves, that we might be next to lose our jobs. But the late-night anxiety is much more than that. This week we will say goodbye to good friends, people who believe as we believe, fight as we fight, and care about community journalism as much as we do. We lie in bed and think about what it means to live in a "post-truth" America. Many of us are plagued by the possibility of journalists losing their place in the world. We are confused about why local storytelling seems like it is dying. It hurts that so many people dislike journalists today.

We worry about the lack of trusted news in the communities where we live. Lying in the dark, we ask ourselves if it is worth all the stress. Then we promise ourselves we will just go find another job in a different field. Then we realize there is nothing else in the world we are called to do. Then we feel a wave of anxiety: if I can't wake up and go to work as a local journalist, if it all ends tomorrow morning, and it could, then what?

Riding up the elevator to the newsroom, Bill dropped his head and said in a soft voice, "I don't know if this is ever going to get any better."

*   *   *

A local newsroom is ground zero for the tsunami of social change that came in the digital age. Many people who don't work in newsrooms feel anxiety over today's media environment too. You may feel like trust in institutions is plummeting. You may sense that modern media have become a game for multibillion-dollar companies and cable-tethered politicians. You may feel like, despite all the advances in communication technology, it has become harder and harder to find news you feel comfortable believing.

This book is a story about why local journalists are becoming forgotten storytellers, why trust in media is broken, and how the weight of that world fell onto the shoulders of working journalists.

The Anthropology of a Newsroom

To explore vexing questions about today's media crisis, I applied to an anthropology program, worked through a master's degree, and became a

PhD student. I continued to work full time as a staff journalist. As journalism and anthropology began to fuse together in my life, I became fascinated with the origins of storytelling and curious about why people tell stories. I came to believe the answers to those questions could be key to understanding the state of media and society today.

One idea: *Homo sapiens* evolved uniquely, somewhere between 20,000 and 40,000 years ago, to be a storytelling animal. That incredible tool helped humans go from small packs of mammals fighting for survival to the most powerful species on Earth.[5]

I explored how that adaptation first served humans thousands of years ago and how it is working out for us today as dramatic storytelling saturates our lives in ways our early ancestors probably could have never imagined. Stories, shared among cooperative groups during the Pleistocene, would have helped *Homo sapiens* survive and thrive. Charles Darwin observed, "There can be no doubt that a tribe including many members who, from possessing in a high degree the spirit of patriotism, fidelity, obedience, courage, and sympathy, were always ready to aid one another, and to sacrifice themselves for the common good would be victorious over most other tribes, and this would be natural selection."[6]

In exploring communal, culture-building storytelling as a survival mechanism, fascinating new possibilities and explanations arise for today's media crisis. Judging by *Homo sapiens*' success in the past 40,000 years, stories told to build united, cooperative cultures may well be the most powerful adaptation in Earth's history. It was not a simple journey, but storytelling animals now rule the planet.

The Stories People Choose

Survival instincts may help explain why humans often choose personal, life-defining story narratives that lack tangible evidence or scientific facts. Those intimate personal narratives may be chosen primarily because they offer a sense of well-being, spiritual connection, and inclusion into a cultural group, or because they will help increase an individual's ability to survive and prosper. Social function may trump facts when it comes to the stories people choose to make their own.

People don't need hard evidence to believe stories. Gallup has been polling Americans about the existence of "God or a higher power" since World War II, and the results are consistent—95 percent of Americans believe.

A 2008 Pew Research Center study found that two-thirds of respondents also believed that angels and demons are at work in the human world today. One-fifth said their prayers are answered directly at least once a week.[7]

But no one can perform a randomized controlled trial for the existence of God. No one can fact check or peer review the power of prayer.

Exploring the wondrous mysteries of religious faith is way beyond this book's purpose. I have my own spiritual beliefs, and they, too, are acts of faith. The point is only that belief in a story does not require tangible evidence. Stories taken on faith have defined societies and cultures in powerful ways that news reports and academic papers never will. Why should modern journalists and media critics be surprised when stories on cable television and social media that are not based on tangible evidence still move millions of people? Why should anyone be surprised that stories today are still, as they have always been, most often about building cooperative communities and creating meaningful connections to a belief system?

Long-Term Interests versus Short-Term Interests

What happens when core beliefs of different culturally cooperative groups collide? What about conflicting stories that just don't get along with each other?

There is a historically important role for spaces that, as Benedict says, make the world safe for those human differences, spaces that listen to and thoughtfully manage all those opposing narratives with benevolent social intentions. Quality local journalism strives to be that kind of space. But today those institutions are under attack. In the five-year span I cover in this book, 2016–2021, I have felt the humanizing media spaces I believe in shrink around me in very personal and often frightening ways.

When humans first started sharing communal stories those many years ago, the stories were likely filled with morals delivered to help them become better humans. At the dawn of culture, the stories, told orally, wired *Homo sapiens'* brains for mutually beneficial communal living. For tens of thousands of years, stories built and served the *long-term* cultural interests of communities.

Today the most successful storytellers are massive enterprises that mostly care only about their own short-term interests, national political agendas, power, influence, and profit.[8] They are global. They don't know or care about individuals. They won't be there for Little League championship games. They won't check the honesty or dishonesty of local government representatives. They won't cover the charitable events sponsored by a place of worship or family triumphs and tragedies or neighborhood concerns.

Maybe stories have always been, on some level, manipulative in how they build culturally cooperative groups. But looking from 40,000 years ago to today, it feels like the recent explosion of communication technology has unleashed the power of storytelling in ways that may not yet be fully explored. It feels like the *long-term* communal interests that defined local storytelling as a public good for thousands of years have been hijacked by powerful, *short-term*, self-serving individual and corporate desires. Healthy human cultures thrived on local, trusted storytelling for millennia. Why is the role of local storytelling in the crosshairs now? What is with all the fake news propaganda and vilification of journalists?

As powerful politicians and media giants say one thing, working community journalists are documenting real, lived human experiences that tell another. Those stories have impact—specific stories about a vanishing middle class, discrimination, corrupt policies that affect vulnerable citizens, and counternarratives to racist and selfish agendas. Collectively, those local stories have the power to help shape history. Society benefits when local journalists sit on porch steps and at kitchen tables, listening to often unheard voices in rural America and chronicling discrimination in historically red-lined urban neighborhoods.

Collectively, local journalism can be more powerful than even a relatively small number of seemingly omnipotent global players. Good local journalism makes powerful people nervous. Those local journalists are not enemies of the people. Their work is not fake. Quality journalism presents daily evidence from members of small communities that often counters self-serving narratives from power-hungry politicians and global media corporations. Local reporting puts human faces on the costs and consequences of selfish political policies and financial agendas. Those granular voices and that one-on-one, rigorous professional journalism process stimulate credible, complicated, and often contradictory public debates.

At its best, local journalism makes safe spaces to report on human differences. That time-honored ethos can amplify the voices of citizens in diverse communities through stories that are balanced, vetted, and professionally produced. The work interrupts narratives that serve global short-term interests that amount to easy profits and political momentum in favor of difficult, complicated, and nuanced long-term discussions that better serve the public good.

* * *

Evolutionary psychologist Jerome Barkow asserts,

> A comparison of the mass media and that of the purveyors of "junk food" suggests itself: In modern market economies, food processors take our strong evolved preferences for salt, sugar, and fat—tastes that in the Pleistocene were indicators of scarce and valuable nutrients—and use them to influence our buying behavior. The mass media, it can be argued, make similar use of the evolved mechanisms that, in earlier environments, would have led to the acquisition of information about important members of our bands. In short, Pleistocene adaptations can lead to profits![9]

Striving to report stories as a public service in ways that are complex, fair, balanced, and in keeping with traditional news values today feels a lot like trying to sell broccoli in a candy store. Media companies, politicians, and social media platforms take strong, evolved preferences for simple, culture-building narratives, rooted in ancient and universal story structures, and serve them up to human brains like candy.

Dangerous untruths and conspiracy theories are shamelessly wrapped into irresistible storylines to create political, economic, and social power. Those stories are about perfect "good guys," horrible "bad guys," unnuanced morality, and dire consequences if "victory" is lost. Stories don't have to be true to trigger ancient survival mechanisms. While storytellers may have always had that power in human societies, today's historically unprecedented explosion of media technology may be taking things to a whole new level.

* * *

Julian Reichelt, former editor-in-chief of Europe's largest tabloid, *Bild*, describes its business model in primal simplicity: "*Bild* is the last national campfire experience in German life. It's the last thing that Germans can come together for. . . . Journalism is basically about emotions, as all of the other news outlets in this country seem to have forgotten."[10]

Other news outlets did not forget. They still practice journalism that embraces complexity and public service.

There is a long and imperfect tradition of news professionals making their best human effort to be fair and balanced. Not so long ago, legacy newsrooms were brimming with journalists who considered themselves public servants. They were good people who dedicated their lives and leveraged their financial futures in an uncertain industry to a fervent belief in that kind of storytelling.

Most of them are gone.

In the digital age, those two opposing storytelling goals, long-term public service and short-term self-interest, have become muddied together into one confusing and untrusted label: "the media."

To survive the current information apocalypse, legacy media would be best served by creating distinct, culturally well-defined digital news spaces. The very existence of legacy journalism in social media spaces and in twenty-four-hour cable news cycles creates cancerous brand confusion. That cultural confusion lies at the roots of traditional journalism's decimated business models.

Storytelling - Trust = ?

Stories can create common worlds, share knowledge, and establish communal morality. They can create social order. Human societies need stories, and people need to trust in them.

Shared stories define religions, nations, families, politics, marriages, high school cliques, corporations, professional fields, armies for war, prophets for peace, online gaming worlds, knitting groups, and individuals' sense of well-being. Because the power of stories got wired into human brains thousands of years ago and created a way to thrive and succeed together, people place trust in them without much conscious thought. Trust is the social glue that holds culturally healthy storytelling together, and in the United States today trust is broken.

A Knight Commission on Trust, Media, and Democracy describes bluntly what many people already know intuitively: "Americans cannot assume that their fellow citizens are operating under the same set of facts. Many of us live inside echo chambers where only our own political sentiments can be heard, and distrust those who do not agree with our particular viewpoint. Provocateurs and hatemongers, foreign and domestic, are fueling disagreements, and media are amplifying the divides."[11] Democracy suffers when Americans don't agree on basic facts, when politicians leverage people's lack of trust in news, and when large swaths of community news organizations die.

*　　*　　*

In this book I explore various solutions that anthropology might offer local media organizations. Modern technology opened access to knowledge and people in amazing ways, yet we cannot seem to find news to trust, and traditional journalists are starting to look like dinosaurs. What will become of society if assaults on truth continue?

In the chapters that follow I consider concrete explanations of how the most fundamental causes of today's crisis are primarily ancient and cultural. What role did stories, and trust in those stories, play for early *Homo sapiens* on their way to buying iPhones and getting Twitter accounts? What role does that history play in explaining my own late-night career anxiety?

Anthropology Theory

A short parable, told by the late American novelist and professor David Foster Wallace, lays groundwork for how anthropological theory may help explore important questions:

> There are these two young fish swimming along, and they happen to meet an older fish swimming the other way, who nods at them and says, "Morning, boys. How's the water?" And the two young fish swim on for a bit, and then eventually one of them looks over at the other and goes, "What the hell is water?"[12]

I love anthropology because it helps me recognize how often-overlooked but ever-present realities make us humans who we are. The anthropology for this book centers on a legacy journalism newsroom, but as I watched fellow journalists struggle with careers and identities, I saw lessons for all who feel confused about media, politics, and our own sense of well-being in the information age. Just what the hell is going on in these crazy new media waters? Who will survive, thrive, or perish? Most importantly, how are these waters changing us all? A newsroom ethnography personalizes those important questions.

The playwright Arthur Miller observed, "Society is inside of man and man is inside society, and you cannot even create a truthfully drawn psychological entity on the stage until you understand his social relations and their power to make him what he is and to prevent him from being what he is not. The fish is in the water and the water is in the fish."[13]

Through anthropological lenses, I explore how fish and water are not two things. They are one thing. Floundering local journalists and the information age are not two things. They are one thing. You and the information age are not two things.

Webs of Culture and the Eversion

There is a definition of culture from anthropologist and literary critic Clifford Geertz that is popular among anthropologists. Geertz contends, "Man is an animal suspended in webs of significance he himself has spun, I take culture to be those webs."[14]

Webs, like water, can be invisible even as one is ensnared in them. Geertz imagined webs of culture in 1973, three years before Steve Wozniak unveiled the Apple I computer. Since then, web spinning and web spinners have become much more complicated.

First came "cyberspace," a term coined by William Gibson in his 1984 novel *Neuromancer*. At that time, digital reality and physical reality were still two separate spaces. You played in the park, or you played a video game. The choice looked something like the 1999 film *The Matrix*, in which a mystical character, Morpheus, offers the protagonist, Neo, a choice: a red pill to experience true reality or a blue pill that would keep him in an all-encompassing cyber fantasy world.

But at the turn of the millennium, those two distinct worlds began to collide. In 2010, Gibson updated his 1984 thoughts about cyberspace. He observed, "Cyberspace, not so long ago, was a specific somewhere, one we visited periodically, peering into it from the familiar physical world. Now cyberspace has everted. Turned itself inside out. Colonized the physical."[15]

There is no longer a clear choice between the red pill and the blue pill. We live in the eversion. There is just one, unavoidable purple pill. And it is being forced down our throats.

We spend our days walking through the physical world, but we also walk through a soup of invisible radio waves that connect technology to our intimate lives. Radio waves swarm around us. Our devices give them life— constant messages, narratives, stories, mysteriously guided algorithms, corporate tricks, and political agendas. They sweep up intimate data about our personal movements. They gather details of our everyday habits and whisk them back to powerful global companies to be bought and sold on the open market.

News feeds and video viewing choices are guided by algorithms so complicated that no single human understands them anymore. Those algorithms are now machine-learned, and they collect more and more personal data. Those details about individuals' behavior are freely shared without their tacit knowledge and automatically reused to refine new algorithms designed to keep humans' storytelling brains ever more engaged on the dominant media platforms.

As Gibson cautions, we should be aware of the powerful ways the eversion colonizes our minds.

So, it was a simpler age, not so very long ago, when Geertz wrote that humankind was suspended in cultural webs of its own making. Today's cultural webs of significance come from a growing cocktail of weavers, human and machine. Many of those webs are not being spun with the well-being of local communities in mind.

Lens, Mirror, X-Ray

When I tell people I am a student of anthropology, they often look confused. They ask me what anthropology has to do with journalism. Isn't anthropology about old bones, strange rituals in odd places, and obscure documentaries?

I borrow an answer from Gillian Tett, chair of the editorial board and editor-at-large at the *Financial Times*, who also holds a PhD in anthropology. Tett explains, "Anthropology really is as much defined by the process of how it looks at the world as its actual subject matter. And the very clichéd images I'd use to try to communicate this to non-anthropologists are the image of the lens, the mirror, and an X-ray machine."[16]

The anthropological lenses taught in grad school help recognize, develop, and communicate empathy for "the other," people who are different from those of one's own group or culture, especially from dominant cultures. With that empathy, observers look in the mirror and ask how their own cultural assumptions are flawed, what they don't see because of their own blind spots, tunnel vision, and blinders.

Anthropologists then try to put the lens and mirror together to make a mental X-ray machine. The goal is to look critically at simple cultural practices that are taken for granted, put those practices into context, acknowledge power structures, look for meaning in social silences, and appreciate how daily rituals and symbols create meaning in powerful, often unnoticed ways.

In each chapter of this book I include, with as much honesty as possible, a lens, mirror, and X-ray examination of my own life and career. The stories are difficult, deeply flawed, and at times embarrassing. I am a white, middle-aged male who came of age in an industry that has a long history of racial and gender inequality. I have looked in the mirror and seen ugliness. I still do. We are all swimming in complicated waters. I share my own unflattering reflections only with a sincere hope of creating discussion and making progress.

What Are Legacy Media?

The idea of "legacy media" didn't even exist on my first day on the photography staff at the *St. Petersburg Times*. On that day I shot an assignment using 35 mm film. I hand-developed the negatives in a closet darkroom in New Port Richey, a small news bureau forty miles north of St. Petersburg. Because I use the term "legacy media" throughout this book, I should define what I think that means. I take "legacy media" to mean news organizations that have been around for many years. Decades, at a minimum. Many, like my own newsroom, have been around for well over a century. When I refer to "legacy media," I am referring to historic institutions under fire and the journalism ethos that defines them. I am also referring to the important role those institutions have played, nobly and imperfectly, to a functioning democracy.

To be honest, when I write about legacy media in this work, I am also thinking specifically about emotionally intense career insecurities and the well-being of coworkers I call friends. Many of them very kindly contributed honest and sometimes difficult perspectives to this work.

I should also try to explain why being a local storyteller means so very much to me. Recently, I was walking down my street when two strangers out walking their dog stopped to pay me a compliment on a story that ran on that day's front page. It was an investigation into mental health abuses and schoolchildren. They said they saw me shooting an event a few years back, liked the picture that ran the next day, and have watched for my byline ever since. I thanked them as best I could, but I hoped they knew just how meaningful their kind words were in these crazy media times. Because just like that, my neighborhood felt a bit smaller and I felt included. They gave me my career narrative back, even if just for a little while. They made me believe that two decades as a journalist here have contributed to my community in a positive way. On a deep and primal level, my career still gives me a sense of place, purpose, inclusion, and direction. It is all rooted in local storytelling.

But these kind neighbors were retirees. They came from a generation that remembers professional journalism as a distinct and well-defined news space. They likely spent the first decades of their adult lives with news habits that engrained a clear narrative of what paid journalists do and why they do it.

The digital age has bred confusion. Professional reporting became lumped under one big umbrella label: "the media." To a digital-native generation, that most often means everything that got thrown at them as information, entertainment, and on social platforms. Legacy journalism got tossed into a soup of social media and unchecked, partisan media channels. Its time-honored narrative drowned in noise. Politicians leveraged the confusion.

I apply anthropological lenses to make a case that journalism will not survive without reestablishing a clear, distinct, and well-defined public awareness of who journalists are, what we do, and the ethical ideals we aspire to. Without focused and intentional efforts to regain that clear cultural narrative in the digital age, I believe we are sunk. A decade of changes in newsroom business models and daily practices has not dealt effectively with that now deep-rooted public reality. It now feels a bit like we've just been rearranging deck furniture on the Titanic.

What Is Ethnography?

I approach this work as an ethnography of a newsroom. The word "ethnography," like "anthropology," was invented in western universities in the nineteenth century. "Ethno" comes from "ethnos," meaning a group of people who share a way of life; "graphy" is writing. In her book, *Alive in the Writing*, Kirin Narayan describes "two faces" of ethnographic writing, explaining, "Ethnography was from its very inception torn between contrary impulses: to present empirical observations gathered through specific methods and processed with theory, or to appeal to readers' imaginations with colorful stories."[17]

I unabashedly embrace both of those two faces. I tell colorful stories of newsroom life, processed with social science theory. As I made my way through grad school, reexperiencing my everyday work life through new theoretical lenses became a magical and rewarding experience. Truth is, as times got tougher and tougher, seeing life through those different lenses also became a kind of therapy. Along with new ways of looking at life, I found reasons to hope.

This book chronicles the lives of local journalists under pressure in a shrinking newsroom, in a society where trust is broken. Then I pull back to consider how anthropologists try to make sense of it all. I explore how looking all the way back to when humans first became storytelling animals helps illuminate today's new cocktail of explosive media technology, politics, power, and big business. I ask questions I hope can help get to the deepest roots of today's media crisis. What happened to legacy news values in today's social media world? Why? How did trust get so broken, and what does it mean for the future of democracy? What can past leaps in communication technology teach us all about human nature, and how can we apply those lessons today? What solutions might all that offer our current media crisis? What might be changed? What can't be changed?

Book 1, "The Fish," jumps into a newsroom to meet journalists struggling to find their way in turbulent times. Chapter 2 revolves around a 2016 staff meeting and how individual journalists were trying to adapt their careers to a swiftly changing environment. Chapter 3 time-warps back 40,000 years to the still-mysterious dawn of culture and storytelling. Chapter 4 is the story of how the *St. Petersburg Times* was born. It is a creation myth about sacred trust and broken trust. The tale embodies a common journalism code of ethics shared throughout the legacy news industry. Beyond that, the story of the newspaper's origins fulfilled a basic human need in me on a personal level.

That timeline leads into Book 2, "The Water," in which I dig into just how public trust in storytellers got so damaged in such a short time. I go deeper into the lives of journalists in today's media crisis and question how new media technology leverages humans' ancient storytelling nature to create politically dangerous media narratives. In the chapters, I consider the consequences of living in a society bereft of trust and explore practical solutions.

Book 3, "Hope," continues the journey through the dark forest of a media career in crisis, a newsroom plagued first by the head-swirling pace of media change, then by a pandemic and sweeping demands for social change. The journey ends, as a good adventure should, back in sunlight, armed with lessons learned and ready for a new, better day. There is every reason to hope that trust in storytelling can be restored, new business models can emerge, traditional media values can find a place in the digital age, and professional journalism can regain its footing as a valued public good. Every age has its challenges. For millennia, dramatic and wonderful storytelling humans have had a knack for somehow coming out just fine in the end. Or so the story goes.

Ghosts and Details

I should also introduce the storytellers in my own head. Two are ghosts and one is a child. This book is dedicated to them in appreciation of all the drama we shared during our journey together.

I never really knew the ghosts personally, but they still managed to shape my life. The child won't be able give feedback on any of this for at least a few more years.

But if dead people are critical to understanding how we got to where we are and children make us care about where we are going, maybe my mental storytellers and I will all manage to get along in the end. Anyway, I can't seem to get rid of them. You will meet them soon.

It is also very important to note that I am not the only journalist in my household. My spouse is a reporter who worked at the *Times* for a decade, covering communities around Tampa, where she grew up. The large and small sacrifices she has made for our family over the years, her continual support, our countless conversations, and her steady stream of thoughtful inspirations are the foundation that made it possible for me to write this book. She has her own strong views about newsroom cultures, but this work, by her choice, is my story exclusively.

The very last thing you need to know is that on January 1, 2012, the *St. Petersburg Times* was renamed the *Tampa Bay Times*. Nothing about the company ownership or structure changed at all, only the name. At different points in time, the company gets referenced as one or the other.

To avoid confusion, I often identify the news organization simply as the *Times*.

The *Times* is a unique place. It is not corporately owned and does not speak universally to the many complexities of the media industry. But it is a canary in the new media age coal mine.[18]

So, let's jump into the newsroom, 2016.

2

2016

Mama told me there would be days like these.

The elevator stuck, paused, jerked upward, paused, jerked again, and opened into the St. Petersburg newsroom of the *Tampa Bay Times*. Balancing two camera bodies, a light stand, a tripod, and coffee, I spilled. The industrial carpet where the coffee landed was made of squares designed so that someone from maintenance could quickly and easily swap musty, coffee-stained squares with fresh, new, pretty squares.

But there were no new squares. Regular rounds of layoffs had left us with a much smaller maintenance budget and staff. One set of stained squares looked like a winking smiley face. Another like two ghosts playing tag.

To the left off the elevator was a hallway to the newsroom. Along the wall hung five gold-framed Pulitzer Prize certificates, signposts of what is still possible if one stays on the coffee-squiggled carpet road.

That road went past rows of 1980s-style cubicles and into the photo department. When I got there, something seemed odd. The usual people were not at their desks.

Weird, I thought. Then I suddenly remembered that everybody was in Tampa for a team meeting. The managing editor and our director of social media were speaking to the photography staff.

At 9:30.

The clock on the wall read 9:02, and that Tampa office was about thirty miles away. I left my coffee on a random desk and sprinted back to my car. In rush-hour traffic, I might make it by 9:40. Hopefully.

Being late for a staff meeting was scarier than it used to be. Rumors were circulating about the next round of layoffs. Everyone worried that their number might come up this time, and it was getting harder and harder not to sweat the small stuff.

After racing around back-road shortcuts to avoid traffic, I finally got to that meeting—at 9:37. Our Tampa office is on the seventh floor, so I ran up the stairs, rounded the hallway corner to the conference room, and walked into a meeting already in progress. I tried to catch my breath as quietly as possible. The director of photography was just introducing our managing editor. Nobody took any special notice when I came in. I smelled fresh coffee brewing, and there were cinnamon raisin bagels with honey almond cream cheese on a plate. A fellow staffer looked at me as if to say, "Look what the cat dragged in, ten minutes late." I pointed to a coffee cup, and she nodded yes. I poured two cups, and we settled in just as Jennifer Orsi, our managing editor, began talking.

> I'm going to narrow my conversation today to one particular thing, and that is what we are looking for in terms of photos for the front page of the *printed* paper. But I don't want anyone to think that because that's what I'm talking about today, that's all I care about, that our digital efforts are not important. I can't emphasize enough how important they are.
>
> I'm going to talk about something else today, but I would love to come back another day and talk about digital contributions as well. Don't take this as any sign that I just care about print, because that's not the message that I'm sending.
>
> I do also care about 1A. It's something that as we balance what we do, have a really great website, have really good projects, have enterprise work, have a good breaking news staff, the front page of the paper is one of the very most important things that we do, and I spend a lot of time thinking about it. The photos on the front page are also very important, and I have some fairly strong opinions on what I want to see on the front page.

Jennifer certainly knew as well as anyone that we were living in a digital age, but as I listened to her address the staff, I thought about a foundational 1955 newsroom study by journalist-turned-sociologist Warren Breed.[1] She was describing what Breed described: a road to success for journalists who built careers when print was king. In her three-decade career at the *Times*, honor, prestige, and recognition within the newsroom were the keys to success.

In a traditional print newsroom, the formula for success had long been to get on the front page (preferably on Sunday), impress the bosses, and win industry-judged awards. Those important, and often unspoken, concepts of symbolic capital and newsroom social control were explored way back in Breed's 1950s newsroom ethnography.[2] Breed notes, "The newsman's source of rewards is located not among the readers, who are manifestly his clients, but among his colleagues and superiors. Instead of adhering to societal and professional ideals, he redefines his values to the more pragmatic level of the newsroom group."[3]

That was the newsroom experience that shaped Jennifer's career. It was the formula I came of age with, too. Her advice to the staff was to win by becoming part of the *Times* brand. It all boiled down to how to impress the bosses and how to get work onto the front side of dead trees on doorsteps. We were solidly into year ten of regular staff layoffs. Was that 1950s model still working for us? I got the feeling other staffers shared my thoughts. At one point a young staffer made eye contact with Lyndsey McKenna, the social media and promotions editor, and rolled his eyes.

As I silently sipped my cup of morning-victory coffee, I looked at reactions around the room and got the feeling that this meeting was about to get interesting. Friction points were everywhere. Older journalists were sticking to their old-school guns. Young journalists were eye-rolling.

After Jennifer finished her presentation, she left directly for another meeting. Then Lyndsey took the podium. Looking confident, she began,

> I know we just spent a lot of time talking about 1A. Well, what makes 1A on the web? The *All Eyes* [photography] blog is something you can contribute to actively. We see the work that you guys are doing, and we want you to have a home for that. Just because something isn't going on 1A doesn't mean it can't go viral. We have a lot of stuff go viral, and we are always glad to service that.

Lyndsey's key to success was to forget Jennifer's advice. She said you really don't need validation within the newsroom. You can find it online. You didn't need to get on 1A in print, win awards, or impress your bosses in the newsroom. You needed to tap into the sea of networks of people outside the newsroom. Lyndsey was delivering a counternarrative. She was explaining how to build a career using social networks, relationships, cooperation, and reciprocity.[4]

Figure 2.1. In a Pinellas courtroom in 1983, an exotic dancer bent over in front of Judge David Demers to defend her outfit in a trial charging her with violating the county's nudity ordinance. *St. Petersburg Times* photo by Jim Damaske.

Lyndsey talked about how to build followers and optimize traffic. She underscored the importance of building a personal journalism brand you could take with you when you changed employers. In a world of connectivity, did you really need to build a career based on just the *Times* brand? There was a huge elephant in the room. Few of us believed in a long-term relationship with our employer anymore. The era of the twenty-year career and a gold watch was gone.

One manager was directing the staff to find measures of success inside the traditional newsroom; another manager was telling them they need to look outside the newsroom. Staffers were stuck, uncomfortably, in the middle.

Lyndsey recapped the top ten posts of the month, bringing each one up on the screen in front of us. First up was a 1983 courtroom photo of a stripper bending over for a judge (figure 2.1).

Lyndsey told a story of how that photo had recently ended up in *Playboy* and linked to our website. She emphasized how an old photo was creating big new online hits. Then she showed us more of the top ten; a photo of Bush reacting to the 9/11 attacks, Cuba welcoming Pope Francis, a photo of two bald eagles fighting, a 2015 Comic-Con photo gallery of people very provocatively dressed, Donald Trump election-rally pictures, and new images of Pluto from space.

Then the questions flew at her:

"Are any of the top ten posts this month considered news?"

"On an assignment, when do we think web first, stop shooting, and send, and when do we cover the whole event, think about 1A, and file for a daily?"

"What hashtag do we use and when?"

"Do we need permission to post on our Facebook page, and will it be curated?"

"Just because Trump gets clicks, should we promote his rally?"

"Do we make any money from social media?"

Lyndsey looked overwhelmed. Her initial confidence faded. She fumbled through twenty minutes of questions about hashtags, ethics, and daily workflow. The director of photography came to her rescue. He assured everyone that this was all a work in progress and the conversation would continue in a productive way. Lyndsey thanked everyone for their time in a rather frustrated and unconvincing tone and sat down.

I could see that the photo staff, both young and old, were stuck in between two distinct silos that represented the thinking of these two managers.

Old school, quality journalism, dead trees, little job security.

New school, crappy journalism-as-clickbait, the digital future, preparation for an economy where job hopping is inevitable.

* * *

That meeting was a turning point for me as an anthropologist—and the birthplace of this book. It was the moment I saw how the dry social theories that professors required students to read and write papers about actually apply to real life.

I had recently learned how the sociologist Pierre Bourdieu reimagined the human social world one evening while watching a Christmas dance in Béarn, a French province, in 1959. Sitting and watching the dancers, he saw how social and economic forces divided the region where he grew up in powerful new ways. He saw how big new social and economic changes made big new cultural silos.

Watching the photo meeting, I wondered, "Is this how Bourdieu felt at the dance?"

Béarn, 1959

Pierre Bourdieu was intrigued by a group of bachelors at the Christmas dance, most of them in their early thirties. A friend described them as "unmarriageable."

They were wallflowers, conspicuously shy, and afraid to dance. They wore the traditional clothing style Bourdieu remembered as a boy. But the dance floor was filled with women in full, modern skirts. The men who were dancing were in slick suits that gave them an urban-chic look. The dancers spoke differently. They moved differently. The music was a new, modern style, jump and jive. It was nothing like music of days past, with names in Gascon, a local dialect distinct from the French spoken nationally, names that reflected generations of culture: *la crabe, lou branlou, lou mounchiou*.[5]

Bourdieu saw how his home region had divided itself into two camps—dancers and nondancers. Marriageable and unmarriageable. He knew the silos were really created by radical economic changes taking place at the time.

Before World War II, farming was the most lucrative work. After the war, agriculture was in decline, and the best-paying jobs moved to the city. Sons who could leave the farms for better city jobs were back home, dancing. Sons tethered by family, tradition, or necessity to farming were being left behind, growing older, and not marrying—or dancing.

Nobody spoke consciously about the scores of cultural symbols that had changed or how quickly they became normalized, but they defined the scene nevertheless. Music, clothing, mannerisms, language, body movement. People drifted intuitively into roles they barely acknowledged or recognized. Bourdieu asked himself why. Why didn't the farmers' sons just go buy suits and learn the new dance moves? Why didn't the women notice (or care) that they were ignoring half the men? Why was everyone falling so naturally into classifications defined by those swiftly moving economic forces?

Béarn, 1959, and our photo meeting, 2016, were a long way apart, but the impact of how sudden economic change siloed communities was striking.

*   *   *

Watching the photo meeting, I also thought about the journalist and anthropologist Gillian Tett, US managing editor of the *Financial Times*, book author, and columnist. She was deeply influenced by that same Bourdieu Christmas dance scene while covering the banking industry in 2007, just before the economic crash of 2008. The crash boiled down to new financial tools such as credit derivative swaps. Tett is credited as one of the few journalists to correctly predict the danger of those new financial tools and the coming crisis. She credits Bourdieu.

Tett first became curious about those new tools after watching siloed banking groups—traditional bankers and a new financial banker class—partying in a hotel during a conference. Something about the scene reminded her of Bourdieu's "marriageable" and "unmarriageable" men at the Christmas dance. Tett considered the root cause of all the swagger, specialized language, tribal bonding, and exclusive camaraderie in the group of financial bankers. Comparing the Christmas dance and the banking conference, Tett observes,

> What these two worlds share in common—along with every society that anthropologists have ever studied—is a tendency to use formal and informal classification systems and cultural rules to sort the world into groups or silos. Sometimes we do this in a formal manner, with diagrams and explicit rules. But we often do it amid thousands of tiny, seemingly irrelevant cultural traditions, rules, symbols, and signals that we barely notice because they are so deeply ingrained in our environment and psyche.[6]

Sitting in the *Times* conference room sipping coffee, I began to feel a heaviness set in my chest. There was one big difference between Bourdieu's Christmas dance and our photo meeting. At the Christmas dance, there was a marriageable group and an unmarriageable group. At this photo meeting, neither silo seemed to have a lock on a good plan for future success.

But I also watched and listened with a sense of wonder. It made me remember how kids feel when they stumble into new adventures. There was so much to learn. So much I couldn't understand. I knew I would do some follow-up interviews with the managing editor, the director of social media, and some staff photographers.

As it turned out, I didn't have to go looking for those interviews. They came to me.

Lara

A few days later, one of the photo staffers, Lara Cerri, pulled me into a room. She was angry about Lyndsey's presentation and wanted to organize a group of us to go talk to Boyzell Hosey, the *Times* director of photography, about her comments during the staff meeting.

"Did you find the crap that Lyndsey showed at the photo meeting as offensive as I did? Seriously, are stripper asses what we want to be known for? Do we need to dig through our archive and find our most offensive material just to get clicks? *Playboy* clicks? Really?"

She slammed a printout of the picture that had been shown at the meeting of the stripper bending over in court for a judge on the podium. There was a stack of other pictures on Lara's lap.

"Before I meet with Boyzell, I just want everyone to be on the same page here," she said. "It's total crap-for-clicks. It has nothing to do with what we do and why we do it."

Lara was angry and confused. Lyndsey was earnest and sincere. Jennifer was just trying to keep time-honored standards high and the ship afloat for a while longer. All three were good journalists, but they were pursuing three different formulas for success in challenging times for journalism.

Lara came to the *Times* photo staff fifteen years earlier. She spent a lot of her free time adopting and helping train guide dogs. She helped organize the Heart Gallery, a Florida Department of Children and Families program that creates portrait galleries of children hoping to be adopted. She played folk guitar, most recently with an Americana band comprised of journalists and their friends. They played at open-mic nights and in friends' garages. One afternoon I took a portrait of the band for their self-produced CD. The graphic designer, a band member who also worked with us at the paper, forgot to give me a photo credit on the CD jacket. Before I could stop her, Lara stayed up late into the night handwriting my name below the photo on each CD cover in careful block letters before distributing them.

Two years earlier, she had taken a sabbatical from the *Times* to teach high school journalism students. She wondered if she could stay connected to her love of journalism without living with all the industry stress. She returned, however, and found continued love for journalism in stories about the environment, community gardening, and children with disabilities. She also played her guitar for sick children at All Children's Hospital once a week.

One night, sitting on my couch, Lara held a glass of wine and cried. She was housing an indigent man who was beginning to require more care than she was able to provide. This man was a friend of a friend whom no one else would help. His growing health needs were intruding on Lara's ability to achieve balance in her life and sustain her own well-being. The man needed hospice care. Lara just dug ever deeper to find time to help him until his passing.

I tell you all of this to reinforce Lara's character and explain why she is a journalist. Lara sincerely wanted to make the world around her a better place. She was always motivated by journalism as a true social newsroom experience. Work, friendships, and relationships were the keys to her drive and her successes. Layoffs of friends, a growing sense of professional isolation, and the grinding loss of purpose in the newsroom had changed her. She explained,

Well, I feel like I'm constantly fighting to stay true to doing photographic storytelling the way it should be done, the way it used to be done, and, let me think of some examples.

When I worked for the *Evansville Courier* in my happiest heyday, I would come back from an assignment. I would soup [develop] my film, and I would sit down with [director of photography] Bryan Moss at a big, long light table, and with a loop, he would go over every single image. It wasn't just click, click, click, click, click, click. But I feel now it is always frantic, frantic. Oh my God, click, click, click. I have to shoot everything, and it's more stressful. Before now, you'd spend time with these people, and you would just take an image or two, you'd watch the light, you'd anticipate the moment. You would get in tune with them. Maybe you'd have a conversation, and then click, and the whole process was so much more thoughtful. Then, I would get feedback from my editor. And we would talk about this story, and he might say, "Wow, this is great but have you thought about this aspect? Why don't you go spend another half a day with this family? Or why don't you go when they're taking the kid out at a park?" And everything was bounced off the story and more directed and more thorough.

Lara had recently returned to the *Times* after teaching journalism for a semester at Lakewood High School. She explained why she needed the break:

Before the opportunity was presented to me to go to Lakewood, I was really more in a slump than I let other people know. I was so down. I was so, so, so down.

I knew I didn't want to teach full time, but I needed a break. I mean, everybody did in some way. I took a pay cut and lost my weekends. And Ted [her husband] and I had to sleep in separate bedrooms because he had the night shift [as a 2 to 11 p.m. picture editor at the *Times*] and I was up before dawn every morning—and I'm a light sleeper.

I learned a lot, but that was so difficult. But you know what? That saved me. I needed that because Ted was coming home with stories about how it feels like a mausoleum in there [the *Times* newsroom].

And then that whole semester that I was gone was when even more people were laid off. It was horrible. I was so busy. It's like people become workaholics because they don't want to see their jobs eliminated. Lakewood was really difficult and really stressful, but I was grateful to have the job, something that was all-consuming because I was so heartbroken and I could not bear to be in the middle of so much heartbreak [in the newsroom]. I knew a lot of friends and colleagues who were right in the middle of that heartbreak. I was grateful to be away from it.

Shortly after coming back, Lara went on an assignment to Flint, Michigan.

We went up there to do a story because Flint has the highest unemployment rate in the country. We went up there to do a business story for like three days. And I remember knocking on a guy's door and talking to him and taking some pictures of him. He lived right across the street from a huge automotive plant that was so gigantic it looked like a city unto itself. He lived on a little street with a parking lot right by the huge plant that had been closed down for decades where he used to work. I remember asking him, "So what keeps you in Flint? What gives you hope for the future?"

And he said, "Well, you know, Ford and GM keep saying they're gonna start this up again, and I believe that's gonna happen."

I sat there thinking I've been in Flint for three days, and this place has been dead for twenty years, and I've told this story before. I keep thinking about it again and again. It's like *we're* becoming that same guy. I remember in my mind thinking, "How can you believe in something that they just keep telling you is going to get better and it's been twenty years?" Because one year becomes two, and two becomes five, becomes . . . ? Yeah, I was sort of like, "You really believe that the auto industry is gonna not bounce back in general but that your job and your identity as an automotive worker and the plant that you can see right out your window is going to come back and be part of your life?"

That's us too, my friend. That's you and me.

Lara's description of how we lost our common narrative as journalists and the ways that loss has affected news production echoed in nearly every interview I conducted for this book.

A few months after that interview, Lara told me she was leaving the paper. She had been at the *Times* and my close friend for sixteen years. She took a teacher's assistant job at an elementary school in Scottsdale, Arizona, and has no plans to ever be a journalist again.

I have no doubt she will continue to make the world around her a better place.

Lyndsey's Graduate-School Dreams

On a pillar above Lyndsey's desk was a large, handwritten sign on white poster board that said,

"Digital Audience Mantra: Content, Engagement, Revenue."

This poster was a blueprint for Lyndsey's personal mission to develop a business model in the digital age. That mission defined her identity as a journalist, and that narrative was deep and personal. She saw "content, engagement, revenue" as her weapons to keep journalism alive for herself and her friends in the newsroom. For at least a decade, that mantra has gotten sticky at "revenue."

Lyndsey grew up in St. Petersburg and worked with *St. Petersburg Times* high school programs at the Poynter Institute for Media Studies, a nonprofit journalism school and research organization. Lyndsey related her personal and professional narrative to me.

I'm from this area originally, and when I was in high school I did the section that was called "By Kids for Kids" [the *Times* high school journalism program]. I always loved journalism. I went to college, and it was like, "I don't know if I can do journalism because this just doesn't seem like it's fiscally responsible in this day and age." But it was the one thing I had always loved. I got a degree in political science because the advice I received in high school was study something that you're passionate about, that you're interested in. But I took on internships in journalism.

In journalism school, there was this sort of running self-deprecating joke of not knowing what you're getting yourself into, that you wouldn't do it if it weren't for some ridiculous ideal which was ingrained in you by the older legacy journalists. That this ideal has permeated your conscience so deeply that you buy into it, yet you know all of that framework is really completely irrelevant now. Journalists? Well, we're all crazy people. No doubt about it.

Lyndsey described those goals and her own personal search for career success.

The clearest path to leadership, the clearest path to actually making an impact in a newsroom, the clearest path to making sure that the organizations that I cherish are still economically viable, is in delving deeper into the digital audience. So that's why I found this role. It was like the social media editor role is the perfect way to get my feet wet in both the hands-on daily and editing social media but also to tackle the more intangible problem. What is our strategy to surround this beast that we can't really tame? And that's what I think we are doing our best to do, tame the beast of social media.

Lyndsey saw her mission as luring people to the *Tampa Bay Times* digital content. She knew there was no money in the first two steps of her mantra, content and engagement. She was concentrating on brand identity and the raw audience. She saw the revenue part of her mantra as being beyond her pay grade. The broken business model was something for those people with years of newsroom experience and enough wisdom to fix. She, like a Pied Piper, would deliver them the audience. She knew how to be the Pied Piper of social media.

She guessed that her delivered audience should find a pay wall or a subscription model or something that could fund journalism.

It's not just that Facebook doesn't pay you. It's the idea that on social media, our content is free. Well, that's a pretty standard model. Social referrals, they get someone to a site. But how do we continue to engage that user that arrives from social? Our content has to be optimized. When someone clicks through onto a site, there has to be something they want to click through to see. That's when they're gonna hit that pay wall. But I think all of that is above my pay grade, making those decisions.

That was the rub. Most older legacy managers did not have the digital mentality to solve the audience and business model problem. Just like Jennifer, they were controlling what they knew how to control and were looking toward the digitally savvy young people like Lyndsey to address all the social media issues. Those young people were looking back at the older ones for guidance.

In 2016 at the *Times*, the social media team was two people. Two Pied Pipers, both under thirty. They went to the news budget meetings, then in actual practice they made all the editorial decisions for the *Tampa Bay Times* digital product. They were the front-page editor, sports editor, photo editor, regional editor, copy editor, and audience development expert.

The possibility of a functional business model fell into the gap between these two contrasting silos, digital and legacy journalists. We could see them clearly in that photo meeting in 2016. These young journalists were pursuing success on social media and making editorial decisions for the digital product above their pay grade. Older journalists were pursuing journalism for the printed page and leaving digital strategy to the younger generation. News producers were stuck in the middle. Lyndsey explained the situation this way:

So we have two people trying to manage something that is admittedly a lot larger and a lot more refined at other places. So, you know, you're being asked to create these digital skills. And when you're discussing it with people above your pay grade, that are above your level on the leadership ladder and don't necessarily have those skills, they don't necessarily know their [the skills'] importance, but they do *recognize* that those skills are important. Still, they don't know how it all fits into the newsroom framework, but they do know it's necessary. It's almost that there is a fundamental disconnect, and maybe that is at least in part why you've got this inherent problem.

Jennifer's Way versus Lyndsey's Way

The opening question during my interview with the *Times* managing editor, Jennifer, was "I'm wondering, since you've taken over as managing editor, what is your greatest challenge in this news environment?"

Jennifer's answer: "I don't think it's social media. I'll tell you that."

Me: "No?"

Jennifer: "No. I think that changes the dynamic. I think that it has people looking at our work in new ways, but social media, on my list of many of the biggest challenges, is not the biggest challenge."

Jennifer knew that social media and our digital efforts are in fact critically important for a sustainable future. But there was an emotional, and justified, feeling that those things were beyond her control, beyond her experience, and beyond her silo. Lyndsey felt the same way but for different reasons. That space that rests between Lyndsey's silo and Jennifer's silo has a name: fear.

As a working journalist thinking about my own future, I knew that fear. I felt it too.

When legacy media mixed with social media, the extremes tore at us and tore our business model apart in ways that felt like a thunderous storm. Our fear was justified. We could not control the storm. Our journalism was caught within that storm and surrounded.

From her position, Jennifer was right and brave to work on controlling what she could as that storm raged. Lyndsey was right to try to bring an audience to the *Times* online, even without a specific business model in place.

Three months after I interviewed Lyndsey, she left the *Times*.

Jennifer's Surprise

Whenever staffers talked about Jennifer's management style, they referenced her ability to multitask the details. A typical description offered was "She can keep all the trains on all the tracks." That was her superpower. We imagine her ability to manage the newsroom came from having grown up in one. She had been at the *Times* for thirty-one years. She didn't just have people skills, she had journalist people skills.

She was a woman in a male-dominated newsroom while parenting her own children and producing stellar journalism in tough economic times.

She got it. She got us. She knew what it felt like to balance family pressures, social pressures, and the financial pressures of journalism with an undying passion for our work. Whenever I went into her office for a career discussion, she sensed my inner scale weighing personal concerns on one side and my passion for journalism on the other. Those were weights on her scale too. I got the feeling she had balanced them longer and better than most.

After starting our interview by saying that social media was not her biggest challenge, she continued on.

> I do not think I could give you a single biggest challenge. I would say that right up there, at the top of the list, are the struggles of the business of doing journalism, which has an effect on the practice of journalism.
>
> We're at this really difficult time for newspapers, especially as an organization, where our whole business model has fallen apart. The money that used to be there to support quality journalism is not there anymore. My challenge is, how do you do quality journalism that continues to serve all the people in your community, who you have always served and want to continue to serve? With fewer people, fewer resources, in terms of technology, because it takes money to buy good technology.
>
> I would say that one of, if not my biggest challenge, is how to continue to keep the quality of the journalism high and do all of the journalism that we want and need to do, in an era of shrinking resources.

Lyndsey saw her job as a social media audience Pied Piper, leading an audience to the *Times* so that management could fix its business model.

Jennifer saw her job as controlling the controllable. She did not spend her energy trying to wrestle with issues that she sensed were outside her control. The field of social media, its extremes, the echo chambers, and how all that affects news consumption was not under her control.

Jennifer continued and answered my first question further.

> Well, I think the biggest thing that people ask me about is the thing I have the least control over, and that is the future of the industry, the future of the organization, the financial stability of the organization.
> [People ask,] "Is this a job that I love, and I really love? Is that going to be here in five years or ten years? Can I make a career here? This is what

I want to do, but will I be able to do it?" I think that's a question that a lot of people have on their minds.

Another question that I hear a lot is "What is the *Times* doing to become a more digital organization and be more competitive with all the other digital organizations?" I think those are two distinct questions, but I think the same people are asking both.

When you talk about career planning, the things that I can talk to people about with ease are "Here's how I think you're doing as a journalist. Here's the type of journalist I think you're becoming. Here's what you need to set as your goal. Here are the skills that you need to get. Here's where you need to improve. Here is where you should focus your time and energy. Here's how to get better."

The kinds of things that have to do with the practice of good journalism I can talk to people about. I can tell them where I think they are on the career ladder and how far they're going to go and how I can help them get there. I can't tell them what our profits are going to be at the end of next year because I don't know. I don't control them. That's what they really want to know, though. They really want to know "How healthy are we going to be as an industry and as a company a year from now?"

I don't have the answer for that. I'm happy to help make them a 50 percent better journalist a year from now, if I can, but I don't have the answer to that question.

"But how about a 50 percent more secure journalist?" I asked her. She responded,

I can't promise that, I really can't. I will say that a message I do preach is that we all got into this business because we love to do journalism. We all want to keep doing journalism. That definitely requires the ability to adapt and to change as to how we keep doing journalism.

She was banking on the idea that many dedicated journalists define themselves personally through their work and the ways we get validated in the newsroom. These are strong currencies, and she knew their power. They kept her in journalism. They keep me in journalism too.

In September 2018, Jennifer shocked the entire newsroom by announcing she would be leaving the *Times* for a communications job at a large financial company. All three of the passionate and dedicated journalists I followed from that staff meeting left the *Times*.

Today, Jennifer is the executive editor of the *Sarasota Herald-Tribune* and Florida/Georgia regional editor for Gannett's USA TODAY Network.[7]

Habitus

Many anthropologists love the concept of *habitus*. It is an idea that goes back to Aristotle, but it was Bourdieu who put it center stage in the social sciences. He offers, in his groundbreaking book *Outline of a Theory of Practice*, a brain-twisting definition:

> The structures constitutive of a particular type of environment (e.g., the material conditions of existence characteristic of a class condition) produce *habitus*, systems of durable, transposable *dispositions*, structured structures predisposed to function as structuring structures, that is, as principles of the generation and structuring of practices and representations which can be objectively "regulated" and "regular" without in any way being the product of obedience to rules, objectively adapted to their goals without presupposing a conscious aiming at ends or an express mastery of the operations necessary to attain them and, being all this, collectively orchestrated without being the product of the orchestrating action of a conductor.[8]

Right now, you are probably thinking what I was thinking after reading that:

"Huh?"

"Structured structures predisposed to function as structuring structures?"

Truth is, habitus is a powerful concept, and interpretations of habitus vary. Here is mine, as it pertains to how I saw the photo meeting.

The historic and time-honored structure of the newsroom stopped working for these three journalists—Jennifer, Lyndsey, and Lara. The economic model, the surety of how to practice journalism, the relevance of our daily meetings and rituals, and so many other small social details that helped us define ourselves were all in complete disarray. Our futures were uncertain, our identities fragile.

All three of these coworkers were searching for new ways to practice journalism in daily life that could help them survive, thrive, and feel whole in all the uncertainty. They were striving for something (a new habitus) that could help them reclaim their career identities. So, the first piece of Bourdieu's definition of habitus addresses how the sum of a person's beliefs, background, and practices gets applied to survival in a new cultural environment. How much and how fast can a fish change in new waters?

My coworkers also wanted that individual way of practicing life, their habitus, to help mold something larger than themselves. They wanted their habitus to help create a new, functional, successful newsroom structure. As in cultures everywhere, they wanted their daily habits to make them a part of a healthy, thriving community, and in return they wanted to be a valued part of building that new culture.

From the podium at the meeting, managers were earnestly laying out their best strategies, best habitus, best choices, for practices that would help them successfully adapt to a new, challenging environment. They wanted to be with the group on the dance floor at the Christmas dance. They also wanted us to dance with them and to dance like them.

They wanted structured habits of how to practice journalism, built from their own backgrounds and histories, to be a positive part of a restructured landscape. Scores of habits and choices build that landscape. They boil all the way down to body language, dress, lingo, daily rituals, and ways to accumulate social capital. As my coworkers intuitively gravitated toward ways of practicing daily journalism to restructure their lives, they also hoped that their habitus would perform a second function: to contribute to a larger, thriving, and successful cultural cooperative group. If they could pull that off, if the structures of their personal habitus (a sum of their beliefs, backgrounds, and practices applied to survival in a new environment) could contribute to building better newsroom cultural structures, there could be a circular cycle of internal and external validation and security.

Going back to Bourdieu's complicated definition, their own personal "durable, transposable dispositions" try with sincerity to "function as structuring structures" to build a newsroom that works again.

As they try to adapt themselves to their new reality, they also try to shape the new reality to themselves. Hopefully, the whole thing circles back around to make it easier for them to adapt to a new, more "me-friendly" reality. It's a feedback loop and an often-complicated relationship between self and social world and back to self.

The habitus in the photo meeting was generational and siloed.

For Jennifer, her efforts to help staffers build meaningful social capital by making the front page, winning awards, and impressing the people on the newspaper masthead no longer worked.

For Lyndsey, the sacrifice of meaningful content for clicks, "engagement, content, revenue," wasn't creating a business model that embraced a traditional news ethos.

Lara could not make her career work in the crossfire of competing agendas.

In anthropological terms, the staff meeting and its aftermath serve as an example of the profound impact of changing social structures on individuals. I know that Jennifer, Lara, and Lyndsey did not just give up on hard-fought and well-deserved careers at the *Times*. I know they loved the *Times* and the journalism it stands for. I know with an emotional certainty because we shared nearly identical struggles.

As dedicated journalists like these three disappear from the newsroom, and there have been so many, it feels like pulling musicians from an orchestra. How many can you pull before the music becomes unrecognizable and people stop buying tickets? And how can you keep musicians in the orchestra if nobody is buying tickets?

The journalists who have not been laid off, the newsroom survivors, walk a tightrope in a storm they can't control. They try to balance the realization that journalism is failing with their own need to embrace career strategies that might keep them in the newsroom.

Routine ritual moments, like the staff meeting, can reveal important truths about today's media challenges. This ethnography digs into those moments, blurry behavioral spots that make newsrooms a unique cultural experience. The next chapters will explore decades-old daily practices, rituals, and traditions. Many are dangerously outdated, but still largely unchanged, in the digital age. Local journalism is often described as a calling and compared to a religious vocation. News producers' deep dedication leaves them vulnerable to power dynamics leveraged by management.[9] We will see ground truths about how sweeping global changes in mass media and individual journalists trying to keep a career alive collide.[10]

To get to the roots of today's media crisis, the next chapter goes back to the beginning. Not the beginning of newspapers, or the printing press, or even the Homeric tradition. It goes waaaay back. Forty thousand years back. The anthropology of a newsroom today really begins at the dawn of human culture, a still-mysterious moment when ancient *Homo sapiens* first became a storytelling animal.

3

Storytelling Animals

Once upon a long, long time ago, *Homo sapiens* began to tell stories.

Nobody knows why.

Stories made it easy to share knowledge. Shared knowledge helped create cooperative communities. Communities created cultures. Cultures created norms and morality for growing social networks of humans. Working collectively, our primate ancestors began to master their surroundings in new and amazing ways.

There is hot debate about exactly when and where human culture dawned. Anthropologist and biologist Richard Klein offers this long view: "In the space of less than 40,000 years, ever more closely packed cultural 'revolutions' have taken humanity from the status of a relatively rare large mammal to something more like a geologic force."[1]

In Darwinian terms, early humans went from being fairly mundane primates to the planet's dominant species very quickly. In broad strokes, anthropologists agree that *Homo sapiens* produced signs of culture by around 40,000 years ago and became fully launched as storytelling, culture-producing animals by 20,000 B.C.

Our planet would never be the same.

In his book *The Dawn of Human Culture*, Klein provides a definitive account of human evolution, beginning six million years ago. The timeline is steady, logical, and predictable until around 50,000 B.C.

Everything before that time left clear and emerging stories in physical fossil records. But the dawn of human culture turned on a dime. Klein describes a stark contrast between "the Upper Paleolithic [50,000–10,000 B.C.] and everything that preceded it, and where we speak of the 'dawn of human culture,' others refer to a 'human revolution,' a 'creative explosion,' 'a great leap forward,' or a 'sociocultural big bang.'"[2]

The authors note a change that has long puzzled archaeologists who study human evolution: "The relationship between anatomical and behavioral change shifted abruptly about 50,000 years ago. Before this time, anatomy and behavior seemed to evolve more or less in tandem, very slowly, but after this time anatomy remained relatively stable while behavioral (cultural) change accelerated rapidly."[3] Strange forces were afoot at the dawn of human culture.

Suddenly there was art, crafted bone, ivory and shell artifacts, and complex graves. An early example, a grave with two children who died 29,000 years ago at Sungir, an Upper Paleolithic site on the outskirts of Vladimir, Russia, contained 10,000 uniformly sized and shaped hand-crafted beads. The archaeologist Randall White estimates that each bead took about an hour to make. So the 10,000 beads buried with the children took around 10,000 human hours to craft. It makes sense that those children occupied a special, socially privileged position in a well-defined society with shared beliefs, norms, and culture.[4]

How? And why?

Some wonder if there was a lucky gene mutation. Some speculate that *Homo sapiens* was under the gun, teetering on extinction, and began trying to communicate with each other in a desperate bid just to survive. Maybe it was God.

In the end, Klein admits, "We must conclude partly inconclusively."[5]

Although 40,000 years may seem like a long time, in the context of six million years of human evolution, it is a blip. And the emergence of media technology is a blip within that blip. The Gutenberg press was invented around 1440, the first telegram was sent in 1844, Guglielmo Marconi invented the radio in 1894, the first television broadcast was in 1927, email developed in the 1970s, and smart phones and social media came into use in the 2000s. This whole storytelling-animal thing is still pretty experimental, and the technology humans use to tell stories is moving faster and faster.

*   *   *

Approximately 42,020 years after the mysterious dawn of human culture, I watch storytelling pervade the daily life of my seven-year-old daughter.

I nag that poor child constantly: put on socks, not just shoes; don't close the cat into a shopping bag; you will eat green beans before you get dessert; put your *whole* body into the bathtub; do your homework. But I never have to nag her to make up stories as she plays. That she does on her own, fanatically, all day long. Her games have all the hard-wired elements of story—scene, characters, conflict, good people, bad people, and resolution.

There was an "aha" moment for me. I was sitting on the edge of a pool at the local Elks Club, toes in the water, reading a book about evolutionary psychology. My daughter started pulling on my legs. I was mid-sentence in my reading and annoyed at the interruption.

She stood rigidly, directly in front of a playmate.

Daughter: "We're dominoes. Knock us over, Daddy!"

Easy enough. I pushed Daughter with my toes. She fell into her playmate.

Playmate (grabs Daughter and falls over): "Oh no, we're falling over the cliff!"

Daughter: "We're falling into the water!"

Playmate: "Dominoes can't swim!"

Daughter: "We can't swim! Help! Dominoes can't swim!"

Playmate: "There are sharks! Sharks are going to eat us!"

Daughter: "We're sinking! The sharks are going to eat us!"

Playmate: "But dominoes can dance! Remember we can dance? Do the domino dance!"

Daughter and Playmate sang together, roughly to the tune of Van Morrison's *Domino*, which had played on the pool radio a few minutes earlier. "Ooooo-ooh, domino! Domino dance! Domino dance! Domino dance!"

They synchronized a dance, placing one arm at a time over their heads. It began to look like flapping. It was pretty damn cute.

Playmate and Daughter, laughing and dancing together: "Bye sharks! You can't get us sharks! Dominoes! Bootie shake at the sharks! Can't bite me sharks!"

Beginning, middle, end. Characters, plot, conflict, villains, resolution, reflection. A two-minute kid play in three acts.

I put the book down, and we played for the next few hours. They did nothing but tell stories. They set scenes, created conflicts, used suspense, defined obstacles, defeated evil, celebrated resolution, reflected, bonded together through the telling of the stories, invented rituals. In short, they intuitively created shared communal story worlds, one after the other.

We all do. All humans, across all cultures.

So What Exactly Is a Story?

Consider this storyline:

At the dawn of time, two young twin brothers must become heroes by outwitting malicious underground Gods of Chaos to convince the benevolent Creators of the Universe that humankind is worthy of this world.

Pop quiz. The above story is:

A) A 1982 Japanese anime film by Hayao Miyazaki.
B) A multiverse young-adult science fiction series published in the 1960s by Australian author Michael Moorhead, based on aboriginal lore.
C) The Popol Vuh, a mythology of the K'iche' Maya people, translated in 1550 by Spanish conquerors.
D) An Egyptian creation story that explains "maat," the separating of chaos into law and order in the human world, translated from the Rosetta Stone.
E) A 2017 logline of a rejected pilot episode created for Nickelodeon by the producers of *Avatar: The Last Airbender* that later garnered a cult following online but never became a series.
F) None of the above. I just made it up.

It could reasonably be any of the above. For reasons that may be forever mysterious, the basic structure of a story seems to transcend space and time. Why do so many humans, across cultures that have had no contact with each other at all, tell such similar stories? The answer will likely never be known for sure. The magic of humankind's first stories left no material trace for archaeologists to follow.

"Occam's razor" is the philosophical principle that the simplest explanation is the most likely one. The simplest explanation for the universality of story structures may be that they were a very early *Homo sapiens* adaptation. Tens of thousands of years ago, at the dawn of human culture, storytelling was a survival mechanism that worked for humans and has traveled with us ever since. Those common story structures continue because they still help us survive and thrive. They are as much a part of humankind as all the other characteristics that define the species.

Because they have been with people for so long and are so deeply ingrained in human nature, the basic and nearly universal story structures across the space and time of humanity may well have migrated with the earliest *Homo sapiens* out of Africa. The shape of stories remains doggedly consistent from culture to culture to culture, from long-lost empires in the East to roaming bands of hunters North and South to major religious texts to modern Western cinema.

I believe that Occam's razor explanation. Some people may believe stories are in God's grand design. Many K'iche' Maya believed hero twins tamed a world created by a pantheon of gods (correct answer to the quiz: "C").

So, we will all choose our own story of stories.

Since we will never know for sure, we could just stick with what we do know. Story structures are as close to universal as anything in our common humanity.

Anthropologist Michelle Scalise Sugiyama studies narratives in humans across space and time and offers this explanation of story structure:

> When the components of narrative are combined, we end up with a representation of human goal-directed behavior and the set of conditions (including constraints and obstacles) under which it unfolds. The basic structure of narrative, then, is SETTING + AGENT + GOAL + ACTION + OBSTACLE + SOLUTION + OUTCOME.

Some Hollywood screenwriters identify fifteen universal plot points. I have found eerily similar explanations of "how to write a good story" in modern screenwriting manuals, in conversations with journalists who write features, in academic literature, and in book-writing manuals. I see those structures in ancient myths, movies I watch with my kid, Maya cosmology, and the Bible.

As I read them, I wondered why the brutal, exacting, and inevitable mechanisms of natural selection would leave such rigid storytelling formulas in place across tens of thousands of years of space and time. I also wondered if this century's idea of "objective" journalism storytelling, the one I grew up believing in, was different than those ancient and persistent ways humans crave stories.

Journalism professor Richard Streckfuss explored where the concept of objectivity in news came from. He contends in a 1990 journal article that the idea originated in a polarized political climate. There are striking parallels to the kind of silos we are experiencing in media and politics today. Streckfuss finds that "objectivity" emerged in the 1920s from a broader cultural movement toward scientific realism "as an antidote to the emotionalism and jingoism of the conservative American press."[6]

Streckfuss offers, "Whatever objectivity may mean now, it had a particular and important meaning at its outset, a meaning created to cope with new information and new conditions. Those conditions . . . are with us still."[7]

Objective journalism was embraced as a sort of scientific method for storytelling as people began to worry that mass media were becoming a threat to democracy in the early twentieth century. Against a backdrop of the Red Scare of 1919 and 1920, labor unrest, and anarchic violence, a media environment emerged that spurred hysteria, nationalism, and superpatriotism.[8] In that social environment, Walter Lippmann wrote *Liberty and the News*, first published in 1920. The essays outline a blueprint for objective reporting to counter his fear that "under the influence of headlines and panicky print, the contagion of unreason can easily spread through a settled community."[9]

Lippmann's concerns resonate with the rise of propaganda in today's digital media age. In what might be the original definition of objective journalism, Lippmann writes about the importance of

> a professional training in journalism in which the ideal of objective testimony is cardinal. The cynicism of the trade needs to be abandoned, for the true patterns of the journalistic apprentice are not the slick persons who scoop the news, but the patient and fearless men of science who have labored to see what the world really is. It does not matter that the news is not susceptible of mathematical statement. In fact, just because the news is complex and slippery, good reporting requires the exercise of the highest of scientific virtues. They are habits of ascribing no more credibility to a statement than it warrants, a nice sense of the probabilities, and a keen understanding of the quantitative importance of particular facts.[10]

For a moment, I'd like to put aside Lippmann's outdated, gendered language about "fearless *men* of science." Just for now, let's also table debates about the impossibility of attaining true objectivity. His larger idea was to create a check-and-balance practice on dangerous propagandists, rising nationalism, and partisan yellow journalism during a time when democracy appeared to be in crisis. Lippmann's obsession with objectivity became standard college curriculum as "journalist" became a more distinct profession.

Ultimately, Streckfuss concludes, "Objectivity had shrunk from a methodology needed to preserve democracy to a practical posture of day-to-day production."[11] Over time, the term "objectivity" stuck. For most journalists today, it is a generalized label for what we strive to achieve. In real-life practice, journalism settled into more practical models of reporting that ideally would embrace fair, factual, multidimensional, balanced news, gathered as a public service that respects complexity, allows contradiction, and invites debate.

Lippmann's concern over the rise of branded patriotism and siloed politics in media during the early 1920s has eerie parallels to today's media environment. It speaks to how stories have long been tools leveraged for power and control and how dangerous historical moments can coincide with advances in communication technology. His era likewise saw storytelling in new forms of mass media that worked against the public good and a healthy democracy.

"Objectivity" was a means to fight against widespread efforts to wield the power of storytelling in ways that did not serve the public good. Objectivity and scientific realism became shields against the use of mass media to manipulate human culture for selfish gain, to promote dangerous nationalism, and to pursue individual power.

That lens puts perspective on today's political attacks on legacy media institutions and the dissolution of public belief in a journalistic pursuit of something like objectivity, however imperfect. Lippmann embraced objectivity to create a clearly defined and better trusted mass media space in defense of democracy, in troubling times. There is an urgent need to reestablish that clear public understanding of professional journalism in today's information apocalypse.

We Are Stories

I read to our daughter most every evening. Then, when the clock strikes bedtime, she pleads with me to make up just one more story while she falls asleep. Then she, like all of us, dreams stories. In the morning she wakes up, and the first thing we do is Daddy Hogwarts Express Piggyback Ride to the breakfast table. Watch out for the tricky witch-cats on the way!

As a leading developmental psychologist, Michael Tomasello, once quipped, "Fish are born expecting water, humans are born expecting culture."[12] Because storytelling is so fundamental to creating culture, human children are born expecting stories. I see it every day in my daughter, it fills my heart to watch, and I feel blessed for it.

My daughter is the child to whom, along with my two ghosts, this book is dedicated. Truth is, I talk everything through with her. Sometimes directly, hoping to hear wisdom "out of the mouths of babes."[13] Sometimes in imagined conversations with some future her.

*   *   *

Journalist and editor Robert Fulford wrote about how mass media and storytelling can be seen as evolving from one technical innovation to the next: the invention of language, then oral history, the written word, the printing press, novels, films, radio, television, and the internet. But in terms of stories and themes and the eternal games of children, new technologies can be seen as circling around the same trail, meeting on their path the same characters and the same stories again and again and again.[14]

Somehow, long, long ago, human brains got wired for those dramatic narratives. It was a turning point in the history of life on earth. United by mysterious forces still unknown, *Homo sapiens*, Earth's dominant storytelling animal, soared up the food chain and became the most powerful species on the planet. Something else strange happened along the way.

More Culture, Less Brain

In his 2014 book *The Domesticated Brain*, cognitive neuroscientist Bruce Hood calls attention to a mystery that took place in *Homo sapiens'* heads 40,000 or so years ago. Just around the time the archaeological record began to fill with signs of human culture, *Homo sapiens'* brains *shrank* by about 20 percent. That is the about same amount of brain loss scientists see in wild animals when they become domesticated.[15]

Hood asserts, "We should not assume that we are fundamentally more intelligent than an individual born 20,000 years ago." It was around that time that the fossil record of *Homo sapiens* explodes with signs of culture—advances in tool technology, cave art, instruments, talismans, ritual burials, and other examples of shared meaning, shared knowledge, and shared experiences. Hood concludes, "We may have more knowledge and understanding of the world around us, but much of it was garnered from the experiences of others that went before us rather than the fruits of our own efforts."[16]

Hood's thoughts raise two riddles.

Riddle 1: How did those early humans begin to accumulate and retain communal knowledge and shared experiences?

Riddle 2: Why might the answer to that riddle suggest why their brains shrank 20 percent?

Neuroscientist Antonio Damasio offers a solution to riddle 1: "The problem of how to make all this wisdom understandable, transmissible, persuasive, enforceable—in a word, of how to make it stick—was faced and a solution found. Storytelling was the solution—storytelling is something brains do, naturally and implicitly. . . . [I]t should be no surprise that it pervades the entire fabric of human societies and cultures."[17]

Putting information in stories works. Literary Darwinist Jonathan Gottschall notes, "The world's priests and shamans knew what psychology would later confirm: if you want a message to burrow into a human mind, work it into a story."[18]

A quick, random example comes from bath time with my daughter, not more than a few minutes after I had read that sentence from Gottschall. I was sitting on the edge of the tub, scratching the shower curtain with my fingernail to see if I could make Luna, our cat, attack the Curtain Monster. My daughter asked me if I could name the planets of the solar system in order, closest to the sun to farthest from the sun.

In exact order? I could not. I'm sure I probably spit that information out on a test at some point, in some science class. But not today, sweet child of mine.

She mumbled something to herself, held up her fingers one at a time, closed her eyes, and said, "Mercury, Venus, Earth, Mars, Jupiter, Saturn, Uranus, Neptune."

I said, "Dang, that's pretty good. How do you remember that?"

She said, "My Very Enthusiastic Mother Just Served Us Noodles."

And now I too will be able to name the planets, in order, for the rest of my days.

It was just a one-sentence story. It has a character, a catalyst, and a small resolution, not exactly a Greek myth or Maya cosmology, but using story to imprint information works.

So, riddle 2, why sharing knowledge and values as storytelling animals shrank *Homo sapiens'* brains. It made human life easier. To Hood's point, a domesticated dog lives a much easier life as part of a human family compared to how her wild wolf ancestors lived. Social networks of storytelling humans with brains all wired for story, cooperation, and collective knowledge were more successful and used less individual energy. Humans didn't suddenly become 20 percent dumber. Working in bonded, cooperative groups, they were just suddenly exponentially more efficient.

*   *   *

An image occasionally seen on T-shirts traces the evolution of humans, as a hunched ape progressively stands more erect to become a modern human. It looks so easy. One might assume the *Homo* genus was on a linear evolutionary path from early primate to modern greatness from the start. The sequence often ends in something like a person jamming out on a guitar or hunched back over a computer.

But if you look back in time, the fate of the *Homo* genus was very precarious. Other branches of the *Homo* family tree went extinct, *Homo erectus* and *Homo neanderthalensis* most famous among them. *Homo neanderthalensis* were group hunter-gatherers, could control fire, were intelligent, stood erect, had opposable thumbs, and were contemporaries of *Homo sapiens*, but they all died out. *Homo sapiens* survived and soared up the food chain.

It may well be that humans thrived by developing common cultures and more advanced social networks. As *Homo sapiens* evolved, we became more personally dependent on accumulated, collective knowledge and some specific small society of other humans. We may never know with any certainty if *Homo neanderthalensis* told stories too, but one thing is clear—we did, and are the only ones still alive to tell the tale.

As humans continued to evolve, our appetite for stories grew. The ways stories got delivered became more efficient. The stories themselves became more efficient. Humans have come a long way, from listening to a trusted elder clan leader weave tales by the fire to politicians bouncing narratives in 280 characters or less off satellites in space to millions of smart phones, but the social functions of storytelling remain the same.

Natural selection is a precision device. There are countless miraculous examples all around and probably millions more to discover. To attract pollinators, the Cuban *Marcgravia envenia* plant uses concave leaves that work like satellite dishes to amplify bat signals as they echo-locate for food and rewards them with sweet nectar. Migratory baby birds stare up to the night sky and imprint the astral center of rotation to guide them in flight when they grow up. Warrior ants use pheromones to signal ants in their own colonies not to attack, except for spy warrior ants, who can imitate the pheromones of another colony and invade them from within. The tiny mind of the *Cataglyphis bicolor* desert ant meanders randomly while looking for food. Once it finds some, it recalculates its original path as a series of vectors relative to the sun and mentally charts a direct path back to the colony.

Evolutionary biologist David Sloan Wilson concludes,

> Our minds are also packed with specialized circuits that enable us to solve our own problems of survival and reproduction as naturally as celestial navigation in birds and dead reckoning in ants . . . whether the common problem is a hostile environment or a hostile group, working together as a group comes naturally in our species, just as celestial navigation comes naturally to migratory birds and dead reckoning to desert ants.[19]

Nature goes to elaborate and amazing lengths to ensure reproduction, survival, and success of a species, but as evolutionary tools go, the human brain's wiring for communal, culture-building storytelling seems to beat them all.

And it's all ours. The queen of all natural selection adaptations may have fallen to early *Homo sapiens*.

Renaming Our Species

I am going to take a shot at renaming the human race. I'm writing a book, so why not go big?

I won't be the first. Storytelling is so fundamental to human nature that several social scientists have floated the idea of reclassifying *Homo sapiens*, post–20,000 B.C., as a new species altogether.

In his book *Homo Narrans*, John Niles describes the title character, storytelling human.

> [T]hrough storytelling, an otherwise unexceptional biological species has become a much more interesting thing. *Homo narrans:* that hominid who has not only succeeded in negotiating the world of nature,

finding enough food and shelter to survive, but also has learned to inhabit mental worlds that pertain to times that are not present and places that are the stuff of dreams. It is through such symbolic mental activities that people have gained an ability to create themselves as human beings and thereby transform the world of nature into shapes not known before. . . . [O]ral narrative is, and for a long time has been, the chief basis for culture itself. . . . [T]he science of mankind, if it is to be complete, must encompass an understanding of human beings as makers of the mental world that they inhabit.[20]

Jonathan Gottschall, author of *The Storytelling Animal*, makes a similar case at a TEDx talk for calling humans *Homo fictus*:

When you call the species *Homo sapiens*, that's an argument. The argument is it's our sapience, it's our intelligence, it's our big human brains that most sets us apart. But other scientists, other philosophers say "no, really we're not all that reasonable, all that logical, most of the time. Really, it's our upright posture, it's our opposable thumbs, it's how sophisticated our cultures are, it's how sophisticated our language is." And I'm not here to argue against any of that, these things are all important. I'm just saying that one thing of equal stature is left off this list, and that is the way that human beings live their lives inside stories. So *Homo sapiens*, that's a pretty good definition for the species—but *Homo fictus*, Fiction Man, is about equally accurate. Man is a storytelling animal. . . . [T]his is what we are doing all the time, every day in our lives. We are trying to impose the order of story structure on the chaos of existence.[21]

As a working journalist, I've learned that effective stories must have drama. Based on that idea, I decided to join Gottschall and Niles and take my own shot at renaming humans. But the thought of making such a lofty contribution to the world made me wonder, who *did* name *Homo sapiens*?

It was Carl Linnaeus, the father of taxonomy. In 1735 he published his classification of living things, *Systema Naturae*. In the first edition he classified 7,700 species of plants and 4,400 species of animals including humans. In that edition, humans were labeled *Homo diurni*, "man of the day."[22] That description lacked a certain gravitas, so Linnaeus eventually went with *Homo sapiens*, "wise human." He used himself as the lectotype, the animal chosen as the single type specimen for a species. To name all humans, he examined only himself.

Linnaeus's system of taxonomy revolutionized science and inspired scientists of his time, among them Charles Darwin. Linnaeus was revered in his lifetime. His fame and infamy persist today. By 1758, he subdivided *Homo sapiens* into six horribly racist and completely baseless hierarchical subcategories with descriptions that flattered Europeans and denigrated all other humans of the world. His taxonomy is criticized for forever branding flora and fauna of the entire Earth through European eyes, a system scientists have yet to wiggle out of. Linnaeus is also the father of index cards, an invention he created to order huge amounts of data in a way that could be quickly alphabetized and shuffled around.

My point is to say that it is all arbitrary. A human put a name for humans on an index card and it stuck.

But how have humans applied their sapience? Much of it has been spent creating common morality through storytelling for ever-expanding social networks. Dramatic stories, with heroes and villains, tears and laughter, moral rights and wrongs, victory and tragedy.

So, just for fun, and to clarify a point I want to make, I am going to rename us all:

Homo dramaticus, dramatic human.

My case is this: stories are definitive to humans, and stories stick only when they stir emotions through drama. People are moved by emotions far more than by facts. In politics, books, television, movies, child's play, and news, the emotional turning points generated by drama move the shared mental worlds of humans. Boring stories do not shape culture. Dramatic ones do.

There are thousands of instructional books on writing stories that highlight the need for drama. It is clear from the Homeric epics to the world's religious texts to Ovid's *Metamorphoses*, to the yellow journalism of the twentieth century, to cable news, to TikTok.

Blake Snyder's book on scriptwriting, *Save the Cat*, points out that all forms of scripts "are intricately made emotion machines. They are Swiss watches of precise gears and spinning wheels that make them tick. You have to be able to take them apart and put them back together again. In the dark. In your sleep."[23] And the emotions that pull us along a storyline must be our deepest emotions—the kind that have driven humans since the dawn of *Homo dramaticus*. Snyder asserts that a scriptwriter must "make it, say it with me now . . . Primal! . . . Primal! Primal! Primal!"[24]

For *Homo dramaticus*, storified emotions must be primal to be effective.

Boring stories that stir no emotions do not work, in Hollywood, religion, literature, or politics.

And here's the thing. More and more, our daily lives are defined by master narratives created by people who leverage the human need for drama. They mostly act in their own self-interest.

Every advancement in media technology has provided better tools to move the emotions of ever larger audiences with greater and greater ease. The digital age provides an arsenal.

Serving *Homo dramaticus* the primal emotional turns we crave is good for business and engaging for politics but, unfortunately, not what democracy and an informed public really need most. The democracy that best protects our liberties is most often boring. The philosopher Friedrich Nietzsche observed, "Democratic institutions are quarantine arrangements to combat that ancient pestilence, lust for tyranny: as such they are very useful and very boring."[25]

Humans have come a long way from existing in small societies listening to intimate stories from a trusted elder or religious leader. The storytellers who have an impact on people's lives today are products of media giants such as Disney, Comcast, and Fox, and the merging of media giants is becoming more and more common. A 2019 report from University of North Carolina professor Penelope Muse Abernathy explains,

> Over the past century, there have been three types of newspaper owners. The founders, who established iconic newspaper brands such as the *New York Times* or the *Chicago Tribune*, dominated the industry in the first half of the 20th century. They were succeeded by corporate newspaper managers in the second half of the century who built large chains, including Gannett and Knight Ridder. Now, in the last decade, investment entities, run by financial portfolio managers, have quickly assembled newspaper groups that dwarf the big chains of the 20th century.[26]

Local storytellers and the idea of news as a public good are getting left behind. That is what my coworker meant in the elevator, exhausted from sleepless nights, as he bowed his head and whispered, "I don't know if this is ever going to get any better."

Stories and Social Control

In their 2017 article "Cooperation and the Evolution of Hunter-Gatherer Storytelling," a group of anthropologists collected stories from different hunter-gatherer communities and considered the role the stories played. Most were about social control:

> We collected 89 stories over seven different forager societies. . . . Of these stories, around 70% were classified as pertaining to "social behavior" (i.e., prescribing social norms or coordinating behavioral expectations), more than any other category. . . . Therefore, storytelling in general may provide a mechanism to coordinate behavior and expectations, transmit social information and promote cooperation in hunter-gatherer camps.[27]

Gottschall notes,

> Throughout the history of our species, sacred fiction has dominated human existence like nothing else. . . . Based on what the sacred stories say, believers regulate the practices of their lives: how they eat, how they wash, how they dress, when they have sex, when they forgive, and when they wage total war in the name of everything holy. Religion is a human universal, present—in one form or another—in all the societies that anthropologists have visited and archaeologists have dug up. Even now, in this brave age of brain science and genomics, God is not dead, dying, or really even ailing.[28]

Religion is only one area where stories are used for moral and social control. Humans' storytelling nature can be seen at play today in increasingly profound ways as people ingest more and more stories, from more and more sources, at a dizzying pace. Cable news, social media, YouTube, blogs, podcasts, traditional media, popular culture, all of them with their own agendas vying for our attention, loyalty, and precious storytelling space in the *Homo dramaticus* brain.

Here lies an important difference to consider for the well-being of a society: the role of trust in storytellers. In a small-scale society, say in a hunter-gatherer tribe of long ago, a storyteller was likely to have the interests of a shared community at heart. In the information age, trusted storytellers are getting harder to come by. The digital age floods our worlds with narratives. It is important to ask if a given storyteller is being manipulative.

Are they pursuing selfish interests? Or are they a trusted voice trying to tell communal stories as public service?

One of the oldest character archetypes in human stories is the trickster. In a paper titled "Literary Prehistory: The Origins and Psychology of Storytelling," Michelle Scalise Sugiyama explains the historic social role of tricksters:

> A powerful testimony to the problem of social control and the use of storytelling to deal with it is the trickster genre, which is dedicated to identifying and condemning proscribed behaviors. . . . Across forager societies, the trickster is widely regarded as a model of bad behavior—as "the incarnation of greediness, lust, cruelty, and stupidity." . . . The traits of the trickster read like a laundry list of antisocial behaviors. He is a liar, a thief, and a cheat, using deception rather than cooperation to get what he wants. Lazy, greedy, and gluttonous, he is always trying to get something for nothing, always wants more than he needs, and always tries to take more than his fair share. He is also arrogant and incorrigible, never learning from his mistakes, and habitually ignoring the advice and warnings of others. Impulsive, short-sighted, and irresponsible, he doesn't think through the possible consequences of his actions, which often end up hurting him and others.[29]

If you put this book down right now and turn on a cable news channel, odds are very good you will quickly find trickster stories. Modern story makers will be self-defining themselves and creating their versions of cultural truth by making tricksters out of others. You will hear them pair the trickster with some primal emotion, most often fear.

For years, Bill and Hillary Clinton have been cast as epic tricksters in right-wing media, precisely as the archetype is defined in the Sugiyama study.

The left employs the archetype too. Maureen Dowd, in the *New York Times*, writes of slithering tricksters, "a vengeful President Trump and his writhing nest of liars slither past the Mueller report—for the moment."[30]

The infamous Republican strategist Roger Stone said the Clintons and the Democrats are the incarnation of greed, lust, cruelty, and stupidity. The infamous Democratic strategist Paul Begala assigned those traits to Trump and the Republicans. Both of them famously called politics "show business for ugly people." Both of them built careers on making political kings by using tricksters and controlling narratives, as *Homo dramaticus* powerbrokers extraordinaire.

*   *   *

I watched a trickster story, in the form of a tweet from the president, and the powerful impact it had on an individual life one day in August 2018 when I ran into Donna Richter at the YMCA. She worked as a copy editor at the *Times* for twenty-eight years and had been laid off a few months earlier during a wave of newsroom cutbacks.

Donna finished a set of leg presses and flipped her Tampa Bay Rays baseball cap, which was on backward, forward. She keeps her gray hair cut short, wears 1950s-style glasses, and almost always has this smile on her face that makes her look like some mischievous all-American teenager. Her face lights up a conversation. I feel like I could just freeze it and insert it into a Normal Rockwell painting of an excited kid with a new baseball glove crouched down in the outfield.

The feeling I get when I see Donna is one of meeting a friend who has gotten my back hundreds of times. In fact, having people's backs was her job at the *Times* before she was laid off. The official title for that is copy editor, and her copyediting skills are impeccable. "Copy editor" is a catch-all title for fact checker, grammar fixer, proofer, second reader, and general ass-saver. She achieved legend status in the newsroom one appreciative ass-save at a time over decades, drop by drop by drop in a huge bucket of ass-save. If a piece of reporting was not a fact, was hazy, was grammatically incorrect, not spelled correctly, or not AP style, it simply did not get past her desk.

That desk was between the elevator and my desk, so I passed her most days I was in the newsroom. We both are huge University of Texas Longhorn fans, so we flashed "Hook 'Em Horns" hand gestures to each other instead of waving. She knows UT football history like the back of her hand.

That day at the YMCA she told me she was staying healthy, working out more, and working part-time driving the range cart at a golf course.

Then I put my foot in my mouth.

"It's so good to see that there is life after the *Times*," I told her.

I saw the beginning a tear in her eye. She quickly shook it off. She told me how much she missed the newsroom and the sense of purpose that comes from being a journalist. What bothered her most was the rise of mistakes in the paper, mistakes that would never have gotten past her desk. It left her bewildered, heartbroken, and deeply concerned about the lack of interest in accurate reporting.

Exactly why is it that after nearly three decades as a fact checker, her iron-clad ability to maintain news accuracy wasn't an employable skill anymore? Was driving a golf range cart really the best use of this amazing journalist's talents?

We talked for a while, and I went to a treadmill. I watched cable news, without sound, on the bank of televisions along the wall as I jogged. This tweet from Donald Trump popped up on one of the screens: "The Fake News hates me saying that they are the Enemy of the People only because they know it's TRUE. I am providing a great service by explaining this to the American People. They purposely cause great division & distrust. They can also cause War! They are very dangerous & sick!"[31]

This was back when tweets like that from the sitting president were still shocking. The phrase "enemy of the people" has been used by national leaders before, by Lenin and Stalin to justify the systemic murder of dissidents, and during the French Revolution and the Third Reich.[32] It implies treason, a crime punishable by death.

I looked over at my former colleague, who had flipped her Tampa Bay Rays cap backward again and was back on the leg press. She has always been a really upbeat person to be around. She believes in peaceful solutions and the power of truthful, accurate information. She is obviously not dangerous or sick in any way. How did her career verifying truth and maintaining accuracy become inviable while a career that flaunted facts, demonized others, and spread social dissent led to the White House?

When I began working at the *Times*, Donna's job was secure, her skills were valuable to society, and the general public understood what she did and why it was important to both the community and a functional democracy. She could look forward to decades of personal growth and job security. But stories change, and when they do, relations between individuals and society change dramatically too.[33]

That day, neither of us really knew how much more destructive those presidential tweets would become.

Hannah Arendt's 1958 "Like" Button

In considering why people tell stories, political philosopher Hannah Arendt concludes that there is a fundamental human desire to take individual experiences and make them part of a larger community narrative. Left by themselves, life events have little meaning. Made public they help people find their place in society. For us humans, finding that place is key to our ability to survive and thrive.

Though Arendt's book *The Human Condition* was published in 1958, her ideas still ring true:

> Compared with the reality which comes from being seen and heard, even the greatest forces of intimate life—the passions of the heart, the thoughts of the mind, the delights of the senses—lead an uncertain, shadowy kind of existence unless and until they are transformed, deprivatized and deindividualized, as it were, into a shape to fit them for public appearance. The most current of such transformations occurs in storytelling.[34]

The power of Facebook's "like" button is that it fulfills that important human desire with a click, publicly affirming the user's private experience as a communal event.

In his book *Radical Technologies: The Design of Everyday Life*, Adam Greenfield considers the emotional power of a smartphone.

> We need to understand ourselves as nervous systems that are virtually continuous with the world . . . fused to it through the juncture of our smartphones. And what keeps us twitching at our screens, more than even the satisfaction of any practical need, is the continuously renewed opportunity to bathe in the primal rush of communion.
>
> Whether consciously or otherwise, interaction designers have learned to stimulate and leverage this desire: they know full well that every time someone texts you, "likes" your photo, or answers your email, it changes you materially, rewiring neurotransmitter pathways, lighting up the reward circuits of your brain, and enhancing the odds that you'll trigger the whole cycle over again when the dopamine subsides in a few seconds.[35]

Confession: if I post something I care about to Facebook, I sometimes leave the page open—ready for me to hit the refresh button to see if my "like" tally is growing. Is that sad, or I am just fulfilling a human need to watch my private, otherwise lonely, event become a more public, more meaningful part of my community?

People I have interviewed in nearly three decades of covering news have expressed that same need to me thousands of times. It is a fundamental reason people talk to journalists after a horrible family tragedy, or winning a Little League championship baseball game. People want to make their stories known to others, to make the stories part of the community, to help give their experiences a meaningful place.

But people don't need newspapers as much as they used to for that, and I find that personally distressing. Didn't *I*, your friendly neighborhood local newspaper guy, used to be the best way to fulfill that human craving to put your story out into your community? As I am out and about covering news, it still feels like people need journalists. They just seem to need us less than they used to.

"Good" Storytelling versus "Bad" Storytelling

Because storytelling creates realities in the social waters in which we humans swim, they inevitably become political. In his book *The Politics of Storytelling: Variations on a Theme by Hannah Arendt*, Michael Jackson writes about just how quickly and intuitively people learn how to "carefully select, censor, and misrepresent one's reality in order to get one's way."[36] In the information age, people are ambushed with stories and narratives, each with its own agenda. Some of those narratives we accept. Some we reject. Ultimately, Jackson contends, those choices form and reaffirm our worldview: "Storytelling fashions images of a 'singular universal': a nation and a person are thought of as one, a person becomes a name, an individual exemplifies an idea, and so on."[37]

But when is that a good thing and when is it a bad thing? If a spiritual leader 10,000 years ago sat people down and told stories to help them fit in with their community, it would very likely be put in the "good" story category. That elder very likely had community members' best interests at heart.

If a politician today promotes fear and exclusion of others, attacks objectivity, degrades institutions of knowledge, fosters a national culture of division for political purposes, and calls journalists enemies of the state, those stories would seem to fit into the "bad" category. But what are they called by people who agree with the politician?

In *Men in Dark Times*, Arendt provides a valuable standard to answer that question. She puts forth the idea that "the meaning of a committed act is revealed only when the action itself has come to an end and becomes a story susceptible to narration."[38]

For Arendt, a story can ultimately be judged as good or bad based on what final goal it is meant to accomplish. She considers whether a story is told in pursuit of individual power, wealth, and influence or to bring a community into a conversation that serves humanity, democracy, and the public good. A good story seeks to strengthen community rather than promote the selfish interests of an individual, company, or institution.[39]

In anthropological terms, a good storyteller tries to build healthy cultures by encouraging multiple voices in humanizing dialogue and debate. Their stories embrace and celebrate social complexity. A good story is told in the spirit of public service.

A bad storyteller tries to manipulate society with dehumanizing, singular truths. They try to push clear-cut protagonists and villains into the human storytelling brain to create a noble "us" versus a dangerous "them." They leverage primal fears of those storified villains to mold behavior. A bad story is told for selfish, greedy, and power-hungry gain.

I think Arendt's definition is a fair way to judge how the culture-building stories we consume may have changed as new digital platforms flooded our lives. It circles around to the question of intent on different media platforms and the power they exert on society. Arendt summarizes the profound social power of stories as they occupy indelible spaces in the social world. She contends, "No philosophy, no analysis, no aphorism, be it ever so profound, can compare in intensity and richness of meaning with a properly narrated story."[40]

It is worth considering whether stories narrated as public service should exist on platforms dedicated to selfish gain. Those different platforms send very different cultural messages and should represent distinct business models.

A Journalism Fairy Tale

Gottschall describes his book *The Storytelling Animal* as being "about the primate *Homo fictus* (fiction man), the great ape with the storytelling mind. You might not realize it, but you are a creature of an imaginative realm called Neverland. Neverland is your home, and before you die, you will spend decades there. If you haven't noticed before, don't despair: story is for human as water is for a fish—all-encompassing and not quite palpable."[41]

As I gained an appreciation for how stories define humans, I had to ask myself what my own person-defining Neverland stories are. There is an obvious one. When I interned at the *St. Petersburg Times* two and a half decades ago, I was told a powerful creation story, a mythic tale that assured me the *Times* was a place that sincerely strived to live up to Arendt's definition of good stories, that is, journalism that served a community in the interests of all. A place that created watchdog stories to act as a check on government power and human-interest stories that brought people and their community together.

It is a tale about sacred trust and broken trust. I can honestly say the story has become a guiding ethical force for generations of journalists. It defined my own professional identity when, as a young intern, I first flew toward the second star to the right and straight on 'til morning.[42]

4

The Ghost of the Sacred Trust

Here is a story that defined me in all the ways stories mold the minds of young *Homo dramaticus.*

It is a creation story about a newspaper. It embodies a legacy journalism ethos in ways that are both admirable and contradictory. Many of the details in this story come from the tireless scholarship of former *Times* journalist and historian Rob Hooker. They come mostly from his comprehensive history, *100 Years, St. Petersburg Times, July 25, 1884 to July 25, 1984.*[1]

*   *   *

Once upon a time, just over a hundred and thirty years ago, three men decided to start a weekly newspaper.

One of them, Dr. J. L. Edgar, owned a pharmacy on a dusty road in a tiny Florida pioneer town named Dunedin. The good doctor purchased a 2,500-pound cast iron printing press, had it shipped from Cincinnati, Ohio, and squeezed it into a 12-by-16-foot storage room.

It was in that room that the three men carefully set, one steel block letter at a time, a very first newspaper masthead—"West Hillsborough Times." It was published July 25, 1884.

Edgar had learned medicine treating wounded soldiers in Tennessee during the Civil War. He was balding with an immense, scraggly beard and mischievous eyes that time had dulled into a tired, solemn expression. He looked something like a cross between a tired wizard and a mad scientist.

The doctor was a hard worker. He often made rounds to patients' homes in a buggy drawn by a clever horse who could find the way home, unguided. This allowed the doctor to catch up on sleep at the end of a long day, slumped in the driver's seat. He never refused medical service and was often paid in chickens, potatoes, and homegrown vegetables.

J. M. "Doc" Baggett was the editor. He attended dental school in Philadelphia, worked as a part-time clerk in Edgar's pharmacy, and planned to open a dentist office next door. The ad for his freelance dentistry business read, "Teeth extracted without pain. A full set of teeth in twelve hours after extracting." Baggett had a sailboat and used it to make house calls up and down the Florida Gulf Coast, extracting teeth in kitchens and porches along the way.

M. Joel McMullen was the youngest, the humblest, and by far the handsomest of the three. McMullen had been trained as a printer in Tampa, and it was he who mastered the iron beast in the back room. He bathed the bed of the press in dark ink, then pulled a wooden lever to lower a heavy metal plate to press paper to ink to typeset, tediously printing one newspaper after another.

The three men were the first of what would become a long chain of important men with abbreviated names, many of whom were very bad at running a newspaper. After just four months, the trio threw in the towel and sold the printing press to a man who ran the general store five miles down the road in a settlement called Clear Water Harbor.

McMullen eventually went into politics. Baggett moved to Tarpon Springs, opened a restaurant, and became a municipal judge. Edgar continued to serve as a tireless doctor until the night of March 10, 1907, when his faithful horse brought him home for the night, stone cold dead in the buggy seat.

The general-store owner who bought the paper, A. C. Turner, had a moustache like Yosemite Sam and a face like Jimmy Stewart. Turner fathered twenty children and dabbled in everything—real estate, farms, a dairy, and shipping. He hired a gaunt-faced log-cabin preacher, Reverend C. S. Reynolds, as editor, and the newspaper struggled.

Turner sold the paper in 1892, about eight years after he purchased it, to another pastor, Richard James Morgan. It was Morgan who moved the paper to St. Petersburg, a little village that sprang up after the railroad reached the southern end of the peninsula in 1888. He eventually changed the name to the *St. Petersburg Times.* He only kept it for two or three years before selling it to a veteran newspaper publisher and politician from Cedar Key named J. Ira Gore, who up and died five years later, on September 7, 1900.

Around that same time, 1,900 miles northwest, in the middle of a bitter Dakota winter, doctors told thirty-four-year-old W. L. Straub he would probably die soon. Straub suffered from a bronchial condition and a crippled leg. On his doctors's advice, he fled south with his family for warmer weather. After a stint in Texas, they landed in St. Petersburg, and in 1901, Straub invested $1,300 in a newspaper. At the time, there were only two ads paid in cash. Both were for saloons. Straub, a fervent Prohibitionist, cut them both. He had two partners—A. P. Avery, a real estate man, and A. H. Lindelie, a fellow journalist from Dakota. Together, the three friends continued the chain of important men with abbreviated names who were very bad at running a newspaper. Straub's own daughter lamented that her father "always said he was the worst businessman in the world—and he was."[2]

In 1912 Straub threw in the towel and placed an ad in trade journals offering the *Times* for sale. It caught the eye of an Indiana publisher.

Risky Saint Poynter

Paul Poynter (full name Saint Paul Poynter) was a risk-taking investor who purchased or started ten newspapers in his lifetime. He was a Christian Scientist and shared Straub's diehard Prohibitionist politics. He was also a fervent newsman. His newsman credo was "The policy of the paper is very simple and easily stated. Our purpose is merely to tell the truth in the pursuit of the truths."[3]

Poynter purchased the paper at the beginning of an era of explosive growth in Florida. The paper grew along with it. He kept Straub on as editor. Together they were described as men of boundless energy and optimism, even in the darkest days of the Great Depression. In 1935, there was a fight over *Times* shares that Poynter had used as collateral on a loan for real estate ventures, causing him to temporarily lose control of the paper. Poynter sued fellow shareholders and managed to keep the *Times*, but eventually lost many of his other business ventures.

The First Ghost

Paul Poynter's son, Nelson Paul Poynter, watched and learned from it all. Nelson Poynter grew up in newsrooms. He had a front-page story in the *St. Petersburg Times* when he was eleven years old and was covering the courthouse for his father's paper in Sullivan, Indiana, when he was fifteen. It never occurred to him to be anything other than a journalist. He became the *St. Petersburg Times* editor in 1939 and its majority stockholder in 1947. The paper he inherited was deeply mired in debt.

Nelson Poynter was the opposite of his father. He loved martinis, disdained organized religion, and focused on one business only—the *Times*. He was a fiscal conservative who routinely made multimillion-dollar purchases in cash. Nelson is credited with building the *St. Petersburg Times* into a fiscally solid enterprise and with securing its future as a unique local news organization.

This whole newspaper tale really boils down to Nelson Poynter. He is by far the most important figure in the newspaper's history. He is the first ghost to whom this book is dedicated.

He is mythic because, upon his death in 1978, Poynter did something unprecedented that became the stuff of legend in the journalism industry.

Death Trick

Poynter was fervent in both his ethical standards for journalism and in his belief that the *Times* must remain locally owned. He wanted the *Times* to be left in the hands of a single journalist, a hand-picked chosen one, a man deemed worthy and someone who agreed that ownership of a paper is a sacred trust. To accomplish that goal, he took the extraordinary measure of giving his newspaper away to a nonprofit school for journalism he created. That school is now called the Poynter Institute.

In the biography *A Sacred Trust: Nelson Poynter and the St. Petersburg Times*, journalist and professor Robert Pierce describes Poynter's vision like this:

> Even more ingenious was Poynter's strategy for protecting his philosophy beyond the grave. He believed a newspaper should be run by one person with the authority but not the wealth of ownership, someone as dedicated to the *Times* mission as Poynter himself. He changed the company's bylaws to require that each succeeding chairman appoint his or her own successor in an inheritance of ideals if not of genes. So confident was he that he vested a monarchical power in those future occupants of his chair; the board of directors would advise but not overrule the chairman.[4]

The sacred trust would be passed to a king and live in a forever kingdom. A book review of Pierce's biography of Poynter helps explain the Nelson Poynter legacy:

> Here, at last, comes the explanation to the beguiling question as to how and why such a successful and acclaimed newspaper as the *St. Petersburg Times*, widely acknowledged to be one of the nation's best, could have emerged in a sleepy little town in Florida. The answer lies in the idealistic vision of Nelson Poynter... Poynter established the institution that bears his name—the Modern Media Institute (since renamed the Poynter Institute for Media Studies)—as a means of introducing higher standards in journalism.[5]

The *Tampa Bay Times* website explains, "Nelson Poynter bequeathed his beloved newspaper, then named the *St. Peterburg Times*, to the Modern Media Institute, a nonprofit school for journalists that would later bear his name. Poynter's gift ensured that the Times would remain locally and privately owned and thereby unincumbered by the pressures chain newspapers face."

Control of the *Times* would be in the hands of one person only, a man anointed to keep the sacred trust.

The founding story of the *Times* reads like a classic fairy tale, a tale of a dying man who created a kingdom cared for by a forever-benevolent chain of valiant journalism white knights anointed to become journalism white kings. It would be a place where the sacred trust that once lived only in Nelson Poynter's own beating heart would live forever.

That kingdom is a place dedicated to preserving truth in storytelling. A place where established ethical journalism standards would serve the local community into the future, safe from national media chains and stockholders.

When Poynter died, leadership of the kingdom passed seamlessly to his hand-picked successor, Eugene C. Patterson. In turn, Patterson named Andrew Barnes as his successor in 1988, and Barnes selected Paul Tash to assume control in 2004.

In a letter to *Times* readers dated December 26, 1999, Barnes explains,

> Having a publishing company owned by a school raises questions of who's in charge. Poynter set it up so one person would have the command, not a committee, because he believed a committee might not

make the necessary tough decisions. As CEO, I also vote the stock in behalf of the Poynter Institute. I was picked by Patterson, my predecessor, and in turn have named Paul Tash as my deputy and successor when the time comes.

"But what," Poynter was asked by his lawyer when he instructed that it be established so, "what if one of those guys wants to take the money and run?" To which Poynter is said to have replied, "You've got to trust someone."[6]

This fairy tale ends with Poynter dying in peace knowing his father's credo, "The policy of our paper is very simple—merely to tell the truth," would be safe from outside influence.

This book digs into the power of stories, and there is power in that one. When I interned at the *Times* as a twenty-three-year-old, that fairy tale guided my future. That kingdom was exactly where I wanted to live.

Unchained

The moral of that fable seems more relevant today than ever. Poynter gave his newspaper away to protect it from chain ownership. At the time, 76 percent of newspapers were chain owned, and he didn't want his to get gobbled up.[7]

That vision seemed even more prophetic in 2019 when a $1.4 billion merger between America's two largest newspaper companies, GateHouse Media and Gannett, sent alarms through the industry. The merger created a media chain that owned over 100 daily newspapers and nearly 1,000 weekly papers in the United States. Eighteen of those papers are in Florida. Large cuts in local staff and management were inevitable. A *Washington Post* article on the merger asserted,

> None of this is positive news for local journalism writ large, which is in an existential crisis. (The local newspaper business, in the blunt assessment of investor Warren Buffett, is "toast.") It's a crisis that threatens American democracy. Local newspapers, despite all their flaws and limitations, have been a trusted—and necessary—source of information for citizens across the country. . . . When local news withers, bad things happen, studies show. . . . People vote less, and they vote in a more politically polarized way. Political corruption has more opportunity to

flourish, unnoticed by the local watchdog. And municipal costs may rise.[8]

The executive editor of the *Tampa Bay Times*, Mark Katches, invoked the Poynter creation story in a column published the day after the merger was announced:

What does all this mean? It means that news is becoming more and more homogenized. Expect more newspapers and websites in Florida to look the same. Watch for more clusters of newsrooms to be run by regional editors, in some cases hundreds of miles away and with a distant understanding of each local market. Brace for more announcements about layoffs and cuts.

It also means that independent, single-ownership daily newspapers like the *Tampa Bay Times* are becoming increasingly rare...

And there you have it: Economies of scale . . .

Here's what you should know about the *Tampa Bay Times*. Life is not easy. Our financial challenges are real. We need subscribers in print and online. Advertisers, too. We also keep a sharp eye on expenses. But we are locally owned and locally made by people who live here and are connected to our communities. We don't send our work to distant places. We do it all here.

Nelson Poynter was the last individual to own the *Times*. He was a visionary who could see the growth of newspaper chains and took pains to keep the *Times* from becoming part of one. He created a school for journalists—now named the Poynter Institute—that could inherit the *Times* and keep it independent long after he died. That was 41 years ago. . . . It's not about economies of scale for us.

Mr. Poynter referred to newspaper publishing as "a sacred trust." To modern ears, that may sound a bit corny, but it still rings true to us. Our mission is to give you complete and lively coverage of this community—the only home we know.[9]

Complicating the Fairy Tale

On October 29, 2019, I was on assignment photographing the unveiling of a plaque at the new police headquarters in downtown St. Petersburg honoring twelve Black officers—Leon Jackson, Freddie Lee Crawford, Adam

Baker, Raymond DeLoach, Charles Holland, Robert Keys, Primus Killen, James King, Johnnie B. Lewis, Horace Nero, Jerry Styles, and Nathaniel Wooten.

When they were hired, those twelve officers could wear the uniform and badge of the department. But they had to drink from a separate water fountain and use a separate locker room. They could not patrol white neighborhoods or arrest white lawbreakers.

So on May 11, 1965, those officers, who eventually became known as the Courageous Twelve, filed an anti-discrimination lawsuit against the department in federal court. The officers put their jobs and families at risk. They paid lawyers' fees from their own paychecks. They endured pushback for three years before they won their case on appeal, on August 1, 1968. The suit was likely the first of its kind, and set national precedent.[10] Leon Jackson became the first Black officer assigned to an all-white neighborhood. Their story went largely unacknowledged and, for years, was not fully celebrated as an iconic local civil rights moment.

Jackson, the last surviving member of the Courageous Twelve, was honored at the dedication. Jackson wrote a book about the civil rights battle, *Urban Buffalo Soldiers: The Story of St. Petersburg's Courageous Twelve*. He explained how the story of their struggle "lay dead for over forty years. Ninety-nine percent of the people I knew didn't know anything about it." In 2007 Jon Wilson, a *Times* reporter, wrote an article that chronicled their struggle. After Wilson's article, surviving members of the Courageous Twelve were formally recognized by the mayor and given keys to the city. They began to get invitations to speak at events, talk to schoolchildren, and had a plaque dedicated to them in the old police headquarters.

Jackson sat with me and explained his feelings about why they did not approach the *Times* or expect coverage from the newspaper back in 1965:

There was lack of coverage of African American history back then. If you would note back in the '60s and so forth, they would cover all your major [African American events]. Like in 1957. You probably weren't born, but you probably read about African Americans integrating the school in Little Rock, Arkansas. That was publicized. Highly publicized. They publicized *Brown v. Board of Education*. To me, the news media would pick and choose what African American struggle they put in the paper. And to us, we thought that they wouldn't be interested in us because they throw a blind eye toward police officers, white police officers. And that's another reason why we were hesitant, because we felt that the news media didn't want to embarrass the police department for racism. . . And like I say, once Jon put it in the paper, it went like wildfire. Everybody was interested in it.

Listening to Jackson, I thought about words from James Baldwin: "The great force of history comes from the fact that we carry it within us, are unconsciously controlled by it . . . history is literally present in all that we do." My personal connection to the Poynter fairy tale suddenly felt complicated.

There were layers of truths.

On one hand, it was not as simple as Jackson's impression that the *Times* wasn't committed to local civil rights coverage. They were.

On the other hand, there was no denying the sincerity of Jackson's feelings about the officer's historic struggle going largely unnoticed.

The *Times* has a strong historical record on civil rights. They promptly endorsed the Supreme Court's 1954 *Brown v Board of Education* decision, apparently the first newspaper in the South to do so. In the early 1960s they dispatched a Black reporter named Sam Adams to cover national civil rights protests throughout the south, making him the only Black journalist covering the race beat for a southern mainstream newspaper.[11] The *Times* was "the South's most liberal daily newspaper" in 1961, according to preeminent southern historian Raymond Arsenault.[12] I know *Times* journalists who are proud of their contributions, and the contributions of their peers, to civil rights issues.

In the *Times'* 100-year history, written in 1984, then-staff member Rob Hooker balanced the paper's complicated history, "The *Times* was almost as segregated as the South, and in ways both subtle and flagrant it had treated Blacks as second class citizens for [its first] 75 years...For all its flaws, however, the *Times* was still ahead of other Southern newspapers. Editorially, no paper in the South called for racial equality earlier than the *Times*, and few covered the civil rights movement as fully."[13]

It can be important to both acknowledge a history of quality journalism and to account for what went missing—silences and exclusions in news coverage of Black communities in a century defined by segregation and racial inequality.

Silence can be hard to measure. For anthropologists who train themselves to identify and listen for social silences, they can be as important to
the construction of culture, power, history and heritage as anything that
can be measured, seen or heard. Sociologist Pierre Bourdieu described
those powerful silences as often unquestioned norms and practices: "What
is essential goes without saying because it comes without saying."[14]

Jackson described how he felt hurt and angry by decades of media silence. After Jon Wilson's 2007 article broke that silence, Jackson described
feeling respected, included, and acknowledged.

I wondered how media organizations that served as newspapers of record in segregated eras might both be proud of what they did cover, as well
as acknowledge legacies of social silences and better embrace how history
is present in all we do. I wondered, "How might I acknowledge those legacies as a journalist, personally?"

In his book, Jackson put the Courageous Twelve's lawsuit in the context
of other local historic events he witnessed: a sanitation strike of mostly
Black workers, which was a watershed event in St. Petersburg history, and
the *Times* Negro News Page, which began in 1939, ended 1967, and cir-
culated only in Black neighborhoods. He wrote, "It would be three more
years before sanitation workers would strike for a higher wage and better
working conditions. It would be two years before the *St. Petersburg Times*
ended its condescending and racist 'Negro News Page.' And it would be six
years before busing for desegregation began."[15]

After talking with Leon Jackson, I looked up as much of the coverage
of the lawsuit, *Adam Baker et al. v The City of St. Petersburg*, as I could
find. The *Times* did publish short stories on significant dates and about
routine court filings in the lawsuit. On May 12, 1965, a story on the bottom
of 1-B headlined, "12 Negro Policemen Charge Bias." On January 18, 1966,
a story on 1-B headlined, "City Denies Racial Bias in Police Jobs." A story
on August 2, 1968, on 1-B headlined, "Don't Confine Negro Police, Court
Rules." Two days later, on August 3, 1968, a story on 3-B headlined, "Ruling
on Negro Police Called a 'Dead Issue.'"

A few months after the historic ruling, on October 14, 1968, the *Times*
published a feature story on the front of the metro section about Freddie
Crawford, who was considered a leader of the Courageous Twelve. It was
packaged with a story suggesting *Adam Baker et al. v The City of St. Petersburg* created a barrier to better policing, and should be reconsidered.

The first story focused only on Crawford's ability to police Black neighborhoods: "Employing what he terms 'firm but fair' technique in his duties as a patrolman in the St. Petersburg Police Department, he has established a rapport with other Negroes." The story made no mention of Crawford's role in the recent historic civil rights case.

The second story was about how the lawsuit filed by the Courageous Twelve created a hurdle that could impede a new computer-assisted police zoning system, "New Deployment of Police Based on Zone Needs Faces Federal Injunction Hurdle." That story read:

Working with city computers and advised by IBM systems analysts, the Florida Bureau of Law Enforcement, the Police Administration Staff of St. Petersburg Junior College, and the International Association of Police Chiefs, local officers have come up with a new zoning system to combat the cycle [of rising crime].

But to go into permanent operation, the plan must first pass a legal hurdle raised by an injunction recently ordered by the U.S. District Court in Tampa.

Stemming from a three-year-old lawsuit filed by 12 St. Petersburg police officers, the injunction followed a U.S. District Court of Appeals ruling that banned racial discrimination in the operation of the department.

In the injunction, Judge Joseph Lieb enjoined Chief Harold C. Smith from practicing discrimination in assigning men or drawing up police zones.

The article continues:

James Sanderlin, attorney for the plaintiff policemen, has asked that no zone be allowed to compromise all Negro residents...But policemen who have worked on the [computer assisted] plan for a year say the drawing of its zone lines is scientific—not discriminatory.

"A computer has no race in it," said Lt. David Robinson. "If the court will take an intelligent, scientific view rather than be dogmatic about it, I don't see how they can fail to approve it."

The plan will be shown to Judge Lieb, and the police expect it to be approved.

The plan was not approved.

Complicated Narratives and Complex History

When he was president of the local NAACP, Darryl Rouson pushed the *Times* to diversify its board of directors. I ran into him on a sweltering July day in 2020 while photographing a Black business expo in the parking lot of a strip mall. As we both dripped sweat on the blacktop, we began talking about the history of the *Times*.

Rouson, who was elected to the state House of Representatives in 2008 and state Senate in 2016, remembered how he was approached by "very passionate African American reporters who said, 'Some of us are tired of being devalued, disrespected in the workplace,' and one of the issues that came up during the lament was the lack of diversity from the top down—not from the bottom up. And the top meant the Times Publishing Company board of directors."

There had been a failed push in 1994 to diversify the board. Rouson told me how one of the reporters gave him a letter addressed to Black staffers by then chairman and CEO Andy Barnes.

A DJ started playing hip-hop, and sweat ran down our brows as Rouson quoted the last paragraph from that letter verbatim:

> "To place a person on the board because of gender, race, or type who lacks substantial organizational responsibility and experience with those of us who have it would be to invite failure and frustration. This is not in the best interest of the *Times*. However, I will continue to push for diversity of race, age, and circumstance the best I know how. Sincerely, Andy Barnes." I memorized it so that as I spoke places, I could see the horror on people's faces when I repeated the words of Andy Barnes in writing. I mean, it's sort of an arrogant kind of thing to say. How dare you say it's not in the best interest of the *Times* to diversify? I still cringe.[16]

Several weeks later, in his air-conditioned office, which was decorated with framed and mounted *St. Petersburg Times* articles, Rouson told me the whole story.

> I was warned, when I was doing that struggle with the *Times*, that one thing you don't do is mess with the people who own the ink and the paper in town. They're like the 800-pound gorilla in the room. And I was warned that taking that on could have been to my detriment.

He explained how, in 2002, he quoted the words of Barnes's 1994 letter back to him and asked him, "Andy, when are you going to do it?" Barnes said he would do it before he retired. Rouson told Barnes that wasn't good enough.

He said the NAACP launched a full court press public campaign. Three months later, the *Times* announced that Karen Brown Dunlap, who was the Poynter Institute dean of faculty, would be appointed as the first African American on the Times Publishing Company board of directors. Rouson recalled, "Now my internal [NAACP] officers and board, we weren't very happy with that because the *Times* got a two-fer. They got a Black woman and somebody who was already there. We would have preferred they brought somebody in from the outside."

As he talked about the *Times* history and the Black community, Rouson also offered a lesson in life's inevitable contradictions.

Nelson Poynter, for all the contradictions, was a good man and touched a lot of Black people. My mother was a writer part-time. She would send columns to the *Evening Independent*, which, as you know, was owned by the *Times*. And I had two sisters who were Nelson Poynter scholars. They got scholarships for college. And one sister who was so impressed with journalism because of her experience with Peggy Peterman [a longtime *Times* writer and columnist] and the *Times* that she majored in journalism in college, became editor in chief of the *Hilltop* newspaper at Howard University, and eventually wrote and worked for *Congressional Quarterly*, which was owned by the *Times*.

I have great respect for the *Times*, great love for the people who work there and the reporters who toil there.

Poynter's ghost itself is as imperfect as the newsroom it haunts.

In Hooker's history of the *St. Petersburg Times*, written to mark its 100th anniversary, he notes,

Poynter was also a man of apparent contradictions. His editorial pages called repeatedly for women's equality, yet he saw no conflict in his membership in private clubs that barred women. ("Most men have very dull wives," he once explained.) He endorsed integration and civil rights, yet rarely, if ever, had Blacks as guests in his home. He championed labor unions and the right to organize, yet worked vigorously to keep unions out of his newspaper. He lamented the ravaging of

Florida's fragile environment, yet contributed to the Suncoast's un-checked growth by publishing lavish special editions that touted the area's virtues while glossing over its problems. He declared that his staff deserved only the best, yet let salaries in the newsroom get so low that some of his best reporters led an unsuccessful union drive in 1974.[17]

*　　*　　*

I was with a group of friends walking down the street on a Sunday morn-ing, just before a buddy's wedding. We were talking about newsroom struggles—financial uncertainty, continued lack of diversity, strained community ties. The conversation hit a somber moment, and we walked in silence. Boyzell Hosey, the director of photography, who is Black and had been at the paper for more than twenty years, broke the silence: "The legacy of the *Times*, by and large, in the Black community is not very fa-vorable. I think people acknowledge the quality of the journalism. I don't think the community feels like the *Times* has been an advocate for them. I hear that often."

We walked another half block. "But," he said, "at the *Times* we can still do work we believe in, and that is getting harder and harder. We do it with a strong code of ethics that hasn't changed, and the work is important. Who else is going to do it if we don't?" Boyzell pointed out a recent inves-tigative report that discovered a historic African American cemetery that had not been properly moved before a housing project was constructed. "Who else but us will do that kind of hard, expensive, local journalism?" he asked.

Despite all contradictions, the Poynter fairy tale fulfills, for many jour-nalists, the basic social functions humans crave. It builds an orderly cul-tural space, establishes norms and values, provides hope and meaning. It is a tribal tale.

In my interviews with *Times* journalists, "Poynter's vision" comes up a lot, often as a staffer explains how journalism became their life calling. The Poynter story explains both why journalists first wanted to work at the *Times* and why they remain committed to local journalism in difficult and financially insecure times. Many journalists in the *Times* newsroom, young and old, flip-flop between the narrative of Poynter as journalism hero and its contradictions. Most are still believers. The ethical standards *are* high. The work *is* uninfluenced. Brave and ambitious reporting *is* appreciated and encouraged. I have witnessed years of evidence that the journalism we practice is well intended on an individual level.

Embracing Contradictions and Complexity

So, there are difficult contradictions in our fairy tale; a set of sacred, fundamental journalism principles that are key to a functioning democracy lie rooted in a kingdom of white male patriarchy and a complicated, racialized history that is being examined more openly in America today than ever.

Fortunately, quality journalism and anthropology deal with contradiction and complexity all the time, ideally in every published work. If there are universal truths, they might be found in the frictions created between opposite worldviews. Media for a healthy society are not built on the simple, one-sided belief in one person's truth or another's lies portrayed in fairy tales and master narratives. Valuable media tackle sticky, complex engagements and the very important contradictions that make us human.

Individual journalists at legacy media organizations like the *Times* are sincere and diligent in their efforts to cover local communities ethically. The contradictions don't diminish all the hard work and real sacrifices that go into producing journalism that creates meaningful change. There is a higher journalism ethos.

In his book *White News: Why Local News Programs Don't Cover People of Color*, Don Heider acknowledges the sincere intentions and earnest work ethic of individual journalists. He worked as a journalist before becoming a media scholar and has observed "few overt dictums or conspiracies" when it comes to planning news coverage. He acknowledges that individual journalists are autonomous, but he also carefully documents how their freedom takes place within constraints of an organizational culture and powerful newsroom structures. His own career experience and subsequent research shed light on how the cultural hegemony of white male ownership often creates unequal, stereotypical, and ultimately racialized daily news coverage. He coined the term "incognizant racism" and describes what he means:

> This is an attempt to explain the consistent behavior of well-meaning journalists who, apparently without intention, continue to participate

in journalistic practice that systematically excludes meaningful coverage of people of color. News workers know there are important issues
in the community, they know the sources they might interview about
those issues, yet no (or few) stories are done. News decisions support
dominant views, reality is defined by the existing social order, and the
exclusionary decisions are routinely ignored... It is no longer accept-
able to produce the majority of stories about people of color in narrative
forms that continually frame them in terms of traditional ethnic festi-
vals or as deviant criminals. These communities are filled with hugely
divergent people, who work and live and love and struggle in the same
wide variety of ways as do people in any community. In these communities there are dozens, hundreds, thousands of stories to tell. It is time,
or past time, to go beyond the usual coverage.[18]

While the *Times* has prioritized diversity efforts in newsroom level hiring, its top executives—the company CEO and the top editor in the news
department—have always been white men. On June 24, 2020, in the midst
of historic social justice marches and calls for greater newsroom inclusion,
the *Times* announced internal executive promotions. A *Times* story published that day read, "The *Tampa Bay Times* on Wednesday announced the
promotions of two executives. On July 1, Conan Gallaty assumes the role
of president, with overall responsibility for the company's business operations, including advertising, circulation and operations. Executive editor
Mark Katches adds vice president to his title." Both executives are white
men. On January 13, 2022, *Times* CEO and chairman Paul Tash announced
his retirement. Gallaty stepped into the role of CEO and was expected to
become chairman when Tash retired on July 1, 2022.

A frequent theme in interviews with journalists and editors in the
newsroom is that there has been a lack of inclusive daily news coverage of the many everyday human-interest stories that are common to all
communities. The *Times* often publishes investigations that highlight in-
justice in vulnerable communities. It is impressive journalism. In 2016,
"Failure Factories" was Pulitzer Prize–winning work. The series showed
how the county school board stood by while five elementary schools in
Black neighborhoods were resegregated and denied promised resources
and then watched as their students failed academically. Boyzell Hosey acknowledges that work but, like Heider, says it is also important to consider
both the broader historic framing and ways in which depictions of African

Americans in news coverage are often skewed toward crime and victimization, rather than routine, inclusive, daily community reporting. It is also important to recognize social silence.

"People I talk to in the Black community point out that that we are also characterizing Black children as failing," Boyzell said. "And it's not just the big projects. These are powerful ways that we cover the Black community as the other, even when we have good intentions."

Heider frames his newsroom studies in hegemonic theory, which examines the ways a dominant culture maintains the status quo in power relations through the consensus of other groups. Hegemony is sometimes intentional but also sometimes unconscious, like the young fish wondering, "What is water?"

The communication scholar James Lull observes, "Owners and managers of media industries can produce and reproduce the content, inflections, and tones of ideas favorable to them far more easily than other social groups because they manage key socializing institutions, thereby guaranteeing their points of view are consistently and attractively cast into the public arena."[19]

In his newsroom ethnography *Social Construction and News Work*, William Schulte concludes that diversifying a newsroom is bigger than the intentions of individual journalists: "The public largely expects that the individuals who collect, produce, and present news are the most influential players in constructing those images as a reflection of reality. But the dominant literature on the pressures and influences on the American news worker over the years has indicated that this is simply not the case."[20]

There is truth to all that. My coworkers and I have absolutely built careers anchored in pleasing bosses and fitting into the newsroom by producing stories that fit the mold. There are strong, siloed departments in newsrooms. They are often headed by strong managers with very certain and established worldviews. Those managers look out for their own members. Those members succeed by fitting in. Upper managers want awards, so we often focus on work that might win awards.

All that said, in more than a quarter of a century working in newsrooms, I have never been told not to pursue a story for any reason other than it just wasn't a very good story. I have never experienced newsroom censorship of my work. I have never been directed toward coverage that would benefit the *Times* economically or politically. I can honestly say that the individual efforts of the journalists I have worked with have been in the sincere interest of serving communities, comforting the afflicted, afflicting the comfortable, striving for balance, diligently trying to be fair, and holding government accountable.

There are clear journalism standards. They are held to be sacred. But they are also deeply embedded in a complex hegemonic history that creates a very complicated present.

So, contradictions are hard.

Bruce Springsteen summed up the importance of mentally accommodating these kinds of contradictions during a keynote address at the 2012 South by Southwest music festival:

> Open your ears and open your hearts. Don't take yourself too seriously. And take yourself as seriously as death itself. Don't worry. Worry your ass off. Have ironclad confidence, but doubt—it keeps you awake and alert. . . . It keeps you honest. It keeps you honest. Be able to keep two completely contradictory ideas alive and well inside of your heart and head at all times. If it doesn't drive you crazy, it will make you strong.[21]

Ultimately, contradictions and complexity may just be an inescapable human reality. Any narrative that says otherwise is probably trying to sell something. Offering simplicity and clarity, good guys and bad guys, may be comforting and popular and profitable, but those narratives can also be dangerous and manipulative.

Reflections

In the end, weirdly and luckily, as facts complicated the fairy tale, the stories Poynter's ghost played in my own mind taught me a valuable lesson. Contradictions are essential to the pursuit of truth. We should make space for them in our heads, and our stories, and our hearts now more than ever.

Is Poynter's vision of fair and objective reporting just objectivity as defined by white men? Is it a white, male-centered tower anchored by a story on some sacred center ground where, from a privileged height, all is surveyed?

Or is the principle of reporting from the center and embracing dissenting perspectives the key to good journalism? Is it essential to a functioning democracy, above its hegemonic history?

Yes. And no. And so many other contradictions journalists should embrace every day.

The stories *Homo dramaticus* seem to need—ancient trickster stories, fables, fairy tales, Hollywood movies, Facebook posts, and cable news drama—rarely embrace contradictions or complexity. They have been structured, for tens of thousands of years, to create heroes (us) and villains (them). But contradictions are an important facet of human reality.

Balancing those contradictory ideas may not have been an advantage for *Homo dramaticus* living in small groups those 40,000 or so years ago as their brains wired for story. Simple social cohesion, clear good and evil, and one shared morality helped them succeed. Today, however, as we face tsunamis of stories and agendas in a globally connected world, accepting contradictions may become much more important to collective success, survival, and well-being.

They keep us honest.

More than that, embracing contradictions and sometimes unflattering historical context can make for better journalism models and better communities. Many journalists openly aspire to write quality "first rough drafts of history," a phrase most often attributed to famed former *Washington Post* publisher and co-owner Philip Graham. The bread and butter of daily journalism is often breaking news, daily coverage, and short feature stories. The immediate impact of that work can benefit when a news organization culture openly and systematically embraces broader, challenging perspectives by historians, social scientists and local community members who feel marginalized. As rapidly changing media technology continues to challenge and polarize the journalism landscape, there is a growing imperative for that context. Kyra Miller, writing for The Lenfest Institute about a project that organizes collaboration between Philadelphia area historians and *Philadelphia Inquirer* journalists, notes, "When reporting on breaking news or shorter pieces, journalists mostly focus on the immediate impact while historians tend to think more of the long-term trends and patterns through time. Without historical context, dominant news narratives can feel more groundbreaking than they actually are . . . This [project] can help readers understand that events don't happen in isolation."[22]

*   *   *

I struggle with a difficult personal truth. In Heider's terms, I may have practiced degrees of incognizant racism for many years. White men made the Poynter myth, and I, as a young white man, embraced it. I felt privileged into that story. I felt a noble purpose. It felt safe and emotionally satisfying. I felt warmly accepted into something special. I did not question. I produced journalism to please the system around me because I wanted to be accepted and successful. The Poynter story welcomed me into a mental tribe. Stories are carefully selective realities. Stories are survival mechanisms. They help humans choose what they want to believe.[23] I chose the Poynter story, hook, line, and sinker.

People create stories, and then our stories create us back. For many years I allowed my career identity, a huge part of who I am, to be made by the story of the Poynter sacred trust.

Poynter Ethics

Contradictory and complicated, Poynter's ghost remains important to a diverse range of staffers. It haunts us with cautionary lessons but also gives meaning and purpose.

So what exactly *is* Poynter's ethical journalism vision? Here are principles drafted at the Poynter Institute in the 1990s. They reflect the history of the Poynter Institute and the values instilled in reporters who came to work at the *Times*. These same principles have been adapted into many professional newsrooms and organizations, including the Society of Professional Journalists.

1. Seek truth and report it as fully as possible.

- Inform yourself continuously so you in turn can inform, engage, and educate the public in a clear and compelling way on significant issues.
- Be honest, fair, and courageous in gathering, reporting, and interpreting accurate information.
- Give voice to the voiceless.
- Hold the powerful accountable.

2. Act independently.

- Guard vigorously the essential stewardship role a free press plays in an open society.
- Seek out and disseminate competing perspectives without being unduly influenced by those who would use their power or position counter to the public interest.

- Remain free of associations and activities that may compromise your integrity or damage your credibility.
- Recognize that good ethical decisions require individual responsibility enriched by collaborative efforts.

3. Minimize harm.

- Be compassionate for those affected by your actions.
- Treat sources, subjects, and colleagues as human beings deserving of respect, not merely as means to your journalistic ends.
- Recognize that gathering and reporting information may cause harm or discomfort, but balance those negatives by choosing alternatives that maximize your goal of truth telling.[24]

That common core of shared ethics keeps the spirit of local legacy journalism alive. They define journalists as people beyond the bounds of their careers.

*   *   *

I remember hearing the news, on June 28, 2018, that a gunman opened fire in the newsroom of the *Capital Gazette* in Annapolis, Maryland, killing five journalists. A *New York Times* article published that same day gave an account of how the surviving *Capital Gazette* journalists responded:

E. B. Furgurson III, a reporter, stood in a blue shirt and khaki pants with his colleagues. He had decided to go get lunch around the time the shooting happened, so he was not in the building at the time.

When asked if they were putting out a paper on Friday, he said fiercely: "Hell, yes."

His colleague Joshua McKerrow, a photographer, said he was going to pick his daughter up for her birthday when he was called about the shooting. He rushed back. He had a hard time finishing sentences.

"Our newspaper is one of the oldest newspapers in the U.S.," he said. "It's a real newspaper and like every newspaper, it is a family." He began to cry. Then he added,

"We will be here tomorrow. We are not going anywhere."[26]

Before the shooting, Furgurson and McKerrow likely felt the same job insecurity that my friends and I have felt for at least a decade. They surely had the same kind of sleepless nights newspaper journalists everywhere have, waiting for the other shoe to drop, worrying that their newspaper will fold or that they will be part of the next wave of layoffs.

In my interviews with coworkers, I always asked, "What is your biggest stressor? What do you worry about at night?"

One version of the most common answer came from Graham Brink, a metro editor. It was not worries over how he would pay bills or that it would be hard to someday retire. It was this: "My biggest fear is that I will wake up one day and not be able to get dressed and go do the only job that I think I could ever really love."

BOOK 2
The Water

5

Brittany's Bowl

Out of thousands of book pages I read about anthropology and media and in more than 150 hours of interviews with coworkers, four sentences stand out. They are from Brittany Volk, a *Times* page designer (and amazing pastry chef).

One morning we were working together in the photo studio on a fashion shoot. We had an hour of down time as the model got into makeup. Brittany began venting her frustration about journalism on Facebook. She compared the quality journalism we produce to gourmet food and social media to junk food, or just plain bad food. Or something even worse than bad food. She dropped this: "We create freaking amazing content here. Facebook is a bowl of shit. When we put our hard work and great content into a bowl of shit, it becomes the bowl of shit. Are we surprised when people don't want to pick it out and eat it?"

Thank you, Brittany. This is your chapter. In it I ask what journalists and anthropologists have to say about culture, trust, and different media platforms.

Facebook doesn't feel at all like Brittany's bowl once a year as all the happy birthday love comes rolling in or while watching funny animal videos, looking at pictures from friends' weddings, and sharing in the life events of friends and family. When otherwise private experiences are shared with a community, they become meaningful. People make warm connections on Facebook.

It's the trust factor that makes Facebook smell bad. Russian ads. Secret algorithms guiding my feed. How did they know to put that ad up? Can they listen to me?[1] How is everyone's Facebook life so perfect? How much data do they collect on me? Who do they sell it to? Hillary Clinton ran a sex dungeon in a pizza parlor? Pope Francis endorsed Trump? Cambridge Analytica?

News media and social media are so very different. Why do they share the same space?

Under the banner of the *Tampa Bay Times*, information is vetted. Stories are produced with time-honored ethical standards from reporter to editor to copy editor. The news business model is based on trust.

Under the banner of Facebook, there are no editors. There has never been a process for reporting truthful information. There is no history of trust or truth-telling. There are no reporters, no accountability, no set standards. Yes, in the wake of the January 6, 2021, assault on the US Capitol, Facebook and Twitter made limited changes to their terms of service, fact-checking policies, and reporting systems, and they banned Donald Trump specifically. But it shouldn't take a physical assault on democracy to take the dangers of a social media–defined mediascape seriously. What about the countless daily micro assaults that came before and continue after?

In defense of Facebook, it wasn't ever set up to be a news media platform. It is a social media platform. Those are just two incredibly different fields. Maybe the lion's share of responsibility for the confusion of news and social media falls on legacy media organizations. It was they who allowed their business model and product to mingle with crap.

It has become very popular lately to beat up on Facebook CEO Mark Zuckerberg. He is often accused of attacking democracy, single-handedly destroying the media industry, and sowing social chaos. Zuckerberg explains his perspective in a 2019 guest column in the *New York Times*: "We've faced a dilemma trying to do more in the main News Feed because most of our community consistently tells us that they want to see more updates from their friends, family and communities, and less other content. For most people, social networks are still primarily about being social."[2]

Zuckerberg essentially said he does not want to be in the news business. Why do some in the news business want to be on social media platforms? It creates brand confusion on both sides.

That confusion is dangerous. One third of the world's people use Facebook, but the difference between news media and social media remains hazy. From Cambridge Analytica mining psychological profiles of tens of millions of Facebook users, to Facebook acknowledging in August 2019 that the company paid hundreds of employees to transcribe private audio conversations,[3] Facebook is not a platform that even pretends to provide news as a public service. The presence of legacy news brands on Facebook creates socially dangerous ambiguity about the very nature of professionally produced news. The merging of "the media" into one field has been a disaster for everyone.

Is broken trust in media now Zuckerberg's mess to clean up? Could he if he tried? If not, whose job is it? Who is going to publicly define the clear and important difference between social media and news media? What if news organizations *stopped* delivering content on Facebook and in 280-character pieces on Twitter? What if news organizations boldly and aggressively declared that those ecosystems do not measure up to ethical standards of trustworthy storytelling? Can news media shift limited time and resources to focus on technology that may benefit unique, independent business models? Is there a way to reassure consumers of news that journalism spaces are trustworthy in a world of greater and greater doubt?

I have put these questions to fellow journalists. The response is usually some version of what I was recently told by a coworker: "It's too late. We can't just ignore social media. You can't put the toothpaste back into the tube."

On a technological level, that coworker is dead-on right. In terms of human culture, I believe organizations can exert much more free will. It can be up to us to define trusted digital spaces more intentionally and rigorously. Ultimately, culture is still a human construction, and when people are intentional, they possess a powerful, and maybe the only, solution to today's media crisis.

Here's what anthropology adds to the ongoing search for solutions: evidence that journalists will survive and thrive as trusted local storytellers only if they clearly define and brand a unique and completely distinct digital local journalism field.

In the current media environment, trust is dead. It feels like if people live there passively, local news organizations lose, no matter what business model solutions they try. Democracy loses. Civilization loses.

That's Our Job!

During an interview, Zack Sampson, who was a metro beat reporter at the time, stopped our conversation to pull out his laptop and show me a graph on his Facebook page that had gone viral. It was an attempt to help people make sense of news sources and credibility (figure 5.1).

Zack told me, "We can't expect everyone on the planet to go to journalism school! We can't ask everyone who wants to read news to take Journalism 101. What, every person needs to stop their busy life and examine what is news to believe and what isn't? That's our job! Why aren't we just doing our job?"

There are significant efforts to teach Journalism 101 to the general public. An example is a flier posted in 2018 on the University of Michigan campus for a free class titled "Fake News, Facts, and Alternative Facts." The teach-out was offered as a public service by a group of journalism professors because they felt the political stakes were rising to dangerous levels. Here is the course description:

> How can you distinguish credible information from "fake news"? Reliable information is at the heart of what makes an effective democracy, yet many people find it harder to differentiate good journalism from propaganda. Increasingly, inaccurate information is shared on Facebook and echoed by a growing number of explicitly partisan news outlets. This becomes more problematic because people have a tendency to accept agreeable messages over challenging claims, even if the former are less objectively credible. In this teach-out, we examine the processes that generate both accurate and inaccurate news stories, and that lead people to believe those stories. We then provide a series of tools that ordinary citizens can use to tell fact from fiction.[4]

While it may be possible to provide Journalism 101 at no cost on a university campus, it is not reasonable to expect every citizen who wants to participate in being a member of an informed society to have the time, resources, and interest to decipher what is and is not trustworthy information.

The world has been here before. Distrust of information coming from new technology is nothing new to modern *Homo dramaticus*. Alberto Ibargüen, Knight Foundation president and CEO, notes,

> For a hundred years after the invention of the printing press, people had trouble figuring out what was true and how to handle so much more information. Today, we're living just that kind of "Gutenberg moment." The Internet has transformed what we know and how we know it and, therefore, how we think about the world. . . . [B]ecause we're just at the

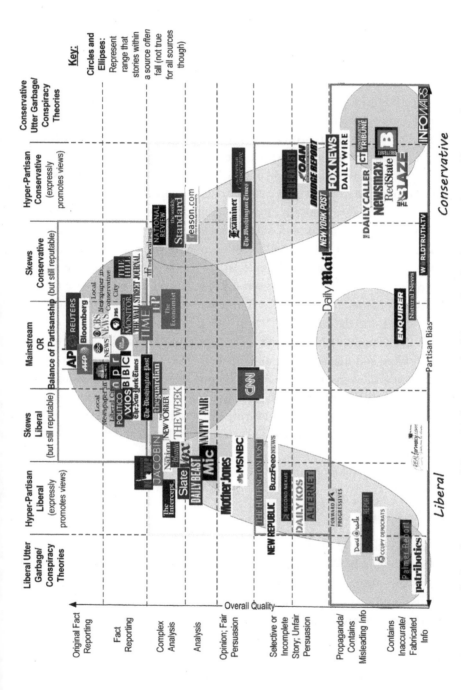

Figure 5.1. Media bias chart, 2018. © Ad Fontes Media Inc. Methodology and updated ratings at https:/adfontesmedia.com.

beginning of the tech revolution, it's not too late. We can still examine the effects of technology on our democracy and actually decide what we—individuals, press, platform, and philanthropy—can, and have the will to do, to shape the future we want.[5]

The death knell for democracy was ringing in the 1930s as well. In a *New York Times* column, Harvard history professor Jill Lepore describes a series the *New Republic* ran in 1937 called "The Future of Democracy."[6] The editors asked each contributing writer, "Do you think that political democracy is now on the wane?" Italian philosopher Benedetto Croce didn't like the question and responded, "I call this kind of question 'meteorological.' It is like asking, 'Do you think that it is going to rain today? Had I better take my umbrella?'" The trouble, Croce explained, was that the social world is not made up of external forces beyond human control; there are forces within people's control. He declared, "We need solely to make up our own minds and to act." Lepore concludes the column with advice for her own contemporaries: "Don't ask whether you need an umbrella. Go outside and stop the rain."

To Zack's point, "That's our job." The urgent need to create those culturally clear and unambiguous news spaces—places that restore trust in professional news as a public good—falls upon legacy news organizations. They are where the rubber hits the road in this age of distrust. It is journalists in these newsrooms who are bearing that weight. The onus is on us, as the pace of technological change today is unprecedented and the need for clarity is pressing.

But we are not doing our job.

On the Sideline

Here is a real-world example from a recent assignment. I had not photographed high school football in about fifteen years. Early in my career I steered away from sports photography to specialize on international news, features, and investigations. But since the latest cutbacks to the staff, we are all shooting everything. So there I was, nervously pacing the sidelines of Jesuit High School for the regional semifinal game against Chamberlain High. I hoped my dormant sports-shooting reflexes would kick in.

So here's how shooting a late game works: I set up a laptop in the press box, shoot pregame pictures, and send those pictures before kickoff, which is at 7:30 p.m. My second deadline to send pictures is 9:15, which should be around halftime. The third deadline is 10:15, which should be about when the game ends.

This game was a running game, which keeps the clock moving but makes for less interesting photography. There were no turnovers in the first half when I hustled up to the press box at 9:02 to send pictures. To be honest, they were pretty mediocre.

I ran back down to the field at 9:18. The third quarter had just started. It was 10–0, Jesuit, but Chamberlain was pressing down the field. In the red zone, on third and two, a solid hit on the Chamberlain running back popped the ball loose. I was standing on the sideline in a pack of Jesuit players, locked on the play, my camera's motor drive hammering rapid fire. A Jesuit defensemen recovered the fumble, held it above his head, and began to jump around. The kids around me started jumping too.

I looked nervously at the pictures on the back screen of the camera to be sure I got the pivotal play when I heard, "Oh that is just sick!" and "Damn, look at that!"

Jesuit players crowded around my shoulders, pointing at the back of the camera. One of them patted my back like I had made a play myself. He made me kind of feel like I did. They asked where the pictures would be posted later.

I had been ordered by my bosses to post to Twitter and Instagram, using a standardized set of hashtags. The idea was that we needed to build a social media following. The theory was that those followers would know the *Times* brand and then go to the website. Someday the newspaper might monetize that content, just like my colleague Lyndsey McKenna's mantra poster "Content. Engagement. Revenue."

But the Jesuit players and I were all having a little sideline moment together, and I just didn't want to give the team a hashtag for Facebook, Instagram, or Twitter. I wanted them to see my pictures on our company's site.

"I'm celebrating with you on the sideline. Come be part of our team too," I thought.

"Go to tampabay.com and click the sports tab, or just internet search *Tampa Bay Times* and Jesuit," I told them. I knew in that moment I was not going to post to social media. I also knew I risked being pigeonholed the next day as the old guy who doesn't get social media. I knew that was a bad label to have in a newsroom that will have more layoffs sooner than later.

But why should I train these students, the very demographic we are trying to reach out to, to go find my cool photos on Twitter of a game-turning point in a championship they will always remember? Twitter wasn't paying me or my employer. Instagram wasn't helping me balance work and family commitments on a late Friday night.

On the other hand, I know there are some really valid short-term reasons to post those pictures to social media, among them my employment status and the metrics my bosses hoped to see. Those reasons boil down to very real and important individual needs. But the long-term goal of reestablishing local journalism's brand as a trusted space gets sacrificed. We can win individual battles and still lose the war.

In the short term, it is in my own self-interest to build social media followers. If I get laid off, future hiring editors would look at my social media accounts. My current employers also want to see "innovation," and success on social media hits that button.

In the short term, social media editors at the *Times* are generally in their twenties. They have acculturated into journalism careers very differently than the generations of legacy journalists who came before them. Employer-employee relations are seen by both sides as short to medium term, or as one social media editor put it, "No one believes in the gold watch anymore." They are here to build skills that will get the next job. Looking outside the walls of the news organization, interacting with the digital audience, and accumulating social capital online is key to their success.[7]

In the short term, for the photo department, the perception of our value in the newsroom, which can translate to preserving staff jobs, is improved when we get good social media numbers.

But in the long term, studies show that if the Jesuit football players go to Instagram for my pictures, most of them will not even remember the *Times* brand, and an opportunity to build their trust in local media will be lost.

Broken Trust and Broken Brands

A 2019 study on news consumers' brand recognition found that "when a news story was arrived at directly, brand attribution was correct 81% of the time. However, correct brand attribution was much lower when news was discovered via search engines (37%) and social media (47%)."[8]

That difference in brand recognition was slightly greater than in a 2017 study that concluded that 78 percent of people who accessed news directly remembered the brand, compared to 52 percent who consumed news through social media and 50 percent for people who clicked on links shared by family or friends.[9]

The study, "based on a survey of news users in 35 countries, shows that using either mainstream or alternative news sources is associated with higher levels of trust in news. However, we find that using social media as a main source of news is correlated with lower levels of trust in news."[10]

The takeaway is that people associate content with the first place they find it. Expectations of trust and accuracy often appear to be set by the first digital platform people click on, whether Facebook or a newspaper's website. Their perception of what is and what is not reliably sourced news does not change as they follow links.

In their 2019 study, the investigators conclude,

We believe that the low levels of attribution from distributed [social media] sources come with two important substantial implications for media and communication research. The first relates to trust in the news. We know that people use news branding (among other things) to assign trust to particular news stories. It seems entirely plausible that if the link between the brand and the user is weakened, people's overall level of trust in the news might begin to fall. Furthermore, when reflecting back on news stories they have read, people might question the content of that story if they are unable to mentally link it to a news brand they believe to be trustworthy. Similarly, for those that inhabit environments that happen to contain lots of untrustworthy information, a weakened link between brand and content might ultimately cause trust to be misplaced. These concerns related directly to the current debates about misinformation in news coverage and their implications for democracy.[11]

It all boils down to more than just bad long-term business-model decisions. Culturally speaking, sending those football players to social media platforms for *Times* content sends mixed messages about who we are and what we do. I worried that I would be sending a message that we are just like everyone else who posts to Twitter. I wondered if our journalism would get lumped in with manipulative politicians, cable pundits, school bullies, and warring celebrities.

In 2018, social media sites surpassed newspapers as a primary news source in America for the first time.[12] That may well mark a worrisome tipping point. It is a trend that is being actively encouraged by today's newsroom practices.

*   *   *

Congrats on the fumble recovery, Jesuit. The very next play was a break-away touchdown run that put the game out of reach. You all went crazy again, and we looked at the back of my camera together to see the end-zone celebration. I also got some really nice frames of you all celebrating your hard-fought season together after the game. Come on over and see them at the *Tampa Bay Times*, a digital news environment with really great photography and ethical rules of storytelling. The rules are clear there. Remember our brand, remember meeting one of us, and know that trusted media spaces do exist. We share a community. It was really cool to be part of your high school memories, and thanks for making the night so much fun for me too.

Platforms and Trust

In the 2018 Edelman Trust Barometer, a 22-year-old annual trust and credibility survey, media became the planet's least-trusted institution for the first time in the survey's history.[13] But two interesting things also happened. Journalists' credibility rose substantially. Trust in media platforms fell. Maybe people were starting to recognize that journalism and social media platforms are not the same thing? Is there something legacy news organizations can do to better that understanding?

The study also found, "Confusion about the credibility of news is connected to the broad, wide definition of media that Trust Barometer respondents now hold. Some people consider all platforms to be part of 'the media'—including social media (48 percent) and search engines (25 percent)—alongside journalism (89 percent), which includes publishers and news organizations."[14]

An independent small media experiment supports the Edelman Trust Barometer findings. In January 2018, the Danish regional television broadcaster TV Midtvest told Facebook to stick it.

The Danish broadcaster ran a test to see what would happen if it stopped posting content to Facebook for two weeks, from January 16 to January 30. A story by Jessica Davies that appeared in *Digiday* explains how, at the time, TV Midtvest was receiving 40 percent of its referral traffic from Facebook, but its directors wanted to take a risk and see if they could wean it off social media platforms. After an initial drop in visitors, it experienced more stable and more engaged traffic:

> Unsurprisingly, the broadcaster saw a 27 percent drop in visitors to its site, a 20 percent drop in sessions and a 10 percent decline in pageviews. But the readers who remained averaged 42 percent more time within articles and read 12 percent more pages per session than they did prior to the test, according to the broadcaster. Readers also read more articles once fly-by Facebook traffic wasn't part of the equation. For example, the broadcaster used to post nine to 16 articles or videos a day on Facebook, and usually it was one specific article that would catch fire on Facebook and cause traffic to spike. When it stopped posting to Facebook, traffic was more evenly distributed.[15]

Nadia Nikolajeva, director of digital strategy at TV Midtvest, called it an eye-opening test and said, "I was expecting a far bigger overall drop [in traffic] after stopping publishing to Facebook. We'd become used to traffic being so unstable. But when we took away the Facebook traffic, our traffic became incredibly stable."[16]

The TV Midtvest experiment reminded me of something a favorite editor used to tell me when things got tough reporting on a story—"Fortune favors the brave."[17]

Know Your "Frenemy"

On October 25, 2019, Mark Zuckerberg suddenly offered to pay for news. A few days after being brutally grilled in the US Congress, Zuckerberg announced he would pay select publishers, including the *New York Times*, *Wall Street Journal*, *Time*, *Washington Post*, BuzzFeed News, Bloomberg, Fox, NPR, Breitbart, and others, for news content. In some test markets, Facebook launched "Facebook News," a tab located off the main "News Feed."[18]

An announcement from Facebook explained,

Journalism plays a critical role in our democracy. When news is deeply-reported and well-sourced it gives people information they can rely on. When it's not, we lose an essential tool for making good decisions. People want and benefit from personalized experiences on Facebook, but we know there is reporting that transcends individual experience. We want to support both.[19]

I question whether it is possible to support both social media and "reporting that transcends" in the same digital space.

The day the news tab test-launched, Mike Isaac and Marc Tracy reported in the *New York Times*, "Facebook and the publishing industry have long been frenemies: Occasionally they teamed up, but mostly they competed. Now the two sides have formed an uneasy truce."[20]

Within hours of Zuckerberg's announcement, there were questions. Facebook's inclusion of Breitbart in the list of "deeply-reported and well-sourced" media outlets that would provide "high quality" and "trustworthy" content spurred protests. Breitbart News is a far-right website. The former CEO, Steve Bannon, has described it as a "fucking machine" to crush political opposition. Bannon also sat on the board of Cambridge Analytica, was central in media coverage of the 2018 Facebook data scandal, and was the chief executive officer of Donald Trump's 2016 presidential campaign.

Questions about the secret algorithms Facebook uses to curate and prioritize news caused immediate concern. In the past, Isaac and Tracy contend in their *New York Times* article, the company's quickly shifting algorithms hurt the publishing industry: "Even small tweaks in Facebook's algorithms have an outsize effect on publishers' web traffic. So when publishers designed their corporate strategies around the whims of the Facebook News Feed, their traffic sometimes plummeted when Facebook changed tack."[21]

Some publishers were being paid, some were not, and details were not public. The payments were described in an NBC report as "millions of dollars over multiple years to select major media partners, including *The Wall Street Journal*, *The New York Times*, in addition to large metro area news outlets."[22]

Zuckerberg had a tough year in 2018. In the wake of the Cambridge Analytica scandal and heading into 2019 with hearings scheduled for both the US Congress and British Parliament, he had been enduring a painful run of bad publicity. His net worth fell $18.8 billion, to just $63.6 billion.[23]

In the wake of the favorable October 2019 publicity about supporting journalism, his net worth went back up to $71.3 billion, $20 billion more than he had at the end of 2018. He was the fifth-richest person in the world.[24]

But Facebook began 2020 by returning to the same defiantly permissive policies of 2018. On January 9 Mike Isaac and Cecilia Kang reported in the *New York Times* that "defying pressure from Congress, Facebook said . . . that it would continue to allow political campaigns to use the site to target advertisements to particular slices of the electorate and that it would not police the truthfulness of the messages sent out."[25] Ellen Weintraub, a US federal elections commissioner, responded the same day by publicly admonishing Facebook, saying its "weak plan suggests the company has no idea how seriously it is hurting democracy."[26]

Zuckerberg could afford whatever millions his company was paying over multiple years for news content on the Facebook News tab. He could probably afford to support independent journalism as a public good on principle.

During the kickoff event for his October 2019 announcement at the Paley Center, Zuckerberg sidestepped a question about how Facebook could make a claim to legacy journalism values, given the platform's sordid history and public unwillingness to fact-check intentional lies.

He said, "This is a different kind of thing" and went on to express the importance of a digital space dedicated to professional news. "People have a different expectation in a space dedicated to high-quality news than they do in a space where the goal is to make sure everyone can have a voice and can share their opinion," he said.[27]

It is telling that the chairman, CEO, and controlling shareholder of Facebook recognized the need for separate spaces in the digital age and that news media are nothing like social media. One shared space does not seem to be compatible with their mostly contradictory goals, individual benefit versus public good. Legacy news organizations should share that conviction.

An optional Facebook News tab, installed during a moment of intense global pressure and negative publicity, did not turn out to be the digital solution that changed the media landscape. It is possible that it was all just an effective publicity move.

But maybe there was some possibility that the effort behind Facebook News was not born out of self-interest during a difficult moment for Zuckerberg. In June 2020, the company opened Facebook News to all accounts in the US and added local news to the feature.

All the same, maybe newsrooms should not count on their frenemies to fix today's media crisis. Maybe those whose business models are broken should boldly cut their reliance on social media platforms and create unique, independent digital spaces for professionally produced news media themselves.

Just in case our frenemies don't come through as promised.

"Tweet or Be Sacked"

Media scholar Stephen Barnard wrote about Twitter and journalism practice in an article titled "Tweet or Be Sacked," a phrase thrown out to staff by BBC global news director Peter Horrocks.[28] Barnard considers the impact of a boss barking an ultimatum out to a news staff and concludes, no shock, that it was stressful. The *Tampa Bay Times* staff has been given that same message consistently in various meetings delivered with much gentler language.

Here is how Lara Cerri, a staff photographer, remembered trying to balance the "tweet or be sacked" mentality on an assignment. She was asked to shoot pictures for the *Times* website and print product as well as images for Twitter and video for Facebook.

Lara was assigned to photograph two back-to-back city candidate forums. A candidate from the Uhuru Movement, which is under the leadership of the African People's Socialist Party, attended the forums but had been excluded from an upcoming television debate. Uhuru supporters were angry. Their issues spoke to the historic community tensions in St. Petersburg. The forum was likely going to get heated. Lara felt that she had to juggle too many deadlines for too many platforms. She recalled,

Well, earlier I was told, "Okay, get something that can be used with the [photo] blog and get it in by this time, but also make sure you have a shot of everybody in both forums, which is a total of sixteen people because we need that for the future." Plus, there's a huge audience, so I wanted to get some audience participation, but at some point, before it was over, I'm on the floor with my laptop trying to get a card inserted because I've got a deadline to make. And then that's when things . . . that's when people started screaming, and I didn't have time to get in place to get any of it. Then, I guess, there was a bit of a shoving match, and some people left. Well, I got some pictures of a guy standing up in a chair from the back, but I didn't even have my right glasses on, and my card was in the computer. And then I get asked an hour later by email, "Do you have any video [for Facebook] of the antics that went on?"

I'm like, "Okay, first of all, nobody talked about getting video beforehand." . . . And so, the whole time I felt like I'm running and running and running. And in the end, I didn't even get what I needed. . . . So there are more and more assignments like that, and compare those to how I used to approach an assignment. I get more assignments now that stress me out, and they're still not effective. And I kind of feel like if I would just not ask people what I'm supposed to be doing and get back to what I know I'm supposed to be doing and focus on either just that photo or just that video or just that person because I'm the journalist who is there to assess the situation. The way we are actually having to do our jobs now has changed what our jobs are. It's really hard to stay true to what I know, being a professional now for almost thirty years. This constant kind of push, pull, push, pull is really difficult.

That is not to say social media is all bad news for journalists. Barnard's study also takes a thorough look at journalists' motivations for using Twitter. He identifies "eight practices employed by journalistic actors on Twitter: information collection, news dissemination, sourcing, public engagement, brief note-taking, field meta-discourse, other professional (inter)actions, and personal (inter)actions."[29]

All of those seem like great ways to use Twitter as a journalism tool—except one. "News dissemination" may well be absolute cancer for local journalism business models. First, disseminating news that journalists produce on other companies' platforms asks news consumers to pick through Brittany Volk's "bowl of shit" to find quality journalism. And to Zack Sampson's point, it requires all news consumers to take Journalism 101 to even know which pieces to pull.

Second, putting news out on various platforms confuses journalists like Lara in the everyday practice of producing journalism and introduces uncertainty in who they are working for, which platform they are producing for and when, and what their priorities and deadlines are.

So far, there is little evidence that social media referrals can be monetized by legacy news organizations. Yes, a platform like Twitter can act as a billboard, directing readers to a story. But as studies show, most readers do not carry brand recognition with them when they link from social media to the original journalism source. The studies also show trust is linked to brand recognition. When that connection is lost, the degradation of trust ultimately undermines journalism business models.[30] While an individual story may benefit from the use of social media as an advertising opportunity, the long-term cost of doing so is worth considering.

The cost raises the question of why legacy news organizations are paying professional journalists to provide other companies with content at the expense of work quality. It begins to feel like a downward spiral if remaining employed at a credible journalism company means having to participate on discredited media platforms.

Context Matters

In 1972, British art critic John Berger walked through a museum and stopped in front of Botticelli's fifteenth-century painting *Venus and Mars*. He took a razor out of his pocket. Placing it above and to the left of Venus, he began to cut. Berger, caught on film, calmly cut a square around Venus and walked away with her.

It was a staged moment and a fake painting. The BBC documentary cuts to an image of Venus among dozens of reproductions of European paintings rolling through a printing press. Berger, looking super-groovy in baby-blue polyester pants and a fat-collared vertical-stripe shirt, comes off like Austin Powers playing a sociologist.

"Tonight, it isn't so much about the paintings themselves," he explains, "as the way we see them now, in the second half of the twentieth century, because we see paintings as nobody saw them before. If we discover why this is so, we shall also discover something about ourselves and the situation in which we are living."[31]

Fade to black. Cue sitar music. Fade up title: *Ways of Seeing.*

But what does groovy 1970s-era sociology have to do with media today? News stories are just like those paintings.

We can bring Berger magically back, Austin Powers–style. In his quote we can just put "news stories" in place of "paintings" and update the sentence to this century: "It isn't so much about the *news stories* themselves as the way we see them now, in the *first half of the twenty-first century*, because we see *news stories* as nobody saw them before. If we discover why this is so, we shall also discover something about ourselves and the situation in which we are living."

Berger explains how the advent of cameras suddenly reproduced and moved works of art away from their intended places to be viewed in all kinds of new and unpredictable contexts. Religious art created to be experienced in cathedrals was suddenly seen on punk-rock T-shirts, refrigerators, and lunch boxes. Each different context redefined a work of art in unpredictable and meaningful ways. "The camera, by making the work of art transmittable," Berger asserts, "has multiplied its possible meanings and destroys its unique original meaning."[32]

Social media today do to professional journalism what the camera did to art. Berger's quote could be updated again: "*Social media,* by making *professional journalism* transmittable, has multiplied its possible meanings and destroys its unique original meaning."

Perceptions of professional news can quickly transform to #fakenews when it is placed on an untrusted platform.

Back in Berger's 1970s documentary, the camera cuts to the painting *Venus and Mars* in the museum, minus the cutout section of Venus. Berger observes,

> Botticelli's *Venus and Mars* used to be a unique image, which was only possible to see in the room where it was actually hanging. Now its image, or detail of it can be seen in a million different places at the same time. You are seeing them in the context of your own life. They are surrounded not by gilt frames but by the familiarity of the room you are in and the people around you. Once all these paintings belonged to their own place. Some were altar pieces in churches. Originally

paintings were an integral part of the building for which they were designed. . . . Everything around the image is part of its meaning. Its uniqueness is part of the uniqueness of the single place where it is. Everything around it confirms and consolidates its meaning.[33]

Art is defined by the context in which it is viewed.

Same with news. The meaning of a news story is defined by where it is found.

Social media companies benefit from professionally produced news on their platforms, but study after study shows that they are not trusted places. The meaning and intent of a news story gets completely redefined and reimagined as it moves from place to place in ways beyond the control of the news organizations that produced it. A story posted on an untrusted platform can easily become #fakenews in the eye of the beholder. Legacy news organizations should not expect otherwise.

Much of the digital resources at the *Tampa Bay Times* have been dedicated to generating success on social media. The goal is to build brand awareness and get click-throughs to the *Times* website as "Content. Engagement. Revenue." For years there have been vague promises of some revenue, someday. One editor described social media as a big funnel filter catching water and bringing it to the homepage. But that water moves through cultural contexts we can't control or predict. It is filtered through cultural spaces known to be untrustworthy, and it is changed along the way. Most of it doesn't funnel all the way through at all, and the bit that does emerges as something completely redefined.

David Fahrenthold started at the *Washington Post* in 2000. He won the Pulitzer Prize for National Reporting in 2017 for coverage of Trump's charitable donations and 2016 campaign. Here is how he describes the movement of journalism from independent legacy to a field tangled in social media:

When I started at the *Post* I tried to imagine my target audience. It was this person sitting at the kitchen table in the morning drinking coffee and reading news inked onto a morning paper. Then it became this person goofing off at work reading news on a computer. Now I imagine my target audience as a person who has just come through a tornado. They are disheveled, their hair is all messed up, and they have pieces of garbage hanging off them.[34]

Fahrenthold is an industry pioneer in effectively using Twitter followers for tips and story input. In investigating Trump, he famously put his reporting notebook out on Twitter and asked for collaboration. The individual story was made better for it. But like many journalists, he is perplexed about how to keep the public's understanding of the news industry's core values from being lost in the modern tornado of information.

Mediadome!

A rite of passage in anthropology grad school is to try to make sense of Pierre Bourdieu's opaque descriptions of social theories, like his description of habitus as "structured structures predisposed to function as structuring structures." Well, Bourdieu also wrote about the field of journalism and offers this complicated definition of "field":

> Here is a simple definition of the notion of field, a convenient one, but, like all definitions, a very inadequate one: a field is a field of forces within which the agents occupy positions that statistically determine the positions they take with respect to the field, these position-takings being aimed either at conserving or transforming the structure of relations of forces that is constitutive of the field.[35]

In terms of legacy media and social media in that definition of the field of journalism, I think Brittany said it much more clearly than Bourdieu: publish high-quality professional work in an online "bowl of shit," and the quality of the work is absorbed, undistinguished, into moral chaos and untrustworthy filth.

The rules and cultural expectations of trust in social media are followed without a lot of conscious thought. When people are put into a new environment, they instinctively do their best to adapt, survive, and thrive.

As I dragged my eyeballs through Bourdieu's theories about media fields and human nature,[36] a scene from a great 1980s movie, *Mad Max Beyond Thunderdome*, kept coming back into my head. I think it is a fair analogy.

Bourdieu himself offers, "I often say that sociology can be a kind of symbolic combat sport that offers a means of defense against the various forms of symbolic violence that can be exerted against citizens, in particular, and very often nowadays, through the field of the media."[37]

Thunderdome takes place in a post-apocalyptic, lawless desert world. Tina Turner plays the ruthless ruler of Bartertown. She is queen of a five-story metal death-cage dome. It is Roman colosseum meets MMA cage fighting. Bourdieu might say it is a field structure very predisposed to structuring social structures. The dome makes for good film drama because it is a literal and primal image of something universal, something like Bourdieu's ideas on how social fields work.

A motley crowd hangs from the girders of Thunderdome. They chant, "Two men enter! One man leaves! Two men enter! One man leaves!" A lanky, creepy emcee introduces the day's death match—Blaster (an iron-masked Goliath beast) versus Mad Max (Mel Gibson sporting long, spikey, metal-band, 1980s hair).

New York Times columnist Charles Blow described to me the current state of media with Thunderdomesque starkness: "People are not looking online for information. They are looking in their echo chambers for ammunition."[38]

Mediadome.

Blaster and Mad Max are suspended in harnesses that let them fly around Thunderdome. They grab weapons hanging from the steel girders—hammers, chainsaws, steel blades. Then they circle around each other and strike.

Thunderdome exemplifies Bourdieu's nearly indecipherable writing. He writes about why and how humans turn professional fields into "a combat sport." He examines the human need to pit extremes against each other in battles for power and control of the field, consciously and unconsciously.[39]

He assesses why people make Thunderdomes and the rules within them. He explores what the field of media has become. Bourdieu's work shows how power struggles in a professional field are as certain as the physical laws of nature.

> To be an agent within a field is to exert effects there which increase with the specific weight one has. As Einsteinian physics tells us, the more energy a body has, the more it distorts the space around it, and a very powerful agent within a field can distort the whole space, cause the whole space to be organized in relation to itself.[40]

Blaster, his face enshrouded in a metal mask, distorts the social space around him. He is the very powerful agent within the Thunderdome field who causes the whole space to be organized in relation to itself. Throngs of ragged spectators chant his name.

In Mediadome, Blaster is cable media and social media, master of partisan narratives, a lord of echo chambers.

In the Thunderdome, Mad Max is introduced by the emcee as "the man without a name." It really doesn't matter what his name is. He is only there to die. This is Blaster's field.

In Mediadome, Max is a wimpy local print journalist. The local journalist looks around, wide-eyed. It is not a place of any local journalists' creation. We did not invent the rules. We wonder how we got here, yet here we fight. This is no Hollywood script. We are getting our butts kicked.

The construction of today's Mediadome was benchmarked by the launch of Facebook in February 2004 and Twitter in July 2006. Maybe the foundations were laid when CNN became the first twenty-four-hour news channel in 1980, or when Fox and MSNBC launched in 1996.

Whatever the dates, Facebook, Twitter, and the emergence of the twenty-four-hour cable news drama cycle are massive gravitational elements in the field of "the media." They now organize the field around themselves, their agendas, their values, and their interests. Those interests are most often not in line with local journalism's time-honored goals of news information as a public good and bettering democracy and long-term civic interests. Their goals often reflect corporate profit, political power, and individual gain.

But it is their Mediadome now. It is the dome where this generation of local journalists epically struggle. Mad Times beyond Mediadome. As in the movie, the winning move is not to survive inside Mediadome. The winning move is to escape and build a better place.

*   *   *

In her resignation letter to the *New York Times*, delivered July 14, 2020, op-ed writer Bari Weiss asserts,

> Twitter is not on the masthead of The New York Times. But Twitter has become its ultimate editor. As the ethics and mores of that platform have become those of the paper, the paper itself has increasingly become a kind of performance space. Stories are chosen and told in a way to satisfy the narrowest of audiences, rather than to allow a curious public to

read about the world and then draw their own conclusions. . . . What rules that remain at The Times are applied with extreme selectivity. If a person's ideology is in keeping with the new orthodoxy, they and their work remain unscrutinized. Everyone else lives in fear of the digital thunderdome.[41]

Journalists living in the Mediadome are not experiencing hypothetical Bourdieu-inspired anthropology theory. Their lives, and the social consequences of that environment, are very real. The impact of social media–inspired tribalism is very real, from the left and the right.

Weiss laments in her resignation letter that "showing up for work as a centrist at an American newspaper should not require bravery."

Information Apocalypse

Mad Max Beyond Thunderdome takes place in a post-apocalyptic land. We may well be headed for a post-apocalyptic media world.

Technologist and media scholar Aviv Ovadya warns of an "information apocalypse."[42] He asks, "Which hurts civilization more: no one believing anything, or everyone believing lies? If we fail to take immediate action to protect our news and information ecosystem, we may soon find out. We are careening towards an infopocalypse—a catastrophic failure of the marketplace of ideas."[43]

Today's Mediadome is not a viable option for the future.

Ovadya, like many of us, worried about the breakdown of trust and construction of reality back in 2016. More recently he has worried about deep fakes, warning, "Advances in technology and artificial intelligence are making it easy to create audio or video content with potentially dangerous consequences, from making it appear that a world leader is ordering a nuclear strike to simulating your spouse's voice on the phone asking for a bank password."[44]

That technology is here today. A quick internet search for "deep fake" videos turns up frightening examples.

Ovadya underscores the importance of reclaiming fundamental legacy journalism goals in today's media world: "As individuals and institutions, we must ensure we trust the trustworthy and disregard the disingenuous. Representative government requires accountability, and accountability requires discerning knowledge. But technology is disrupting that edifice of knowledge, and if we don't act quickly enough, it may soon bring us past the point of no return."[45]

My journalism coworkers and I feel those dangers in very real and personal ways. If trusted digital media spaces are not created—and created soon—the social fabric of *Homo dramaticus* that evolved through stories and is reliant on trust could begin to unravel just as surely as newsrooms and journalists' careers and identities are unraveling now.

6

Master Narratives

Children grow into adults by learning stories, and so do nations and communities.
ROBERT FULFORD, *THE TRIUMPH OF NARRATIVE*

One young fish turned to the other and asked, "What the hell is water?"

Master narratives are water.

Master narratives order nations, empires, marriages, corporations, religions, political parties, homeowner associations, the mafia, tribes, and teenage social cliques.

In his book *The Triumph of Narrative*, journalist and critic Robert Fulford describes them.

> A master narrative always speaks with the confidence of unalterable and unassailable truth. . . . A master narrative that we find convincing and persuasive differs from other stories in an important way: it swallows us. . . . A master narrative is a dwelling place that encompasses our ideas about the history of our culture, its possibilities, and our own identity. We are intended to define our lives by it.[1]

People soak up these stories intuitively, and their emotional truths become far more powerful than facts. They are a means to grapple with a world that is far more complex than any human ability to understand it.

Plato wrote a famous allegory that describes the challenge of interpreting the immense complexity that surrounds us. We live as if we are chained in a cave facing a blank wall. There is a fire behind us, and we are forced to interpret reality from shadows projected on the wall as the real world passes behind our backs. I imagine master narratives as the stories we tell ourselves about those shadows.

As a young journalist I looked at the wall and imagined my world in terms of an emerging career identity. In the flickering firelight, I saw

Nelson Poynter's ghost, a tribe around it, and a noble life purpose. The shadows came together as a play in my mind, and I was the hero. That play is a fairy tale of the sacred trust, a master narrative that molded my perception.

Those master narratives work on a larger level as well. Master narratives make a shared morality feel normal, from an Egyptian citizen casually watching slaves build pyramids, to ecstatic dancers between church pews, to Joseph McCarthy shouting down alleged communists in the 1950s, to cheering one team's jersey color over the other's, to murdering priests in the Spanish Crusades, to a Virginia plantation owner raising his whip, to Native American potlatch ceremonies, to a Nazi with a hand on the gas valve, to a young intern at the *Times* dedicating himself to a career in journalism after hearing a fairy tale about sacred trust. The narratives are sacred and profane.

Fulford contends,

> A story that matters to us . . . becomes a bundle in which we wrap truth, hope, and dread. Stories are how we explain, how we teach, how we entertain ourselves, and how we often do all three at once. They are the juncture where facts and feelings meet. And for those reasons, they are central to civilization—in fact, civilization takes form in our minds as a series of narratives.[2]

Civilization takes form for individuals in a mix of storified facts, context, perceptions, and emotions. Here are three narratives about Thomas Jefferson, a founding father of American master narratives, and his relationship to Sally Hemings.

Narrative 1: Sometime between 1787 and 1789, Thomas Jefferson, author of the Declaration of Independence and two-term US president, initiated sexual relations with Sally Hemings, who was enslaved, when she was fourteen to sixteen years old. Jefferson was around thirty years older than Hemings. She became pregnant. Hemings had six children in her lifetime; four survived to adulthood. DNA evidence has linked descendants of the surviving children to Jefferson.

Narrative 2, from Jean Zimmerman's radio review of Stephen O'Connor's novel *Thomas Jefferson Dreams of Sally Hemings*:

> I have often fantasized about meeting the author of the Declaration of Independence, but after reading this novel I would love to know Sally

Hemings, the person who fascinated and beguiled him. She is one of history's numberless mystery women, but she comes thoroughly and thrillingly alive in O'Connor's telling. "I want us always to be as we are here," she tells her lover, "where we are only our eyes, our hands, those parts of us made for each other by nature, where our only words are the ones we whisper in the little caves we make between pillow, cheek, and lips." . . . Strip away the history in any historical novel and judge what is left. Stephen O'Connor's comprehensive research provides a scrupulous underpinning for the world of *Thomas Jefferson Dreams of Sally Hemings*. But more importantly, he succeeds in dramatizing a "joy of such terrific intensity that it is barely distinguishable from sorrow . . . out of the simultaneity of two contradictory impressions." The agonizing crashing together of love and slavery. O'Connor has the insight to put them side by side, and the result is searing and even sometimes beautiful.[3]

Narrative 3, from Michael Coard's opinion piece "President Jefferson: A Pedophile Rapist" in the *Philadelphia Tribune*:

Jefferson, the third president of the United States and the man given credit for drafting the Declaration of Independence—which hypocritically proclaimed "All men [and women] are created equal"—was not only a slaveholder. He was also a pedophile rapist. You want proof? OK . . . As U.S. Envoy and Minister to France, Jefferson began living there periodically from 1784–1789. He took with him his oldest daughter Martha and a few of those whom he enslaved, including James Hemings. In 1787, he requested that his daughter Polly join him. This meant Polly's enslaved chambermaid, 14-year-old seamstress Sarah "Sally" Hemings (James' younger sister), was to accompany her. . . . Both Sally and James were among the six mulatto offspring of Jefferson's father-in-law, John Wayles, and his enslaved "domestic servant" Betty Hemings. Sally and James were half-siblings of Thomas' late wife, Martha Wayles Skelton Jefferson (meaning Thomas and Sally were technically related). . . . Thomas Jefferson, after repeatedly raping Sally while in Paris, impregnated her. Her first child died after she returned to America. But she has six more of Thomas' children at Monticello. . . . The next time your children's or grandchildren's or nieces' or nephews' teachers lie to them about the great Thomas Jefferson, ask those teachers this: "How could a slave-owning racist pedophile (incestuous) rapist be a great man?"[4]

Could Hemings and Jefferson have loved each other? Or was he simply a racist pedophile rapist, not worthy of the glory bestowed on him? Belief in one story over others does not change what happened; it does something far more powerful, Fulford contends:

> The "master narratives" by which our society traditionally guided itself, from the Bible to the agreed-upon stories of beneficial British imperialism and European ascendancy, have been challenged and largely discredited . . . and yet humanity clings to narrative. We may distrust large-scale narratives that attempt to shape society, but our narrative drive persists. For all the reasons that fill this book, we cannot do without it.[5]

So, Jefferson the rapist or Jefferson the lover? Should NFL quarterback Colin Kaepernick stand or kneel during the national anthem? Republican or Democrat? Jewish, Christian, Muslim, Buddhist, Hindu, Sufi, or agnostic? CNN or Fox? People make those master narrative choices, and then those choices begin to make them back.

Culture, Narrative Shapes, and Kurt Vonnegut, Failed Anthropologist

In his book *The Invention of Yesterday*, Tamim Ansary writes,

> What any of us humans see as the whole world is just the world as we see it, whoever "we" might be. What we know as the history of the world is actually a socially constructed somebody-centric world historical narrative. There's a Euro-centric one, an Islamo-centric one, a Sino-centric one, and many more. How many more depends on how many collections of people on Earth think of themselves as "we" distinct from "others." Any two world historical narratives might have the same events and yet be different stories because the shape of the narrative depends on the teller of the tale. . . . The shape of the narrative is what it all comes down to in the end.[6]

Kurt Vonnegut, failed anthropologist, loved the shapes of narratives. He also recognized their power.

In World War II Vonnegut was held as a prisoner of war in Dresden, Germany. His war experiences were the basis of his classic novel *Slaughterhouse-Five*. When he returned home, he attended the University of Chicago and tried to get a master's degree in anthropology.

Here is how he has explained his thesis idea:

> What has been my prettiest contribution to my culture? I would say it was the master's thesis in anthropology which was rejected by the University of Chicago a long time ago. It was rejected because it was so simple and looked like too much fun. One must not be too playful. . . . The thesis has vanished, but I carry an abstract in my head, which I will here set down. The fundamental idea is that stories have shapes which can be drawn on graph paper, and that the shape of a given society's stories is at least as interesting as the shape of its pots or spearheads.[7]

Vonnegut was enrolled in a joint undergraduate and master's program, so when the university sent him packing, he had no degree to show for the years of coursework. He worked for General Electric as a technical writer and publicist and struggled for years to support his family, all while freelancing and writing future classic novels that helped define his time.

Vonnegut set out to graph stories across cultures, space, and time and developed a system for graphing the shapes of stories. The graphs in figures 6.1–6.6 are reproduced from Vonnegut's autobiographical book *Palm Sunday*. In the graphs, the X-axis is labeled "B" for "beginning" and "E" for "end." The Y-axis is labeled "G" for "good fortune" at the top and "I" for "ill fortune" at the bottom (figure 6.1).

This story line is about a person who is getting along fine until life throws bad luck their way. They find strength, learn an important life lesson, and overcome adversity. In the end, they are better for the journey (figure 6.2).

Vonnegut discovered that creation stories from many diverse cultures look like a staircase. Humankind begins in a wretched state, then divine forces bestow one blessing after another to raise people up (figure 6.3).

He depicts a Judeo-Christian story shape that differs from other creation stories, explaining, "Our own creation myth, taken from the Old Testament, is unique, so far as I could discover in looking like this" (figure 6.4). Vonnegut's story shape begins with a human created alone and helpless. God gives Eve to Adam, showers them with gifts, love, and the

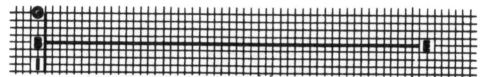

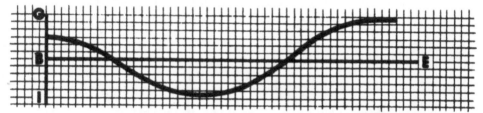

Figure 6.1. Kurt Vonnegut's "Shapes of Stories" graph 1. Illustration from Kurt Vonnegut, *Palm Sunday: An Autobiographical Collage*, © 1981 by Kurt Vonnegut. Used by permission of Dell Publishing, an imprint of Random House, a division of Penguin Random House LLC. All rights reserved.

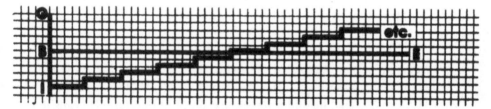

Figure 6.2. Kurt Vonnegut's "Shapes of Stories" graph 2. Illustration from Kurt Vonnegut, *Palm Sunday: An Autobiographical Collage*, © 1981 by Kurt Vonnegut. Used by permission of Dell Publishing, an imprint of Random House, a division of Penguin Random House LLC. All rights reserved.

Figure 6.3. Kurt Vonnegut's "Shapes of Stories" graph 3. Illustration from Kurt Vonnegut, *Palm Sunday: An Autobiographical Collage*, © 1981 by Kurt Vonnegut. Used by permission of Dell Publishing, an imprint of Random House, a division of Penguin Random House LLC. All rights reserved.

bounty of the Garden of Eden. He explains, "The sudden drop in fortune, of course, is the ejection of Adam and Eve from the Garden of Eden."[8]

Then something blew Vonnegut's mind.

He saw that the story of Cinderella has a nearly identical shape as that of Adam and Eve, only with a big, redemptive swoop at the end. Cinderella begins forlorn, and a divine agent, her fairy godmother, bestows gift after gift. Midnight comes, and it all goes to pot. But in Cinderella a prince comes, and the story ends with a big swoop up to good fortune (figure 6.5).

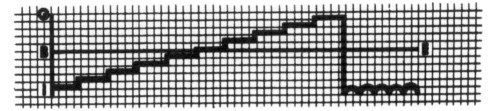

Figure 6.4. Kurt Vonnegut's "Shapes of Stories" graph 4. Illustration from Kurt Vonnegut, *Palm Sunday: An Autobiographical Collage,* © 1981 by Kurt Vonnegut. Used by permission of Dell Publishing, an imprint of Random House, a division of Penguin Random House LLC. All rights reserved.

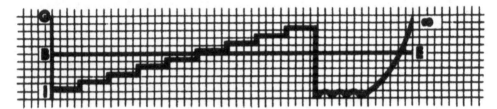

Figure 6.5. Kurt Vonnegut's "Shapes of Stories" graph 5. Illustrations from Kurt Vonnegut, *Palm Sunday: An Autobiographical Collage,* © 1981 by Kurt Vonnegut. Used by permission of Dell Publishing, an imprint of Random House, a division of Penguin Random House LLC. All rights reserved.

Vonnegut became fascinated. He theorized that the story shape was an anthropological equivalent of spearheads and potsherds. It was a template for Western storytelling and a representation of our culture. He calls it "Western civilization's most enthusiastically received story."[9] Someone is born to misfortune, accumulates gifts from fate or a supernatural being, has a moment of reckoning, falls to their darkest hour, and finds the hero within, or a hero comes to redeem them. Their happiness returns, and they are wiser and transformed by the journey.

Then he realized that in the New Testament, Jesus is the swoop at the end: "The rise of bliss at the end was identical with the expectation of redemption as expressed in primitive Christianity. The tales were identical. I was thrilled to discover that years ago, and I am just as thrilled today."[10]

That swoop is a nearly absolute prerequisite for any Hollywood script. It is deeply embedded in Western narrative story shapes that we all encounter most every day.

Maybe Vonnegut was on to something. Perhaps story shapes do reflect civilizations as much as ancient potsherds and arrowheads. We humans make the story shapes, but do those story shapes also make us humans?

Master Narrative Formulas

Hollywood films follow strict formulas. Almost all feature films still follow the very same Cinderella story shape Vonnegut graphed. Its pervasiveness is not a huge surprise, as cinema is the West's most iconic story form.

There are tons of books on how to write to that formula. Screenwriter Blake Snyder has broken down scriptwriting and most every movie plot into fifteen predictable, sequential "beats." Each one is a primal emotional turning point designed to keep us humans hooked.[11]

The beats are listed below. Anyone can take them and watch a Hollywood feature, any Hollywood feature. The beats will be there, in order. For quicker proof, do this. Look at the total running time of the movie. Divide it in half. Go to that point and watch five minutes on either side for beat 9, the midpoint. It is a scene in which an event happens to the main character that makes them realize they are all in. It is the point when they become fully invested in whatever the adventure is. After that event, there is no turning back. It is the point of no return scene. It will be there.

Blogger Tim Stout has summarized Snyder's fifteen formulaic beats.[12]

1. Opening Image—A visual that represents the struggle and tone of the story. A snapshot of the main character's problem, before the adventure begins.
2. Set-up—Expand on the "before" snapshot. Present the main character's world as it is and what is missing in their life.
3. Theme Stated (happens during the Set-up)—What your story is about; the message, the truth. Usually, it is spoken to the main character or in their presence, but they don't understand the truth, . . . not until they have some personal experience and context to support it.
4. Catalyst—The moment life as it is changes. It is the telegram, the act of catching a loved one cheating, allowing a monster onboard the ship, meeting the true love of your life, etc. The "before" world is no more; change is under way.

5. Debate—But change is scary, and for a moment or a brief number of moments, the main character doubts the journey they must take. Can I face this challenge? Do I have what it takes? Should I go at all? It is the last chance for the hero to chicken out.

6. Break into Two (choosing act 2)—The main character makes a choice and the journey begins. We leave the "Thesis" world and enter the upside-down, opposite world of act 2.

7. B Story—This is when there's a discussion about the Theme, the nugget of truth. Usually, this discussion is between the main character and the love interest. So, the B story is usually called the "love story."

8. The Promise of the Premise—This is when Craig Thompson's relationship with Raina blooms, when Indiana Jones tries to beat the Nazis to the Lost Ark, when the detective finds the most clues and dodges the most bullets. This is when the main character explores the new world and the audience is entertained by the premise they have been promised.

9. Midpoint—Dependent upon the story, this moment is when everything is "great" or everything is "awful." The main character either gets everything they think they want ("great") or doesn't get what they think they want at all ("awful"). But not everything we think we want is what we actually need in the end.

10. Bad Guys Close In—Doubt, jealousy, fear, foes both physical and emotional regroup to defeat the main character's goal, and the main character's "great"/"awful" situation disintegrates.

11. All Is Lost—The opposite moment from the Midpoint: "awful"/"great." The moment that the main character realizes they've lost everything they gained, or everything they now have has no meaning. The initial goal now looks even more impossible than before. And here, something or someone dies. It can be physical or emotional, but the death of something old makes way for something new to be born.

12. Dark Night of the Soul—The main character hits bottom, and wallows in hopelessness. The *Why hast thou forsaken me, Lord?* moment. Mourning the loss of what has "died"—the dream, the goal, the mentor character, the love of your life, etc. But, you must fall completely before you can pick yourself back up and try again.

13. Break into Three (choosing act 3)—Thanks to a fresh idea, new inspiration, or last-minute thematic advice from the B story (usually the love interest), the main character chooses to try again.

14. Finale—This time around, the main character incorporates the Theme—the nugget of truth that now makes sense to them—into their fight for the goal because they have experience from the A Story and context from the B Story. Act Three is about Synthesis!

15. Final Image—opposite of Opening Image, proving, visually, that a change has occurred within the character.

Snyder's fifteen beats can be charted as they fall in Vonnegut's Western story shape (figure 6.6).

Do the beats feel familiar? You have undoubtedly experienced them thousands of times. If you were born in a Western country, that pattern likely shaped some master narratives that helped you grow from a child to an adult. They form narrative patterns that have defined citizenship, built nations, and codified communities. They are also used every day in media and politics to manipulate people.

But actual life events don't follow a story pattern. Sometimes a hero isn't chosen. The villain isn't pure evil. The mysterious character who will change your life doesn't show up on page 12 of the script. A new, exciting world to explore doesn't open up. A love relationship doesn't show up on time to save you. There is not a definitive midpoint where you become

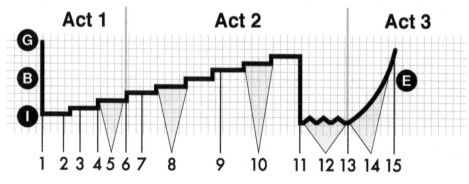

Figure 6.6. Blake Snyder's beats applied to Vonnegut's "Shapes of Stories." Adaptation of illustration from Kurt Vonnegut, *Palm Sunday: An Autobiographical Collage,* © 1981 by Kurt Vonnegut. Used by permission of Dell Publishing, an imprint of Random House, a division of Penguin Random House LLC. All rights reserved.

certain of your path. When you hit your darkest hour you may not get the advice you need from a perfect friend. A new, ingenious plan doesn't come clear in act 3. That last swoop on the graph, the one that carries you back up to victory and redemption, the one the New Testament added to our story expectations, may not come at all. You might get cut off mid-swoop. Did you fail in some way? Should you sit and wait for a prince to arrive? Do we start inventing princes? Do we get depressed if we don't fit the curve?

Story Slaves

Documentary legend Ken Burns recognizes that all humans are under the power of what he calls the "laws of storytelling." In a video interview he explains, "Jean-Luc Godard said cinema is truth twenty-four times a second. Maybe. It's lying twenty-four times a second, too. All the time. All story is manipulation."[13]

The laws of storytelling manipulate primal emotions and story patterns to control people. The storytelling rules taught in how-to books and university scriptwriting classes were born in human social evolution. Raw emotions, emotional truths, and perceived facts mix together in the shapes of the stories people make and in the way those stories make people in return.

Burns's documentaries are up to nine hours long and take on sweeping topics. It is fair to say he is intentionally tackling master narratives. Like Hannah Arendt's definition of good and bad stories, some master narratives may be bad if aimed at accumulating personal power and individual glory. Some might be good if aimed at long-term betterment of a community of people. Burns is unabashedly manipulative. He claims that his intentions are good, that the ends justify the manipulative means. But it is Burns, the storyteller, who gets to make that call.

Be Aware

Here is why the Western story shape, emotional beats, and master narratives matter more than ever in today's media crisis.

First, now that you know the formula, you can write a script, manipulate Western minds, make millions of dollars, or try to grab political power. But beware that others are doing the same. Story shapes, genres, and emotional beats are blueprints for *Homo dramaticus* minds. Watching *Pirates of the Caribbean* or a reality TV show about chefs may not be a problem. But in today's media and politics, when stories are used to recycle dangerous historical master narratives, we all need to be aware.

Second, please know that if your life does not follow the Western story shape, be kind to yourself. It is not you who needs fixing. Narrative scholar Gretchen Busl explains in a campus TED talk,

> Humans are socialized into stories both fictional and nonfictional. . . . That mental framework, it's built on the stories we are told— yes, by our friends and our family, of course, but primarily by the stories that are sold to us, right? By the mainstream media.
>
> We are storytelling animals. We love coherence, we love fidelity. That is why the media is able to tell us the same stories over and over again. In fact, we kind of like it when they do. . . .
>
> Over time, over a lot of exposure to different stories, you start to understand that if your lived experience does not match up to these stories being told and sold to you, that *you* are what's not normal. There's nothing wrong with the stories. There's something wrong with *you*. And then in that case it is very easy for politicians and for corporations to sell you something to fix you.[14]

When the reality of life as it unfolds does not fit Vonnegut's graph of the Western master narrative, if Blake Snyder's beats don't come on cue, it is not you that is mixed up.

Third, please think about master narratives as you consume media today.

There are more questions to explore. How did the rules of storytelling get made? Do people who know the rules take advantage of the rules?

What happened at the beginning of the twentieth century offers some answers as the birth of cinema created new media possibilities for *Homo dramaticus*.

Spoiler: it was an example of "bad" master narrative making.

The Birth of a Nation, Birth of Cinema Narrative

Many believe that modern filmmaking began with D. W. Griffith's *The Birth of a Nation*. The 1915 epic film is an overtly and purposefully racist rewriting of US history post-Reconstruction. It was written, crafted, and produced to promote a culture of white racial superiority. Problematically, it was also a masterful and undeniable singular force in the evolution of cinema.

Journalist Rachel Janik notes that *The Birth of a Nation* was "by all accounts the first American blockbuster, the first historical epic, the first Hollywood film to resemble what movies are like today. . . . It inspired the revival of the KKK but also galvanized what was then a nascent NAACP into action. It helped define what cinema means for American audiences. It was the first film ever shown inside the White House."[15]

Griffith has been called, by himself and others, "the man who invented Hollywood." The film was an epic leap that invented or perfected the use of the close-up, establishing shots, flashback, dissolve, continuity editing, parallel editing, and staging of actions on multiple planes. It was the first film to be shot at night, and the battle scenes were grander in scale than anything that came before.

Beyond his formative role in establishing the grammar of cinema, Griffith was key in creating the narrative scriptwriting formulas that became the cinema genres still seen today. In 1920 he established United Artists with Charles Chaplin, Douglas Fairbanks, and Mary Pickford. Together they were central creators of Hollywood's business model. They applied a three-act narrative formula that became film genres—the western, the horror film, melodrama, comedies, and action-adventure films. Those formulas made safe bets for film investors and are still used today.

It was those screenwriting standard structures and business practices that Walt Disney adapted to a tried-and-true sure-bet story, Cinderella, as he adapted it for the silver screen. Those structures embodied what Vonnegut recognized as "Western civilization's most enthusiastically received story."

After *The Birth of a Nation* was screened in the White House, President Woodrow Wilson reportedly declared that the film was "like writing history with lightning."[16] A closing slide in the film declares, "The former enemies of North and South are united again in defense of their Aryan birthright."

Birth of a national master narrative.

The shape of that Western narrative continues to self-perpetuate and define what it means to live in America. Hollywood may have removed the Klansmen from the horses and replaced them with less controversial heroes, but the narrative structure embodied in cinema, and all the ways it creates what becomes accepted as true, remain.

The Birth of Digital Politics

The early twentieth century brought technology to make movies, and that technology was immediately leveraged on an epic scale for purposes of political power and promotion of a racist and dangerous master narrative.

New technology in the early twenty-first century has also been leveraged for political power. Donald Trump, who ran a reality television show for fourteen seasons, adopted and applied new technology to historically known and well-tested political narratives. Trump knows the power of nationalistic storytellers. He hung the Presidential Medal of Freedom, intended as the highest civilian honor for people who have made "an especially meritorious contribution to the security or national interests of the United States, world peace, cultural or other significant public or private endeavors,"[17] around the neck of Rush Limbaugh, a politically biased, controversial, dogged master-narrative-weaving conservative radio talk show host.

Trump built upon his reality-television scripting skills to leverage new media technology to promote an effective political master narrative constructed largely on what came before in America.

The greater danger is just how easily a politician can hitch their wagon to master narratives on social media and ride to power today—and tomorrow. The presence, power, and persistence of a master narrative is greater than one person and one political cycle.

New York Times writer at large Amy Chozick put that same idea to Mike Fleiss, a pioneer of reality television as the creator of *The Bachelor* and *Who Wants to Marry a Multi-Millionaire*. She reports,

> These days, Mr. Fleiss does what American TV viewers are doing in record numbers—he sits glued to cable news, watching a panel of experts discuss the latest developments in the sprawling, intricate, unpredictable 24/7 show that is Donald Trump's presidency.
>
> "This is the future of the world and the safety of mankind and the health of the planet," Mr. Fleiss told me. He paused. "I should've thought of that one." . . .

Mr. Fleiss and other TV producers have watched—equal parts entranced and horrified—as Mr. Trump has taken the gimmicks of reality TV that he picked up on "The Apprentice" and applied them to daily governance.[18]

As I read Chozick's article, I remembered hearing about a group of teenagers in Veles, Macedonia, who made tens of thousands of dollars a month during the 2016 election creating fake news. I thought of how an analysis by BuzzFeed concluded that "top fake election news stories generated more total engagement on Facebook than top election stories from 19 major news outlets combined."[19]

In their 2018 book *Like War*, Peter Warren Singer and Emerson T. Brooking write about speaking to one of those Macedonian teens. This teenager directed fifty fake-news websites. Those sites created 40 million page views that made him $60,000 in Google ad revenue in six months. Singer and Brooking report, "There was one cardinal rule in the business, though: target the Trumpkins. It wasn't that the teens especially cared about Trump's political message, but, as [the teen] explained, 'nothing could beat' his supporters when it came to clicking on their made-up stories."[20]

The small-town teenager was basically just being a kid. He wanted money, girlfriends, and popularity. He had no interest at all in politics. Singer and Brooking relay the young man's point of view:

> "I didn't force anyone to give me money. . . . [P]eople sell cigarettes, they sell alcohol. That's not illegal, why is my business illegal? If you sell cigarettes, cigarettes kill people. I didn't kill anyone. If anything, the fault lay with the traditional news media, which had left so much money on the table. They're not allowed to lie," [the teen] noted scornfully.[21]

On some level, the Macedonian teenager is right. Yes, technology changed. But that doesn't fully explain the powerful shift in narrative forces that have moved some 300,000 local news workers out of their jobs since 2001. It doesn't explain the media-fueled rise of extreme politics. Something more powerful than just changing technology did that.

It could be that even the playwrights of master narratives are surprised at their power. Griffith claimed, "A terrific power lies in the motion picture. It's a power that is only too leanly recognized in these days. I'm constantly amazed and sometimes almost terrified by it."[22]

It could be that a cocktail of new technologies, *Homo dramaticus*'s hard-wired appetite for master narratives, and manipulative, self-interested storytellers large and small are to blame.

Ethical Storytelling

Kurt Vonnegut writes in the introduction to his novel *Slaughterhouse-Five*,

> I think about my education sometimes. I went to the University of Chicago for a while after the Second World War. I was a student in the Department of Anthropology. . . . [One thing] they taught was that no one was ridiculous or bad or disgusting. Shortly before my father died, he said to me, "You know—you never wrote a story with a villain in it." I told him that was one of the things I learned in college after the war.[23]

Ethical storytelling doesn't have to use emotional tricks or villains to lead people to believe something is right, wrong, good, or bad. That does not mean ethically told stories do not provide color wheels of emotion, show life's trials, or keep us on the edge of our seats. Ethical stories just avoid telling people how to feel about what happens in them. Vonnegut's story shape for Shakespeare's *Hamlet* and much of his own work again has the Y-axis marking ill fortune to good fortune and a dead straight line on the X-axis from beginning to end.

Good luck and bad luck are not charted for the reader or an audience. They are not told what is good fortune or bad fortune and are not told how to feel or behave. There are no tricksters. No sanitized heroes who will grow perfectly after overcoming their darkest moments. There are no built-up villains who become the only characters who cannot change or grow. There is no agenda. The stories tell of life events in all their contradictory, unexplained, dramatic glory. Ethical stories can deliver mystery, murder, love, and pain. But they don't say whether the events are good news or bad news, which characters are protagonists or villains, or whether this team or that one should win. Vonnegut holds that masterful works accomplish something that manipulative master narratives do not. They celebrate the truth of human complexity.

In a 2004 lecture, Vonnegut said, "We are so seldom told the truth, and in *Hamlet* Shakespeare tells us we don't know enough about life to know what the good news is and the bad news is, and we respond to that. Thank you, Bill!" He continues, "We pretend to know what the good news is and the bad news is. . . . If you think about our training in this matter, all we do is echo the feelings of people around us."[24]

In the information age more than ever, people echo feelings from stories all around them. Those stories manipulate us for all sorts of reasons that boil down to various political, economic, or social agendas.

In addition to being a failed anthropologist, Vonnegut worked as a local journalist at the Chicago City News Bureau. I would like to think legacy journalism values influenced his line of thinking because it feels like his ideas circle back around to explain the difference between the local journalism ethics that used to define my career and the broken trust in the media landscape today.

In his 2004 talk, Vonnegut said, "I don't believe in Heaven, but I would like to go to such a place and ask what is the good news, and what is the bad news just so I can be sure."[25]

If he were alive today, he could have his choice of cable news channels and social media silos to give him those emotionally simple and satisfying answers.

7

Unicorn-Killing Broken Trust

On October 7, 2019, First Avenue South in St. Petersburg, Florida, became a dividing line over impending impeachment proceedings against Donald Trump.

On the north side, outside Democratic congressman Charlie Crist's office, about two hundred Trump supporters waved signs and led chants supporting the president. Facing off with them on the south side, about three hundred people waved signs and led chants calling for the president's impeachment.

Maybe I shouldn't love covering protests, but I often do. Throughout my career, they have felt like democracy at work. I have found there is a lot of passionate and often optimistic energy in the air. When I started my career, walking around a fired-up crowd as a member of the news media felt like being on a border between clashing worlds and having a passport to easily jump from one side to another. Strangers would passionately open up to me about their core beliefs. I could walk right up to anyone and just start talking. People would generally be friendly because they understood I was neutral. I was there as a journalist. For most of my career, people seemed to trust that it was my job to be fair and listen to everyone.

I was there to make a single picture that represented the event as fairly as I could. Visually, I had a problem. There was a wide, busy street separating the protesters. The two sides were too far apart to easily put them together into one picture. If I only featured protesters on the north side, that sent a biased message. Same if I just shot on the south side.

I could go with two pictures for the print paper, but then which would run as a lead picture and which would be secondary? There might not even be space for two pictures in the paper. Two protest pictures also might be visually redundant. I needed one.

I decided I would start shooting protesters on the north side, then protesters on the south side—just to be sure I had something. I tried shooting from the north side of the street with a long lens, through protester signs, looking toward the south side. Then I crossed the street and did the same from there, shooting from the south side to the north side. Every picture had the same problem: visual bias.

This is the part I usually enjoyed most. I would roam, talk to strangers, and wait for something surprising or unexpected to happen. I hoped opposing protesters would move into a space that fit into a single camera frame. But that day was different. The rally just didn't have that exciting protest energy. When I talked to them, most of the protesters seemed sort of—grumpy. Approaching people felt awkward and strained.

I was jeered on both sides of the street.

"Who are you with?"

"The Tampa Bay Times."

"Oh, I don't have a parakeet. I don't need your lamestream newspaper!"

Pretty good line, actually.

A man cursed at me aggressively. I walked away.

I asked another protester for her name.

"I don't talk to the *media*."

"The media" sounded like it tasted bad on her tongue.

I asked a protester I photographed for her name. I was referred to a public relations specialist for their group.

"When did protesters get public relations specialists?" I wondered.

Eventually, an anti-impeachment protester crossed the street and stood next to a pro-impeachment protester. It made a solid photo of the two sides in one frame. They both were willing to give me their names.

I felt exhausted. Not from the heat but from having to justify my job over and over. I walked back to my car wondering if people we report on trust us at all anymore. I felt like the kid in PE class nobody wants to pick to be on their team.

It wasn't always this hard. I remember a time, not so long ago, when people at a rally respected how I was making my best effort to report from the center. I remember not being distrusted on both sides of the street. I remember not having to repetitiously convince people of my intentions. I don't know what happened to my passport to talk to anyone and have them trust me.

This happens all the time now, and not just at rallies. I justify myself and try to explain that centrist journalism is alive and well. I make my case sitting at people's kitchen tables, in emails requesting interviews, on assignment in schools, at the state fair, to people at parties when they ask me what I do for a living. Local newspaper ethics and my approach to my job haven't changed, but how I am publicly perceived has changed radically.

More than ever, people don't want to participate in stories because they don't trust "the media." That is a huge problem. It's a problem because people who don't trust media are self-selecting out of news coverage, perpetuating a cycle of distrust and exclusion. And it's a problem because the foundation of a future business model for local media outlets will need trust and inclusion from the communities they serve.

Newseum Plaque

Covering that protest reminded me of a day when I sat staring at a plaque that was on display at the Newseum in Washington, DC. The plaque says,

> The United States "maintains some of the world's strongest legal protections for press freedom," thanks to the First Amendment, says Freedom House. But more news outlets are aggressively partisan in their coverage of political affairs and the financial decline of long-established media organizations has diminished coverage of local news.

I stood and looked at the plaque for a long time. Seeing the words etched into a permanent museum marker was sobering. The plaque tells two truths:

One: "More news outlets are aggressively partisan in their coverage of political affairs."

Two: "The financial decline of long-established media organizations has diminished coverage of local news."

I stood and reread the plaque several times. Were those terms cause and effect? National media became partisan, and local media that did not change their ethical standards became guilty by association?

To the general public, news organizations have all become "the mainstream media." To the local journalists I work with and to me, the plaque might be more complete if it read, "More news outlets, *primarily national cable networks, talk radio stations, and internet platforms,* are aggressively partisan in their coverage of political affairs. *As a result, public trust in local media plummeted. That broken trust contributed significantly to the* financial decline of long-established media organizations and has diminished coverage of local news."

The breakdown of trust in national media quickly spilled over to local media markets and into the daily lives of working journalists. Local newspapers like the *Tampa Bay Times* got branded by a sweeping stereotype of "the media." I got branded, too, and it feels very personal.

The ethical foundations that define how I do my job have not changed since long before I was hired in 1997, but public perception of what I do for a living has changed radically. Most people no longer believe in balanced, centrist local reporting. They don't believe in me anymore.

The decline of trust is a disaster for local journalism business models. The Pew Research Center's "State of the News Media 2016" report describes a turning point:

> Though the industry has been struggling for some time, 2015 was perhaps the worst year for newspapers since the Great Recession and its immediate aftermath. Daily circulation fell by 7%, the most since 2010, while advertising revenue at publicly traded newspaper companies fell by 8%, the most since 2009. At the same time, newsroom staffing fell by 10% in 2014.... Coming amid a wave of consolidation, this accelerating decline suggests the industry may be past its point of no return.[1]

The decline continued. A Pew Research Center fact sheet states that newsroom employment at US newspapers dropped 51 percent between 2008 and 2020 (figure 7.1).[2]

The US Bureau of Labor Statistics paints a similar picture of the enormous shift in newsroom employment in the new millennium (figure 7.2).[3]

Another Pew report says that in 2018, US newspaper circulation hit its lowest level since 1940, while cable news revenues for national and partisan networks (Fox, CNN, and MSNBC) rose 4 percent that year. Digital revenues for all platforms were up 23 percent. More than half of that went to just two companies; Facebook took 40 percent of all digital revenue, and Google took 12 percent.[4]

The cultural impact of those legacy media losses and digital media gains could be profound on public perception of media as a whole. Following the money, it becomes clear that profits are most often not being made by providing news as a local public good. Profits are made by promoting partisan agendas on television and with algorithms that encourage echo

Number of US newsroom
employees by news industry

80 *(thousands)*

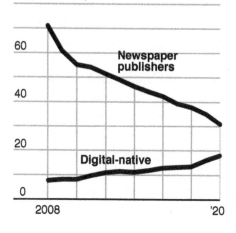

Figure 7.1. Newsroom employment at US newspapers has plummeted since 2008 as online news jobs have increased. *Source*: Elizabeth Grieco, "U.S. Newspapers Have Shed Half of Their Newsroom Employees since 2008," Pew Research Center, Washington, DC, April 20, 2020, https://www.pewresearch.org/fact-tank/2020/04/20/u-s-newsroom-employment-has-dropped-by-a-quarter-since-2008/.

Employment in selected information industries, 1990-2016

500 *(thousands)*

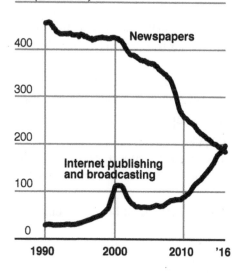

Figure 7.2. In 2016, employment in internet publishing and broadcasting surpassed newspaper employment for the first time. *Source: Employment Trends in Newspaper Publishing and Other Media, 1990–2016*, Bureau of Labor Statistics, June 2, 2016, https://www.bls.gov/opub/ted/2016/employment-trends-in-newspaper-publishing-and-other-media-1990–2016.htm.

chambers online. Fostering partisan drama is far more profitable (and easier) than producing public service journalism, but that partisan drama embodies Hannah Arendt's definition of bad storytelling: media that prioritizes the short-term interests of individual power and corporate profit. Today those stories flood the mediascape. The long-term interests of local communities and public understanding of centrist journalism are getting washed away.

Economically, the winners can hardly be blamed. Media profits are media profits. The social functions of stories, impact on democracy, legacy news values, and dissolution of public trust don't factor into their equations.

So yes, these are really dark economic times for local media. Yes, journalists are having much less fun doing their jobs since being lumped into a media stereotype that was created and is perpetuated by global and national media platforms. In this newsroom ethnography I consider a reality the charts and profit margins and circulation numbers do not—local journalists' deep commitment to their calling. There is no questioning the challenges and realities, but an ethnography of newsroom employees is an assurance that a commitment to local journalism is in no way past its point of no return.

Unicorn BBQ

In 2018, I was holding a plate of delicious potluck mashup at a family barbecue and talking to an engineering professor who was in his early thirties about the messy media times we live in.

He suggested, "How about a website that balanced news by topic?"

A reader could click a topic. A story from "the liberal press" and a story from "the conservative press" would come up together. That way, a reader could get both sides of the issue in one place.

I joked with him, "Yeah, man! That is such a good idea, they should have one journalist talk to both sides. Then they could just put them both into one fair and balanced story."

Without a hint of irony, his face lit up. That would be a great business model!

"And just to show how important it is to do that kind of work, they should not just put stories like that online—they could even print them on paper and put them on people's doorstep every morning!" I joked.

He got it right away and the topic shifted to navigating the information age. I gave him my "I've lost my journalist identity" spiel, that it is hard to do a job that many people don't even believe exists anymore.

He said newspaper reporters are centrist journalism unicorns.

Being a unicorn made me feel special again. But do unicorns have jobs?

He talked about how he sees "the media" as everything that gets thrown at us, social media, cable, and local legacy news media together. He is not alone. To anyone just going about their day and trying to make a living, it is one, big, noisy, confusing field full of self-interested and competing agendas.

The perception that it is all one field creates dangerous confusion. It is not one field. Social media are not local legacy journalism. National partisan cable news networks are not local legacy journalism. Sadly, centrist, balanced journalism efforts become lost signals in all that noise. In the heat of battles between the extremes of left and right, time-honored journalism ethics and the centrist narrative that defines local legacy journalists are lost to most of the public under forty. So is my personal identity. Lost readers, lost revenue, and technological challenges become symptoms of an underlying disease in our communities: broken trust.

Unicorn-killing broken trust.

The Immune System of Democracy

There is a journalism mantra about the press being the immune system of democracy. At the barbecue in 2018, it felt as if that immune system was going down. On January 6, 2021, democracy was openly attacked by a mob of Trump supporters.

In a 1972 Gallup opinion survey, 68 percent of respondents expressed "a great deal or a fair amount" of trust in media. In a 2018 poll, 42 percent of people polled said they trusted media. But that is not the whole story; 76 percent of Democrats expressed trust in media, but only 21 percent of Republicans did.[6]

Traditional media's shared ethical guidelines have been boiled down to the idea that you can put six reporters in a courtroom and they can sit through six hours of court verbiage and they'll come out with the same story.

Of course, perfect objectivity is impossible. But reporting can be a fact-based, honestly executed human endeavor to be balanced and fair.

But that kind of consistent reporting would be unlikely today with Fox, MSNBC, CNN, the *New York Times*, Reuters, and NPR in the courtroom. How their stories would play on Twitter and Facebook would be another matter.

Media scholars Pablo Boczkowski and Eugenia Mitchelstein write, "Journalists occupy a bridging position between two worlds that are structurally unconnected: the sources of news and the members of the audience."[7]

That perspective of traditional journalism is a lot like Hannah Arendt's explanation in *The Human Condition* of why humans have always told stories. We crave a way to take something that happened to us privately and make it a part of our community. Local journalism builds those bridges.

Thing is, we have Facebook for that now, right? Problem solved?

No. Social media do not fulfill critical social functions. Those platforms do not respect the power and importance of trusted information as a public good. A bridge made by professional and trusted journalists matters in the construction of healthy communal cultures.

Boczkowski and Mitchelstein describe how the decay of that bridge challenges "three fundamental roles of the news media in democratic polities: acting as watchdogs of the powerful in the public and private sectors, setting a common agenda for the citizenry, and serving as a space for public deliberation. . . . [T]hese roles are tied to the notion of information as a public good, in that it is nonexcludable and nonrivalrous, and thus potentially obtained through collective action."[8]

That millennia-old cultural value of storytelling pursued as collective action and a public good is critical. It is why the death of trusted storytelling lies at the heart of so many of today's challenges.

The late Supreme Court justice Ruth Bader Ginsburg told the BBC in an interview, "I am optimistic in the long run. A great man once said that the true symbol of the United States is not the bald eagle. It is the pendulum. And when the pendulum swings too far in one direction it will go back."[9]

But a pendulum needs a strong fulcrum in the center to function. A free press operating for the public good using time-honored ethics, one whose mission and ethos are well understood by the public, is that strong center. To Boczkowski and Mitchelstein's point, that fulcrum is also decaying.

Most small communities in the United States have 60–75 percent fewer trained journalists than they did in 2000. Many have none. There is simply less raw material to support the swinging pendulum democracy requires.

There is less raw material for the bridges that quality journalism builds. The remaining working local journalists are stressed, tarnished, and uncertain.

In an online journalism master class in 2017, *Washington Post* associate editor Bob Woodward, of Watergate fame, framed the stakes: "This is a time we're being tested. Let's tell the truth. Let's not be chickenshit about this. . . . This is the final exam for democracy."[10] Woodward points out that this test is not just of reporters and writers but of everyone—scientists, businesspeople, laborers, lawyers, public officials, consumers, and parents. Quality journalism is critical to the social health of the communities in which everyone lives and fundamental to the checks and balances in society.[11]

Reporters Without Borders, an international nonprofit organization that monitors press freedom around the world, ranked the United States 45th out of 180 countries in its 2018 World Press Freedom Index, just below South Korea and Romania. The accompanying report, "Hatred of Journalism Threatens Democracies," notes, "More and more democratically elected leaders no longer see the media as part of democracy's essential underpinning, but as an adversary to which they openly display their aversion. The United States, the country of the First Amendment, has fallen again in the Index under Donald Trump, this time two places to 45th. Trump has referred to reporters as 'enemies of the people,' the term once used by Joseph Stalin."[12]

Same Story, New Technology

Media turmoil is nothing new. The idea that people in power do not like being under a critical media lens is nothing new. But the communication technologies available to adversaries of centrist journalism are new, and they present real dangers.

Journalists are fond of Thomas Jefferson quotes that defend freedom of the press, but Jefferson's contradictions on press freedom are as real as his contradictions on democracy, human rights, and slavery. A *New York Times* editorial describes a difference between Jefferson as an upstart rebel signing the Declaration of Independence versus Jefferson under pressure from the media as president:

In 1787, the year the Constitution was adopted, Thomas Jefferson famously wrote to a friend, "Were it left to me to decide whether we should have a government without newspapers, or newspapers without a government, I should not hesitate a moment to prefer the latter." That's how he felt before he became president, anyway. Twenty years later, after enduring the oversight of the press from inside the White House, he was less sure of its value. "Nothing can now be believed which is seen in a newspaper," he wrote. "Truth itself becomes suspicious by being put into that polluted vehicle."[13]

People in power have never liked watchdog journalism. I wonder what America would be like today if Jefferson had a Twitter account.

Bees in a Bottle

In January 2020, *Orlando Sentinel* journalist Scott Maxwell was offered a buyout of eight months' salary. A large hedge fund had just bought a sizable stake in the Tribune Company, which owns the *Sentinel*. Maxwell put his choice like this:

> So this buyout comes with an extra, not-so-subtle incentive: *Take a pile of money . . . or risk getting canned in a few months anyway. . . .* [W]ith new clouds looming, this offer to leave is probably the most attractive yet.
>
> Yet I have no plans to take it.
>
> For a simple reason: I love this job with a ridiculous, white-hot passion.
>
> It's both a blessing and a curse.
>
> My coffee pot is set to start percolating at 4:50 each morning. By 5, my computer is usually fired up, and so am I.
>
> I like diving into local issues, asking questions and sharing information.
>
> Let the rest of the world obsess over Donald Trump and Hillary Clinton. I want to know who's cutting deals with the mayor, who's trying to get a no-bid contract at the airport and why the state has a 10-year waiting list for therapy and other services for special-needs children.
>
> I relish meeting the people who work tirelessly to make this community a better place to live and sharing their stories.
>
> And here's the thing you should know: I am not alone.[14]

Maxwell's decision may seem like an odd choice, given all that is going on in the media industry. CareerCast rated newspaper reporter as the third worst of 224 jobs in its 2019 annual survey, just ahead of taxi driver and logger.[15]

Community journalists are not foolish martyrs or desperate unemployables. They stay in spite of it all because they believe there is a basic, primal, and important need for local storytellers in their communities. They are motivated by a millennia-old human instinct that was born in the still-mysterious dawn of culture. There are so many local journalists who simply won't quit because that drive is too deeply embedded in their human nature to be hijacked by short-term-focused, greedy national and global forces. Those journalists' very real, very primal local storytelling instinct is far stronger than eight months' salary, all the fear, and all the uncertainty.

In his 1901 book *The Life of the Bee*, Nobel laureate Maurice Maeterlinck describes an experiment that illustrates how difficult it can be to overcome hard-wired instincts.

If you place in a bottle half a dozen bees and the same number of flies, and lay the bottle down horizontally, with its base to the window, you will find that the bees will persist, till they die of exhaustion or hunger, in their endeavor to discover an issue through the glass; while the flies, in less than two minutes, will all have sallied forth through the neck on the opposite side.... [T]urn the transparent sphere twenty times, if you will, holding now the base, now the neck, to the window, and you will find the bees turn twenty times with it, so as always to face the light. It is their love of light, it is their very intelligence, that is their undoing in this experiment.... They evidently imagine the issue from every prison must be where the light shines clearest; and they act in accordance, and persist in too logical action. To them the glass is a supernatural mystery they have never met with in nature; they have no experience with this suddenly impenetrable atmosphere; and, the greater their intelligence, the more inadmissible, more incomprehensible, will the strange obstacle appear. Whereas the feather-brained flies, careless of logic as of the enigma of crystal, disregarding the call of light, flutter wildly hither and thither, and meeting here the good fortune that often waits on the simple, who find salvation there where the wiser will perish, necessarily end by discovering the friendly opening that restores their liberty to them.[16]

Wave of layoffs after wave of layoffs, I smack against the glass. It hurts my head. I shake off confusion and ask myself the same question—"Why don't I just quit?" There are so many easier ways to make a living. I, like many journalist friends I care deeply about, have been slamming against that invisible glass for years now. We see light on the other side of the bottle as freedom of the press, healthy democracy, and a deeply rooted societal need for local storytelling. There is something primal in our nature that tells us to steer by that light and to fight in vain against the mysterious barriers that surrounds our careers.

My heartfelt purpose in examining the bottle—vexing problems that trap well-intentioned local journalists—is to seek solutions to today's media challenges. The hope is to be a bit more like the flies in Maeterlinck's experiment, simple and exploratory. And free.

8

The Damned-Dirty-Trick Story

An American Master Narrative

The great force of history comes from the fact that we carry it within us,
are unconsciously controlled by it in many ways, and history is literally
present in all that we do.

JAMES BALDWIN

Lying on my couch on a bitterly cold Michigan winter day, I dragged my
eyeballs through one of the densest and dullest books I have ever read.
Unexpectedly, tears streamed down my cheeks.

The book was *From Prescription to Persuasion: Manipulation of Seventeenth Century Virginia Economy*. It was written by my uncle, John C.
Rainbolt, a historian and the second ghost to whom this book is dedicated.
He died from spinal cancer just after completing the book. I was three
years old at the time. He was only thirty-three. My mother named me after
him.

The index for that book was finished by his wife, my aunt Martha, as he
lay in hospice care. With all due respect to my uncle's last efforts on this
earth, it is so very boring. I had picked it up once as a teenager, read a few
pages, and was mind-numbed. It is an academic work, not written with
a general audience (much less a teenager) in mind. To my young eyes, a
book on colonial Virginia macroeconomics was a black hole.

The day before I rediscovered the long-forgotten book, I listened to a
podcast series called *Seeing White* by John Biewen. In an early episode,
Biewen talked about the importance of colonial Virginia economics and
politics to how race became legally codified in America. I remembered
the title of my uncle's book, the one that sat untouched on a bookshelf in

my childhood home. Was my uncle exploring the roots of race in America too? Maybe colonial macroeconomics isn't dull?

Early the next morning I was in the basement of the undergraduate library at the University of Michigan, heart racing unexpectedly, reaching for HC 107.v8 R16. The book had an old-fashioned library stamp card still glued inside the cover. There were only two stamps: "Jan 5, 1998" and "Jan 7, 1998."

My mother teared up whenever she talked about her brother. I learned as a boy not to bring him up. So who was he? Would I see anything of myself in his writing?

I brought his book back to a house our family had rented for eight months in Ann Arbor. It was 2017, and I was four months into a Knight-Wallace Fellowship for journalists at the University of Michigan. The fellowship gave me time to do things like research a master's thesis, go to lectures, and get sidetracked reading my dying uncle's work.

It was a Monday. I was on the couch in jeans recycled from the hamper and a My Little Pony sweatshirt featuring Rainbow Dash. My daughter and I had taken advantage of the extra fellowship time to debate and conclude that Rainbow Dash is, by far, the coolest Little Pony. We bought shirts to honor Rainbow's awesomeness.

A cowlick stood up in my hair from the wool cap I pulled off when I got home from the snowy walk back from the library. I had reclaimed half a cup of cold coffee from the sink after deciding time at the coffeemaker was less valuable than getting my uncle's book open. I scoured the chapters for clues on what to read first. There was only page after page of exacting historic detail. Sensing no shortcuts, I flipped back to page one.

As it ends up, my uncle spent his last days writing about a pivotal moment in US socioeconomic and racial history. He wrote about Bacon's Rebellion in 1676, when Nathaniel Bacon led hundreds of protesters, including enslaved Blacks, white indentured servants, and a mix of other economically oppressed people of all classes and races, against the economic tyranny of the Virginia colonial government. In his book *Stamped from the Beginning*, Ibram X. Kendi captured the historic moment:

> By summer [of 1676], the frontier war had quickly become a civil war—or to some, a class war—with Bacon and his supporters rebelling against [Governor William] Berkeley, and Berkeley hiring a militia of mercenaries.

By September 1676, a defiant Bacon had "proclaimed liberty to all Servants and Negroes." For Governor Berkeley's wealthy White inner circle, poor Whites and enslaved Blacks joining hands presaged the apocalypse. At the head of five hundred men, Bacon burned down Jamestown, forcing Berkeley to flee. . . . Rich planters learned from Bacon's Rebellion that poor Whites had to be forever separated from enslaved Blacks. They divided and conquered by creating more White privileges.[1]

Fear of a united class of multiracial bonded-servitude people working together to rebel against inequality struck fear into both Mother England and the Virginia legislature. That fear defined the times. Military costs soared.

Ultimately, fear of united cooperation between oppressed races and classes led to a cost-effective strategy that would create an enduring American master narrative: legalized socioeconomic-racial manipulation. Because united action is a far greater threat than divided action, the Virginia House of Burgesses worked with intent to legally define a race-based caste system—slavery for Blacks and a claim to social privilege for working and indentured white poor. The policy's overt intention was to prevent organized rebellion by dividing the economically oppressed of the colonies into racialized, siloed castes.

Those efforts culminated in the Virginia Slave Codes of 1705. The slave codes marked the political and legal birth of race as class in America. My uncle wrote that the legislation was "an early—perhaps the first—instance in colonial history of a kind of white solidarity in the face of real, exaggerated or imagined threats" of united rebellion.[2]

I read those words, and a hollow sadness swallowed my chest. For slavery and the manipulation of impoverished whites by an aristocracy, for master narratives that endure, for the seekers of money and power who still use them, for what my country has always been, and for an empty space in my own family I had never noticed before—where I had an uncle who would have told me all about these things himself. For how little has changed.

Months later, as I quoted my uncle's words in this book, I choked up again. I imagined him typing them. I was a baby. Nixon was president.

I wept on the couch because it is a myth that this is a nation created of, by, and for all people. I wept because, in a steady chain from colonialism to industrialization to finance capitalism, my country's aristocracy has endeavored to keep the most vulnerable members of its population under one heel or the other.

Retired Air Force colonel Curtis Milam, son of an Air Force brigadier general, describes himself as a person who has served his country all his life, as either a supportive family member or in the military himself. He writes in a 2020 opinion piece, "America was the first modern nation, created of, by, and for the people—supposedly a nation with no class structure, where anyone could reach their potential. But that was a myth. America had classes: slaves at the bottom—treated not as people but property—then poor and working-class whites, and atop it all our original aristocracy of landed gentry and traders in the South, merchants and industrialists in the North."[3]

Milam points out that the nation is experiencing the greatest wealth disparity in more than one hundred years, in a tax system that is regressive, pushing the burden to a shrinking, anxious, and struggling middle class. I believe new digital platforms help enable that aristocracy, today's 1 percent, to maintain class division with weaponized storytelling, using powerful new communication tools in a media environment that goes largely unchecked and unbalanced.

But it is the same old damned-dirty-trick story told to create and maintain caste.

Isabel Wilkerson, in her 2020 book *Caste: The Origins of Our Discontent*, meticulously details the trick:

> In America, race is the primary tool and the visible decoy, the front man, for caste. . . In the same way that *black* and *white* were applied to people who were literally neither, but rather gradations of brown and beige and ivory, the caste system set people at poles from one another and attaches meaning to the extremes, and to the gradations in between, and then reinforces those meanings, replicates them in the roles each caste was and is assigned and permitted or required to perform. . . . Thus we are all born into a silent war game, centuries old, enlisted in teams not of our choosing.[4]

She offers that it is "as if everyone were in the grip of an invisible playwright." In the tricky story, "None of us are ourselves."[5]

For me, my uncle's work began to build an intimately personal bridge from our nation's colonial history to the times in which my uncle lived to

my own present. From the Virginia Slave Codes to the civil rights movement to me on the couch, listening to cable news political coverage in the
background. The fix was in long before any of us were born.

My uncle wrote about rising white anxiety as the Black population increased in the late 1600s. He documented that in 1630 just 2 percent of the
population of Virginia was Black.

> By 1700 blacks comprised over 28 percent of the total population. Before
> the end of the colonial period the proportion would increase to over 40
> percent, but in no other decade did the ratio increase so rapidly. . . .
> [A]pprehension regarding insurrections deepened as the number of
> slaves grew. In the three decades after 1688 the legislature provided
> elaborate restrictions on the movement and congregation of slaves.
> This generation laid the basic foundation for Virginia's slave codes that
> would serve until the Civil War.[6]

My uncle's voice spoke to me on a personal level. There is, of course, a
pantheon of clearer, wiser, contemporary Black voices who chronicle that
American master narrative. Carol Anderson has observed that white anxiety and rage historically rise in periods when people of color gain greater
access to positions of power and authority. In her book *White Rage: The
Unspoken Truth of Our Racial Divide*, Anderson writes about white reaction to a growing Black population in America.

> [W]hite rage is not about the visible violence, but rather it works its
> way through the courts, the legislatures, and the range of government
> bureaucracies. . . . The trigger for white rage, inevitably, is black ad-
> vancement. It is not merely the presence of black people that is the
> problem; rather it is blackness with ambition, with drive, with purpose,
> with aspirations, and with demands for full and equal citizenship.[7]

That white anxiety and the blatant and intentional political purpose of the
Virginia Slave Codes was stated directly in 1848 by former US vice president John C. Calhoun, who laid down this founding piece of storytelling:

> [W]ith us the two great divisions of society are not the rich and poor,
> but white and black; and all the former, the poor as well as the rich, be-
> long to the upper class, and are respected and treated as equals, if hon-
> est and industrious; and hence have a position and pride of character of
> which neither poverty nor misfortune can deprive them.[8]

Calhoun knew that was a dirty-trick story when it left his mouth in 1848. He and so many others systematically wove a dark fairy tale of two castes in America to preserve power for a third, aristocratic, caste. That master narrative was dirty trickery after Bacon's Rebellion in 1705. A dirty trick in 1848. The story is still dirty-tricking us today.

The caste narrative is an example of how the human need for story was used as a powerful, weaponized sociocultural tool to cast the nation into castes to serve the selfish interests of aristocratic power. That narrative, repeated over time, wove Godless enslavement and shameless economic lies into an American story that not only created castes but also pitted them against each other to protect the wealthy from the oppressed.

Martin Luther King noted in 1965,

> [T]he southern aristocracy took the world and gave the poor white man Jim Crow . . . and when his wrinkled stomach cried out for the food that his empty pockets could not provide, he ate Jim Crow, a psychological bird that told him that no matter how bad off he was, at least he was a white man, better than the black man. . . . And when his undernourished children cried out for the necessities that his low wages could not provide, he showed them the Jim Crow signs on the buses and in the stores, on the streets and in the public buildings. And his children, too, learned to feed upon Jim Crow, their last outpost of psychological oblivion.[9]

To correct Calhoun's narrative, as if it's not too late, the two greatest divisions of American society, now more than ever, *are* the rich and poor.

Dividing and pitting poor whites and Blacks as a master narrative was a forthright damned-dirty-casting trick. It set the stage for depths of evil for Blacks in America, plain and bare—legalized rapes, public lynchings, whip wounds, broken families, segregations, mortgages denied, unjust court systems, prisons past and present, broken public school systems, lack of intergenerational wealth, and other daily reminders of America's depravity. For poor whites the damned-dirty-casting trick is different. It is a psychological monster lurking, unspoken, in dark mental corners. It must be their own fault they are not rich and successful. Given the oppressive sins committed in plain sight on the lowest caste in the name of white hegemony, can there be any excuse for those still-impoverished white people in the middle caste (huge swaths of the country) who are still struggling to make ends meet? For people of European descent in America who can't break out of poverty, the fault must lie within. Not in predatory finance banking, not in colonial history, modern income inequality, lack of living wages, underemployment, a health care system that will break people before it saves them, and not in social and economic structures built long ago to intentionally exclude them, too.

In the American master narrative, no middle caste is written into the story. So those who live in the unacknowledged reality of that middle caste have to just take it on the chin. But they can't flinch. The Calhouns of the American story say they have a pride of character that neither poverty nor misfortune can deprive them of.

But it does.

There is no acknowledgment of very real historical, social, and economic forces that discriminate across the board. It must be that they just didn't pull up on their bootstraps. The inexcusability of being unable to make it from paycheck to paycheck runs deep in white families, in quieter, more desperate, more demoralizing ways. I know them, too, and I know there's very little psychological room for that experience in the old, dark fairy tale.

So, it's complicated. Black advancement historically creates white anxiety. But that is not the only driver of psychic stress in the middle caste.

In a 1965 debate with William F. Buckley Jr., James Baldwin expressed thoughts on the poor white American experience.

> They've been raised to believe, and by now they helplessly believe, that no matter how terrible their lives may be, and their lives have been quite terrible, and no matter how far they fall, no matter what disaster overtakes them, they have one enormous knowledge in consolation, which is like a heavenly revelation: at least, they are not Black.
>
> Now, I suggest that of all the terrible things that can happen to a human being, that is one of the worst. I suggest that what has happened to white Southerners is in some ways, after all, much worse than what has happened to Negroes there.
>
> Because Sheriff [Jim] Clark in Selma, Alabama, cannot be considered—you know, no one can be dismissed as a total monster. I'm sure he loves his wife, his children. I'm sure, you know, he likes to get drunk. You know, after all, one's got to assume he is visibly a man like me. But he doesn't know what drives him to use the club, to menace with the gun, and to use the cattle prod.

Something awful must have happened to a human being to be able to put a cattle prod against a woman's breasts, for example. What happens to the woman is ghastly. What happens to the man who does it is in some ways much, much worse... Their moral lives have been destroyed by a plague called Color.[10]

The capacity of Baldwin to empathize with a blatantly inhuman man like Clark through the lens of his own humanity was humbling.

Princeton economists Anne Case and Angus Deaton noticed that working-class white men and women without four-year degrees in America were dying at staggering rates from what they termed "deaths of despair"—suicide, drug overdoses, and alcohol-related illness. In their 2020 study they found the numbers rising year after year, decade after decade. They calculate that in 2017, there were 158,000 deaths of despair in the United States. They compare that to three Boeing 737 jets crashing from the sky every day for a year.

Returning to Wilkerson's point, in a caste system, "none of us are ourselves." To find real monsters, look to the playwrights.

The impact of the damned-dirty-trick on working-class and poor white Americans, who often live piled with debt from pulling on booby-trapped bootstraps, illustrates the power of politicized human storytelling, and they are an important American demographic. They are an angry, reliable voting bloc. They are a dedicated media audience. They were told their work ethic, good moral choices, and a story-based sense of nationalized privilege would give them a life better than their parents had. They were duped. Their experiences are not even written into the dirty-trick story. Someone must be to blame. There are politicized and leveraged story narratives, many not based on facts, that provide simple, emotionally satisfying explanations.

Most of them are not new. More than three hundred years after the Virginia Slave Codes, Steve Bannon, then Donald Trump's chief campaign strategist, was still pulling the damned-dirty-caste trick codified into law in 1705. Bannon told Robert Kuttner of the *American Prospect* in August 2017, "The Democrats, the longer they talk about identity politics, I got 'em. I want them to talk about racism every day. If the left is focused on race and identity, and we go with economic nationalism, we can crush the Democrats."[11]

If he's right, the nation may remain trapped in Calhoun's psychologically devastating two-caste fairy tale. The population will remain divided, like crabs in a bucket. The falsely inclusive narrative of economic nationalism will be the bucket, and the collective American lower and middle castes will remain crabs inside, pulling each other down.

Conspiracy Theories and the Storytelling Mind

There are people who scorn partisan media outlets and politicians who push out stories that do not hold up to fact checks. Those people look down on unfactual stories as foolish products consumed by weak-minded people. Maybe they even call them "deplorables," as Hillary Clinton famously did in the 2016 campaign. They may be missing the point.

In his book *Darwin's Cathedral*, David Wilson points out that, considering the evolutionary purpose of storytelling, accepting a story as part of a cultural belief system is not mental weakness. It is the healthy functioning of a biologically and culturally well-adapted human mind.

> Rationality is not the gold standard against which all other forms of thought are to be judged. Adaptation is the gold standard against which rationality must be judged, along with all other forms of thought. Evolutionary biologists should be especially quick to grasp this point because they appreciate that the well-adapted mind is ultimately an organ of survival and reproduction. If there is a trade-off between the two forms of realism, such that our beliefs can become more adaptive only by becoming factually less true, then factual realism will be the loser every time. . . . We know this is the case for patriotic versions of history, which are as silly and weak-minded for people of other nations as a given religion is for people of other faiths. Many intellectual traditions and scientific theories of past decades have a similar silly and purpose-driven quality, once their cloak of factual plausibility has been yanked away by the hand of time. If believing something for its desired consequences is a crime, then let those who are without guilt cast the first stone.[12]

Wilson mostly examines religion in the book, but enter someone like Alex Jones, who built a commercial empire by spewing tales of outlandish conspiracy theories that explain, to a largely white, right-wing audience of millions, how evil global elites are taking elaborate measures to take over planet Earth and dominate good people.

In conspiracy theories, the storytelling mind is operating at its "glorious worst."[13] Jones shamelessly feeds his audience ridiculous explanations for why they are anxious and insecure in today's America. More importantly, he builds a united, cooperative counterculture. Jones offers a master-narrative-hungry voting demographic.

For Jones, 9/11 was a federal conspiracy. The Sandy Hook school shooting never happened; the parents of the slain children were actors. When the personal email account of a former White House chief of staff and chair of Hillary Clinton's 2016 US presidential campaign were hacked, Jones identified the words "cheese" and "pizza" as code words for a child-pornography ring. He accused Clinton and high-ranking Democratic Party officials of involvement in a child sex ring based in the basement of a pizza parlor. That narrative inspired twenty-eight-year-old Edgar Maddison Welch to drive from his home in Salisbury, NC, to the Comet Ping Pong restaurant in Washington, DC, with three guns to free enslaved and abused children in the basement of the restaurant. There were, of course, no such children. There was no basement at all.

The Jones lies are epic and span decades. They have also built a culture. They did it by blatantly exploiting the human need for stories and belonging. Jonathan Gottschall, in his book *The Storytelling Animal*, points out, "Conspiracy theories are not, then, the province of a googly-eyed lunatic fringe. Conspiratorial thinking is not limited to the stupid, the ignorant, or the crazy. It is a reflex of the storytelling mind's compulsive need for meaningful experience. Conspiracy theories offer ultimate answers to a great mystery of the human condition: why are things so bad in the world?"[14]

In the case of Alex Jones, he offers explanations for why the damned-dirty-trick left American working families behind. Jones leverages psychic stress for his own profit.

Who is to blame for your middle-caste American struggles? Some kind of evil, pure and simple.

Who could be heroes? We could.

Gottschall sums up, "For this reason, conspiracy theories—no matter how many devils they invoke—are always consoling in their simplicity. Bad things do not happen because of a wildly complex swirl of abstract historical and social variables. They happen because bad men live to stalk our happiness. And you can fight, and possibly even defeat, bad men. *If you can read the hidden history.*"[15]

Conspiracy stories are dramatic and exciting. They present a call to band together into a united, cooperative group against evil. They are candy to the human brain's story wiring.

* * *

What worries me, personally, is not who will win the next national election. It is the damned-dirty-trick dividing narrative and the power of stories created to leverage it. Maybe the next election won't change anything. Maybe politicians will use those stories again and again to ride to power on the left and right. I'm afraid that year after year, election cycle after election cycle, we the people living in aftermath divisions of the 1705 slave codes will continue to be living pawns in centuries-long political leveraging of a racialized caste system.

Bannon knew with certainty how a campaign strategy that kept Democrats focused on race and Republicans pushing economic nationalism would work because that old damned-dirty-trick has worked for centuries to make sure poor and working-class Americans across the board exclude each other in the common fight for social and economic inclusion. Moreover, Bannon had historically powerful new media tools at his disposal.

Jones is still raging his ludicrous conspiracy stories on infowars.com. He also knows they will continue to work as long as they build culture.

Using identity politics and compelling narratives to prevent unified opposition to economic power is not historical, archaic, or outdated. It is streaming and posting today, reimagining old, tried-and-true master narratives using new technology.

New Weapons

In March of 2018, the Cambridge Analytica story broke. The company harvested personal data from more than 50 million Facebook users, then allegedly used their data to influence the 2016 election. According to whistleblower Christopher Wylie, who served as the company's research director, "Steve [Bannon] wanted weapons for his culture war, that's what he wanted. . . . We offered him a way to accomplish what he wanted to do, which was change the culture of America."[16]

But really, it is possible Bannon wasn't working to change the culture of America. He was also reinforcing the culture of America, to ensure that the song remained the same. With new tools and greater efficiency, Bannon manipulated narratives to divide and dehumanize the electorate in 2016 just as surely and intentionally as Calhoun in 1848 and the Virginia lawmakers in 1705.

Ultimately, responsibility for the worst damage to legacy journalism's business model does not boil down just to new technology; it boils down to not successfully questioning the ways new digital platforms become tools for old-school colonial efforts in the digital age. It boils down to powerful interests leveraging *Homo dramaticus*'s storytelling nature for short-term individual gain. Community journalists are drowned out when their work complicates those narratives as they seek complexity and amplify seldom-heard voices. We have recently been labeled (again) by people in power as enemies. We aren't. We are threats to their dangerous narratives and to their roles as playwrights in a national caste system.

Politicians no longer need Virginia's legal code. Today's politicians use identity politics to divide and manipulate working class Americans every day, in most every news cycle, with simple tweets.

Virginia Slave Codes are to John Calhoun and colonial power politics what Cambridge Analytica is to Steve Bannon and 2016 power politics.

Virginia Slave Codes are to historical colonialism what social media is to modern social colonialism.

The Damned Russians and Pink Rain Boots

I was reading news on the *New York Times* app in short spurts as I got my daughter ready for school on Thursday, November 2, 2017. That was the day after "Lawmakers released scores of political ads . . . purchased by Russian agents on Facebook and Twitter that showed the extent of the Kremlin's attempts to polarize the American voting public on issues like race, police abuse and religion."[17]

These were the very ads that would inform a historic federal investigation, but the story was the fourth headline in the *New York Times* news play I saw on my phone app (figure 8.1). Just before midnight Trump tweeted about a suspect in an alleged New York terrorist attack: "He killed 8 people, badly injured 12. SHOULD GET DEATH PENALTY!" The dramatic tweet dominated the morning news coverage.

With Tweet, Trump May Add Burden to Prosecution of Attack Suspect

• Just before midnight, President Trump tweeted: "He killed 8 people, badly injured 12. SHOULD GET DEATH PENALTY!"

• The president's message could complicate the case against the man accused in the Manhattan truck attack before it even heads to trial.

31m ago 🔖 ⬆️

Mr. Trump's tweet capped a day in which he sought to turn the Manhattan terrorist attack into a political talking point.

The president suggested the truck attack suspect be sent to Guantánamo Prison, an unprecedented step.

How Russia Got Americans to Turn Against One Another

• Accounts with names like Blacktivists and Back the Badge were aimed at specific voters. One account published an illustration that equated Hillary Clinton with Satan and Donald Trump with Jesus.

• The sampling of ads, some of which had been made public earlier, came during a second day of congressional hearings with the top lawyers for Facebook, Twitter and Google.

Figure 8.1. *New York Times* online news feed, November 2, 2017. © 2017 The New York Times Company. All rights reserved. Used under license. https://www.nytimes.com/.

Figure 8.2. Social media advertisements funded by Russian organizations. *Source*: US House of Representatives Permanent Select Committee on Intelligence, https://intelligence.house.gov/social-media-content/social-media-advertisements.htm.

I wondered if Trump's tweets were effortlessly manipulating us on social media to overshadow news coverage of Russians manipulating us on social media. In that morning's coverage, it felt to me like Trump's dramatic late-night tweet overshadowed early questions of Russian interference in democratic elections. Those ads seemed to be designed, like the Virginia Slave Codes of 1705, to intentionally polarize the American voting public (figure 8.2).

The ads would be included in former FBI director Robert Mueller's report ("Report on the Investigation into Russian Interference in the 2016 Presidential Election"):

Defendants, posing as U.S. persons and creating false U.S. personas, operated social media pages and groups designed to attract U.S. audiences. These groups and pages, which addressed divisive U.S. political and social issues, falsely claimed to be controlled by U.S. activists when, in fact, they were controlled by Defendants. Defendants also used the stolen identities of real U.S. persons to post on ORGANIZATION-controlled social media accounts. Over time, these social media accounts became Defendants' means to reach significant numbers of Americans for purposes of interfering with the U.S. political system, including the presidential election of 2016.[18]

The indictment notes,

[The Russian Internet Research Agency] had a strategic goal to sow discord in the U.S. political system, including the 2016 U.S. presidential election. Defendants posted derogatory information about a number of candidates, and by early to mid-2016, Defendants' operations included supporting the presidential campaign of then-candidate Donald J. Trump ("Trump Campaign") and disparaging Hillary Clinton. Defendants made various expenditures to carry out those activities, including buying political advertisements on social media in the names of U.S. persons and entities. Defendants also staged political rallies inside the United States, and while posing as U.S. grassroots entities and U.S. persons, and without revealing their Russian identities and ORGANIZATION affiliation, solicited and compensated real U.S. persons to promote or disparage candidates. Some Defendants, posing as U.S. persons and without revealing their Russian association, communicated with unwitting individuals associated with the Trump Campaign and with other political activists to seek to coordinate political activities.[19]

The ads themselves seemed like a modern example of the old, colonial damned-dirty-trick narrative: sow division among socially and economically vulnerable Americans in the interest of political power. The Russians used Facebook like a fiddle to play that American master narrative, divide by race to conquer.

Trump seemed to reach for his fiddle, too. With a single tweet, he pushed a historic story down the page.

There on my mobile device, the *New York Times* seemed to take the bait.

I was frustrated by that particular morning's news decisions. More than that, I was frustrated by the nagging feeling that Trump's Twitter antics were being embraced by legacy media companies. Eventually, media critics would write about the "Trump Bump." In 2017 the term was added to the Macmillan Dictionary and this definition was suggested for the Collins English Dictionary: "A sudden rise in stock market share value or revenue as a result of the election of Donald Trump." *Washington Post* writer Paul Farhi was among many critics who questioned how the Trump presidency improved media revenues across the board. In 2021, he wrote that:

> In 2014, the year before Trump announced his candidacy, the three leading cable news networks collectively attracted an average of 2.8 million viewers a night during prime-time hours. By 2019, Trump's third year in office, that number had nearly doubled to 5.3 million each night . . . a handful of leading newspapers can likewise thank Trump, at least in part, for a sharp rise in digital subscriptions over the past five years. The *New York Times* began his term with 3 million such subscribers and ended it with 7.5 million. The *Post* tripled its subscriber base to more than 3 million during his administration.[20]

That morning, in 2017, uncaffeinated and grumpy, I fumed at my iPhone screen. I grumbled to myself, "Why do we consistently let Trump's dramatic antics push important news down the page? How do newsrooms take the bait so easily, and where the hell is my daughter's left pink rain boot?"

It was a crazy family morning. Our daughter had been up in the middle of the night. We had all slept in too long and were running behind. My wife was half listening to my rant while cutting an apple for a school lunch and getting herself ready for work. She correctly pointed out that I had put sneakers on our daughter when it was raining outside. I started trying to cajole my daughter out of a fort made of string to get her sneakers off and rain boots on so we wouldn't be late for school.

I feel all that made for a very telling ethnographic moment about how stories are being socially manipulated and how news is consumed in the digital age. We were one busy family trying to process a whirlwind of politically loaded information on an iPhone screen. We were passively navigating a media field politically mined by dangerous narratives that manipulate, divide, and rule the American public. On the fly.

If news morning editors won't think critically about social context for us, who else has time to sort it all out? Shouldn't that be their job? I want my job to be to get my kid in the right shoes and out the door to a society safe from blatant manipulations from a former reality-show host and foreign powers.

I finally poured a cup of coffee and grumbled some more, to no one in particular: "How's about news editors do their job, and I'll do mine?"

*   *   *

Pulitzer Prize–winning American playwright and essayist Arthur Miller once said, "A good newspaper, I suppose, is a nation talking to itself."[21]

When a news organization accomplishes that task, it is producing news as a public good. The more difficult that national conversation becomes, the more urgently news sources that embrace Miller's advice are needed. In the long game for journalism's survival, no business model will be sustainable once faith in that role is lost.

On June 7, 2020, James Bennet resigned as editorial page editor of the *New York Times* after running an opinion piece from Arkansas senator Tom Cotton that advocated deploying military troops to quell social justice protests that were taking place across the nation in the wake of the murder of George Floyd. The pros and cons of publishing the conservative senator's viewpoints were laid out in the days that followed.[22] The debate largely boiled down to core values, a push for truthful and socially responsible reporting versus publishing newsworthy viewpoints in the interest of public debate.[23]

Two arguments emerged.

On the side of running Cotton's views, opinion pieces are designed to promote conversation. They are an often difficult necessity to ensure, as Arthur Miller suggests, that legacy media remain a place where a nation's differing opinions remain in conversation with each other. They are supposed to present all viewpoints so people are informed about what others are thinking. Readers are not expected to agree with everything they read in the editorial section. The point is to explicitly present voices outside of readers' own silos, to encourage public debate and inform them about the world. Senator Cotton was newsworthy. He was a member of Congress with presidential ambitions. His opinions, regardless of what they were, had consequence.

On the side of not running Cotton's views, they were not fact-based. They were perceived as incendiary, conservative propaganda. He proposed that "nihilist criminals are simply out for loot and the thrill of destruction, with cadres of left-wing radicals like antifa infiltrating protest marches to exploit Floyd's death for their own anarchic purposes." There was no proof that Antifa was even a structured organization or involved in any sort of coordinated planning. Cotton's views were seen as biased political dogma that could incite violence.

Tom Jones, a senior media writer at Poynter, made the point that the issue boils down to something deeper than just one controversial opinion piece.

Bennet appears to have been caught up in this debate between what journalism is and what it should be and it cost him his job. However, [chairman of The New York Times Company and publisher of *The New York Times*] Sulzberger told *New York Times* media columnist Ben Smith on Sunday to not interpret Bennet's resignation as a philosophical shift.

Still, Smith wrote, " . . . the shift in mainstream American media—driven by a journalism that is more personal, and reporters more willing to speak what they see as the truth without worrying about alienating conservatives—now feels irreversible. It is driven in equal parts by politics, the culture and journalism's business model, relying increasingly on passionate readers willing to pay for content rather than skittish advertisers."

If Smith is correct—and I do think there is evidence to suggest that he

is—the *Times* could be headed down a slippery and potentially dangerous road that might make staffers and some readers happy, but it is the
antithesis of what objective, but contextualized, journalism is supposed
to be.[24]

When the editorial page editor who embraces sharing controversial viewpoints leaves journalism, I worry that the industry, like our hunter-gatherer
ancestors, will begin creating tricksters of others who do not share the values of its own cooperative group. Journalism could be in danger of using
storytelling as a means of culture building by defining appropriate self and
inappropriate others. That kind of storytelling uses narrative as a tool for
social and moral control, for its own interests, at the expense of professionally produced journalism that embraces complexity and open dialogue as
a public good.

                    *   *   *

As a much younger man, I once drove across Texas to meet the parents
of a woman I was dating. They were quiet, devout, small-town Baptists.
I was a long-haired, rebellious, twenty-one-year-old anthropology student.

Religion quickly became an important topic. Her father and I went
around and around for hours. We both really wanted to get along, but we
just could not see eye to eye on matters of faith. Eventually I asked, "Can
we talk about being Baptist in the context of religions?"

The father immediately replied, "No, but we can talk about religion in
the context of being Baptist."

We fell silent and shared a moment in which we recognized we both had
a right to our own beliefs. They were just different. Neither of us had any
problem with the other's perspective as long as we respected and understood each other.

The social forces behind Bennet's resignation ask a similar question. Is
the industry today leaning toward pursuing social justice in the context of
journalism or journalism in the context of social justice? There is no wrong
answer. There is a huge difference.

Listen to Maya Angelou

In 1705, the Virginia legislature had to draft and enforce legal slave codes
in order to manipulate and divide the people of Virginia. Today, politicians

and special interests divide us and distract us from collective organization with tweets gobbled up and legitimized by legacy media organizations.

Venture capitalist Chamath Palihapitiya, who joined Facebook in 2007 and served as its vice president for growth, warns about politics and new media tools: "I think we have created tools that are ripping apart the social fabric of how society works. . . . The short-term, dopamine-driven feedback loops we've created are destroying how society works. . . . No civil discourse, no cooperation; misinformation, mistruth. And it's not an American problem—this is not about Russians ads. This is a global problem." He continues, "Bad actors can now manipulate large swathes of people to do anything you want. It's just a really, really bad state of affairs."[25]

I began to ask myself, and my ghosts, difficult questions. What role is the journalism I believe in assuming in a dehumanizing and increasingly dangerous media ecosystem? How complicit are we in the manipulation of political identities? Is it reasonable for the public to believe we can be truth-tellers in a digital media world full of lies? Am I still called to be a journalist? Is there still a place in society for journalism that strives to make safe spaces for human differences? Does anyone under forty even believe in what legacy journalists claim to do anymore? Or am I just kidding myself? If media are failing society in the digital age, where do I stand? Who have I become? What has journalism become?

I asked those questions in 2018 to Joshua Johnson, then host of the NPR program 1A, and he offered some hope. At the time, the show was fairly new. Johnson had taken over a beloved and critical time slot left by The Diane Rehm Show, which ran from December 1970 to the end of 2016.

Johnson said today's polarized media environment leaves people feeling confused and negative about how they consume news. He explained that his guiding principle came from Maya Angelou, who is credited with giving this advice, "I've learned that people will forget what you said, people will forget what you did, but people will never forget how you made them feel."

Too many people do not feel good about how they consume information today, Johnson told me. To him, that was a defining human problem facing news organizations as they struggled to redefine their business models. He said, "The first thing, the very first, that people need is to feel like they are welcome to the conversation no matter who they are and what they believe."

A Reuters Institute survey of more than 70,000 people worldwide found that "almost a third of our sample (29%) say they often or sometimes avoid the news. For many, this is because it can have a negative effect on mood. For others, it is because they can't rely on news to be true."[26]

There are real consequences to the news business when media deliver stories in ways that isolate and dehumanize people. Investigative journalist Amanda Ripley describes what happens when pushing easy emotional buttons becomes more important than embracing fairness, balance, and complexity.

> Deep in their bones, talk-show hosts (like journalists generally) understand certain things about human psychology: we know how to grab the brain's attention and stimulate fear, sadness or anger. We can summon outrage in five words or less. We value the ancient power of storytelling, and we get that good stories require conflict, characters and scene. But in the present era of tribalism, it feels like we've reached our collective limitations.
>
> As politicians have become more polarized, we have increasingly allowed ourselves to be used by demagogues on both sides of the aisle, amplifying their insults instead of exposing their motivations. Again and again, we have escalated the conflict and snuffed the complexity out of the conversation.
>
> In this dynamic, people's encounters with the other tribe (political, religious, ethnic, racial or otherwise) become more and more charged. And the brain behaves differently in charged interactions. It's impossible to feel curious, for example, while also feeling threatened. . . . In this hypervigilant state, we feel an involuntary need to defend our side and attack the other. That anxiety renders us immune to new information. In other words: no amount of investigative reporting or leaked documents will change our mind, no matter what.[27]

Ripley concludes, "The goal is not to wash away the conflict; it's to help people wade in and out of the muck (and back in again) with their humanity intact."[28]

I am not certain how much professionally produced journalism is accomplishing that goal today. I am worried that the short-term business gains that come from embracing political dramatics are killing the long-term needs of producing news as a public trust. I am worried about the questions history will ask when the consequences of today's political manipulations and dehumanization are examined from a distance.

Which is to say I am not sure I am living up to my own personal moral obligations. Should I be explicitly standing up to political and cultural manipulation on social media platforms? Is that part of my job? Does the presence of my professional work and the work of my peers on those platforms validate them? Does it contribute to public confusion of what professional journalism values?

I am asking these questions to my two ghosts and my child.

Nelson Poynter, can we build a digital newsroom today that will survive financially, atone for the past, and still champion your values?

Uncle John, how do we deal with history repeating itself?

Daughter, when you are grown and you look back at my professional work, will you be proud of me?

BOOK 3
Hope

9

Four Black Holes

This chapter is about my personal thoughts on what I think are four significant black holes in the newsroom and how they relate to this book's two main ideas: *Homo dramaticus* as a storytelling animal and how we might repair broken trust in media. The first black hole is the Fiscal Black Hole. The second is the Get Off Your Butt Black Hole. The third is the Bull's-Eye Black Hole. The last is Metric Black Holes.

The Fiscal Black Hole

The Times Publishing Company sold its building in St. Petersburg in 2016 and remained as a tenant, but we no longer had access to a conference room large enough for staff wide meetings.

But the Florida Holocaust Museum had a big enough meeting room. The museum is right across the street from the Times building, and they kindly provided space for the quarterly forums that update staff on the state of the company. The forums got shorthanded in the newsroom: "You going to the holocaust?"

For a company forum in 2019, we all walked across the street to the museum and through metal detectors. The museum exhibit included a boxcar used to transport Jews and other prisoners to killing centers. The meeting room walls were lined with portraits of children who were killed during the war. The state of journalism described at the meetings could often be described as dismal.

After one of the forums, a group of us walked slowly back across the street and bantered about the challenging state of the industry: attacks on the press seeming more frequent, loss of trust in our profession, shrinking newspapers that save on newsprint costs, job insecurity, pay cuts, and uncertainties about retirement. For the group, the somber venue set a tone. The museum felt like a metaphor for feelings of helplessness about forces outside our control. For years, newspaper business models in crisis have pulled on our careers, identity, and well-being like gravity around an apocalyptic black hole.

To address specific questions about imminent company changes, individual departments scheduled smaller staff meetings in the week that followed.

The photo department did not need a conference room for our small group, so the meeting was held in the still-abandoned office of Jennifer Orsi, the managing editor who left the *Times* in 2018 and had not yet been replaced. There were nine of us. The topic was survival. This meeting contrasted the one in 2016 when we discussed how to elevate good journalism. We were a fraction of what we used to be, so no more large conference room. No more coffee, bagels, or doughnuts. But the two meetings, nearly four years apart, offered striking parallels. The messages were eerily familiar.

Boyzell Hosey, the deputy editor of photography, was blunt: "You need to take care of yourselves now, emotionally and financially. I don't want to lose anybody. I don't want to lose a single one of you. But you can read between the lines and hear what I'm saying to you."

Department heads assured us photo would be key to developing ad revenue strategies. We would focus on building audience on YouTube and Facebook. Right then we weren't seeing any significant revenue, but we were assured there would be a tipping point. Photo in particular was being encouraged to be aggressive about social media.

The message felt unchanged in the years since that earlier photo meeting. Questions from staff seemed the same, too.

Staffers asked about work flow. When do we post to social media on deadline, and when do we slow down and cover an event to prioritize our own product? Do we share the password to the company social media accounts with the whole staff? Can everybody post? Do we want a few posts a day or a lot of posts from everyone? What about Instagram stories, how do we coordinate so two people aren't telling stories on the *Times* account at the same time?

Other staffers wanted to know how much of our time on assignment we should spend building social media and when the financial payoff would come.

The guest speakers looked as uncomfortable as our former director of social media Lyndsey McKenna did in 2016. Boyzell jumped in and said that this was all a work in progress. We were all just going to have to find new workflows.

There were more questions about workflow and more debate. Eventually, a digital content manager summed it up like this, "Ever since social media and news media merged in what, like, 2000? — this is just the world we live in."

I thought back to Lyndsey's mantra poster: "Content, Engagement, Revenue." It was gone, but it hung over her desk for more than a year after she left. That mantra hasn't worked yet. And a lot had changed since the 2016 meeting.

But the black hole described by Lyndsey's poster hasn't changed. It is still sucking up human resource hours and pulling our business model deeper into darkness.

The Fiscal Black Hole was our dismal financial situation, but it was also all the human hours we were putting into trying someday to get a meaningful financial payoff from social media. Those platforms did not share our values. They weren't invested in us or our specific community. It seemed more and more unlikely that they would support us financially. Even if they did, it would come at what cost?

Those human hours might be better spent practicing local journalism that works toward building our own public service–based business model.

Freedom

The best coping skill for all that newsroom stress was to get out and do the job I love.

The day after the photo staff meeting, Lane DeGregory, a beloved co-worker, and I spent the day with an amazing family on a really promising story. Lane is left-handed. She drags her hand across the legal pads she uses to take notes as she writes. On a great reporting day when she has taken a lot of notes, her left pinky turns blue with smeared ink. Today was a blue inky pinky day, and we were in high spirits.

Lane and I have worked on many stories together and agreed that we had the best job in the world, certainly the best job in the world for us.

On the car ride home we decided to just embrace the stories we love until the end. In fact, we said, let's love them more.

Lane is a Pulitzer Prize–winning feature writer. And, true story, she has also won every other major journalism award I can think of. But that's not what makes Lane amazing. What makes her amazing is how warmly and sincerely she cares for people. Her interviews are much longer and go deeper than most reporters. For any story, she wants to know the name of their first dog, what their first car was, what it was like where they grew up, and important life moments unrelated to the reporting she needs. She will listen and care about whatever they want to tell her for as long as they want to talk, and she values building relationships above all else. She invests so much more time and so much more of herself than she needs to, always and on every story.

"We are the fiddlers on the *Titanic!*" she laughed.

I offered, "Right? Like Janis says, 'Freedom's just another word for nothing left to lose.'"

We pulled the song up on her playlist and started singing "Me and Bobby McGee."

There was still journalism left ahead for us at the *Times*, and neither of us will stop telling stories when the music stops.

Freedom is just another word for nothing left to lose, so I am going to dish straight dope on what anthropologists and media scholars have to say about three more newsroom black holes. The next one is Get Off Your Butts.

Newsroom Journalists, Get Off Your Butts!

Journalists spend more time than ever before in the newsroom sitting, looking at screens. That creates black holes in the communities we serve. People don't have personal experiences with journalists like they used to. Less public contact with journalists is a downward spiral for our business model.

In his 2013 book about newsrooms, *The Life Informatic: Newsmaking in the Digital Era*, Dominic Boyer's biggest takeaway is "The news journalist is increasingly a sedentary screenworker."[2]

Not only are there far fewer working local journalists, but those who are left are spending less and less time out in their communities. Fewer personal interactions means less communal trust is being built. We are less acknowledged as local storytellers. That hurts our business model. Why should you trust people you've never met?

Boyer noted a 2008 study of five German newsrooms, by media scholar Thorsten Quandt, found that journalists spent 32.1 percent of their time on screen-based search-related activities, 21.5 percent of their time on screen-based text production, 14.9 percent of their time on communication via media, and only 1.8 percent of their time "Moving/walking around."[3]

Since Quandt's research in 2008, aggregating news and reporting events by watching livestreams has become increasingly commonplace. Travel for stories used to be routine, but years of budget cuts have taken most out-of-town trips off the table.

The impact of journalists becoming more sedentary has a profound impact on our relations to our community. We can't build public trust if people barely ever see us. There are stories that can't be found surfing emails, watching livestreams, and monitoring social media on a desktop. Our business model suffers when people meet fewer and fewer local journalists face to face. Communities who don't know who we are may stop choosing local legacy media as their trusted storytellers.

*   *   *

Lane told me about the first story a new editor asked her to check out.

This woman had gotten arrested for abandoning her little, little kids while she went to work at McDonald's at night. The neighbors had called, and their house was filled with feces all over the place, and they had just taken the kids. So I got in the car and I drove up to the apartment on the address on the police arrest report, and I got in there while they're pulling feces-covered couches and shit out the door. Then I drove to the McDonald's and I talked to the co-workers of this woman at McDonald's, and I got up to the office and [the editor] said, 'Where were you?' And I said, 'I went to this apartment to check this out and then I went to the McDonald's.' And [the editor] goes, 'Oh, I would have started with the documents.' You know, it was the whole idea of, if I had waited for another two hours, they would have had all the crap out of the house. I wouldn't have been there to cover that. But [the editor's] whole gut initial reaction was check out the documents. . . . To me, that felt like a huge shift in the way that we're reporting. . . . And I just felt like, that's not how I want to do my job. It's not effective in that situation.

The emergence of "screenwork" as a dominant means of producing news has profound cultural implications to media and society.[4] It completely changed what I saw as I sat at my desk and watched the newsroom around me. One of today's most important journalism skills can be to artfully aggregate multiple, rapidly evolving news situations from livestreams and Twitter feeds quickly and accurately. Another is to add that content back online and push it out for clicks.

Data Reporting: The Good, the Bad, and the Bull's-Eye Black Hole

A good data set can set a journalist up for success, but not all important stories have data sets. Journalists should be careful not to become limited to what gets measured, particularly because important truths sometimes go intentionally unmeasured.

A well-worn saying among statisticians, often attributed to Albert Einstein, is "Not everything that can be counted counts, and not everything that counts can be counted." Sometimes people don't want to count important things that should get counted.

Here's an example. People who are deemed to be dangerous to themselves or others can be locked up even though they have committed no crime. Every state has a law that allows for civil commitment. Because the person has not committed a crime, it is the most extreme legal deprivation of liberty possible. Once in custody, a person may be subjected to forced medication, seclusion, restraint, and personal trauma.

But nobody is accurately counting them. A 2019 study highlights how, in most states, thousands of people who have committed no crime are taken into custody but not counted. In an age defined by data collection, accurate data are not being gathered on the most extreme deprivation of liberty.[5] When data are available on everything from criminal incarceration to marriages to speeding tickets to everyone's shopping habits, it seems unfathomable that civil commitments would not be accurately counted. A likely reason is that it is not in anyone's interest to count them. When journalists wait to report on what others decide to measure, no good data can easily amount to no investigative news coverage. The complex topics journalists need to tackle don't always fit reliably and validly onto neatly rowed spreadsheets. Many needs of society's most vulnerable members exist in social silences, unmeasured.

Reliability and validity

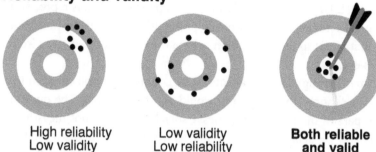

High reliability	Low validity	**Both reliable**
Low validity	Low reliability	**and valid**

Figure 9.1. Understanding the complexities of the social world is vital to determining whether a data set is both reliable and valid. Illustration by Steve Madden.

Even when journalists do stumble on a data set that fits newsroom investigative models, anthropologist Vincanne Adams warns about the ways that those aggregated data sets create "an illusory sense that there is firmness and stability in the intrinsically messy social world."[6] She convincingly argues that the pursuit of evidence-based reporting creates an "unnatural laboratory" out of a naturally complex social world. I see that in journalism today. Data sets become gospel, and the gospel lies in data sets.

In their 1979 book *Reliability and Validity Assessment*, Edward Carmines and Richard Zeller explain an important challenge. Reliability and validity are very different. Reliability is about accuracy. Validity refers to how well a study actually measures something real.

An analogy often used is shooting bullets at a target. Reliability is how closely the shots get clustered; a cluster can be nice and tight but nowhere near the bull's-eye. Those tight clusters, even though they are nowhere near a bull's-eye, are still very reliable shots.

Validity measures whether they hit the bull's-eye. On a target, it is marked in red. In the real world, that bull's-eye is much harder to spot. Validity is the Bull's-Eye Black Hole (figure 9.1).

Confusion between reliability and validity can be common in newsrooms. A thermometer can measure to three decimal places reliably. If a working thermometer reads a body temperature of 100.786, it is accurate. But it can't determine if someone just drank a cup of coffee, if it was placed on a lightbulb to fool a parent, if someone just got out of a hot shower, or a person's immune system is fighting infection. On election day November

9, 2016, a 7 p.m. *New York Times* "poll of polls" predicted an 86 percent chance Hillary Clinton would be elected president. It was a precise average of all evidence-based reporting polls nationally. Reliable polls, but like the first target in the illustration, where the data clustered away from the bull's-eye.

Later that night, as actual votes were counted, the poll changed to a 96 percent chance Donald Trump would win the election. The question of what part of the intrinsically messy social world was not measured will ultimately be debated by historians, as will the role media played in the surprising election-night results. *New York Times* reporter Jim Rutenberg led a story the next morning, "All the dazzling technology, the big data and the sophisticated modeling that American newsrooms bring to the fundamentally human endeavor of presidential politics could not save American journalism from yet again being behind the story, behind the rest of the country."[7] Reliable data missed the hard-to-find bull's-eye.

The polling methodology was solid. In the 2016 election the polls measured *something* reliably. They just missed the validity bull's-eye by a mile.

In the social world, validity is really hard to confirm, especially in a newsroom where shoe-leather journalism feels old-school. Validity is nearly impossible to find without closing the spreadsheet, turning off the computer, leaving the newsroom, and talking to real people.

So the Bull's-Eye Black Hole is a very close neighbor to the Get Off Your Butt Black Hole.

Finding both, reliability/accuracy and validity/bull's-eye, is much harder than just finding a big set of reliable numbers. Newsrooms often do not take that into account when a reporter scores a great data set. There are two dangers.

First, a lot of reliable and time-consuming reporting is not completely valid reporting. That is, the numbers on the Excel sheet are not gospel truth in the real world. They don't reflect a holistic social world, might miss the most pressing story angle, and might not recognize the most important issues. The numbers may not even measure what an editor thinks they do.

Second, important issues that do not have existing data sets just do not get investigated like they used to. They may never even be visible in today's newsroom.

Carmines and Zeller's work cautions that to establish meaningful social validity there needs to be a very specific question. In journalism (and anthropology) the roots of that question should come from direct knowledge of a community. We should look for data in response to something we learn in the real world, not vice versa.

Validity becomes a very real and common challenge when journalists pick a story in response to an available data set. Those stories aren't wrong or unreliable, but they are a huge time investment and sometimes will never hit a bull's-eye.

For a local newspaper, those stories often do not connect intuitively with readers. From a cultural standpoint, there is also this—data and flowcharts are not how *Homo dramaticus* processes stories. If the goal is really public service, policy impact, reliable and valid reporting, big-data journalism alone too often leaves gaping holes.

Metric Black Holes

"What happens when you have a fire hose of data, measuring a lot of just a few criteria that don't reflect a question in the social world well enough? You can easily miss what has been described as 'metric black holes,'" explains University of Michigan professor Avik Basu.

Basu teaches a class on quantitative small experiments in data gathering. The model has been taught and practiced for nearly thirty years and can be of real benefit to newsrooms. Rachel Kaplan, who developed the model in the early 1990s, explains it like this: "They are 'small' in cost, in number of participants involved, and, especially in their intention. A manageable study, however, need not be conceptually sloppy. To be useful, even small experiments need to be thoughtful and disciplined."[8]

Their small-survey method is an achievable way to get valid and reliable data on specific questions, data that hit the bull's-eye. They are a great way to answer the kinds of questions that old-fashioned shoe-leather journalists stumble across out in their communities. The surveys can also be a good way to get out into a community.

*   *   *

In an article criticizing the gold standard of data collection, randomized control testing (RCT), for not measuring the world accurately, psychologist Jonathan Shedler explains the dangers.

Here's an example: Some people wrongly concluded that tooth flossing lacks scientific support, after a review of RCTs found little evidence of benefits. But flossing is beneficial in the long run, and the RCTs followed patients for only brief periods. They found exactly what you would expect—pretty much nothing. Knowledge about flossing's benefits comes from other sources, including dentists' observations over more than a century, and an understanding of the mechanism of action—how it works. . . . [S]ome people, primarily in the social sciences, would have us believe that RCTs are the gold standard of scientific knowledge, and all else can be ignored. This is misguided, and it doesn't require a science degree to understand why. No RCT has ever shown that the sun causes sunburn, sex causes pregnancy, or food deprivation leads to starvation. We know these things because we can observe cause and effect relationships and because we understand the mechanisms of action. Ultraviolet radiation damages skin cells. Sex allows sperm cells to fertilize egg cells. People die without food. Copernicus, Galileo, Darwin, Einstein, Niels Bohr, Marie Curie, Stephen Hawking. What do they have in common? None of them ever conducted an RCT.[9]

Shoe-leather reporting and in-the-field research are necessary to measure validity—to find the bull's-eye—in complex systems. When a "great data set" is represented as definitive reality without real-world reporting, the results can cause harm.

The ways in which the black holes of increased screen time, decreased community time, a trend toward big-data reporting, reliance on aggregation, and overconfidence in the validity of data sets affect journalism may not be directly measurable. They may have to be considered in terms of what went missing. It is important to consider the cumulative effects of journalists having fewer human interactions on media business models and communal trust. Perspectives not gained and ground truths underreported can't be measured. We may not know how often reporting misses the bull's-eye. Important stories are floating out there, unseen and unmeasured. There are many unacknowledged dangers, social silences, and vulnerable populations that can't be seen in Excel.

Real Newsroom Examples

I was standing with Lane at her desk in 2016. Lane had mentored an intern into reporting what would be a cover story. She had taken the intern to meet the family to be featured, introduced everyone, and set the story on course.

She was looking at a printout of the intern's story. Everything was reported from social media posts. The intern had not talked to a single person. None of it was confirmable.

Lane was upset. "I walked her from family member to family member, we got everyone's phone number, contacts for everyone . . ."

She should have been checking in periodically with the intern, but they were both already overworked because of staff reductions. She had assumed the intern's reporting would be what reporting had always been for her—in-person interviews, time invested developing relationships with the people in the story, coordinating time with a photographer to get with the family and document their lives.

They still had three days before deadline, time to help the intern get off her laptop and into the real lives of her subjects. She went into an editor's office and shut the door to call her.

Lane later recalled the event:

"And in the end, you have to call these people and talk to them."
    "Well they won't return my Facebook messages."
    "Well call them! Go see them!"
    I think there's a weird split between the forty-, fifty-somethings and the twenty-somethings, the way that we converse and the way that we do the job. . . . And I think that's not just affecting journalism but affecting us as people.

The episode and others like it have left Lane, a thirty-year-veteran with a heart for teaching younger journalists, feeling unappreciated as a mentor with experience to share. She said,

But there's also the thing about hierarchy, if that makes sense. I don't feel like the interns who come in want to learn from their elders who have been there. It's almost like the older people are having to rely on the younger people for weird technical skills, but the whole art of what we do as craftsmen or artists or writers and artists is not being passed down.

It makes you feel unappreciated. It makes you feel archaic. It makes you feel like you have to question what you're doing, even though you really do know what you're doing.

It makes you feel a little bit dismissed. I don't want to be freaking revered by the damn newsroom, but it would be nice if somebody was like, "Oh, Lane, can I get your help on something?"

*   *   *

The first question I asked Graham Brink, who was a metro editor at the time, was about how young reporters approach journalism differently than veteran journalists. He responded,

I mean when I'm talking to younger reporters, there's some very simple things. One, go talk to some people. That hasn't changed. Whether it was twenty years ago, fifty years ago, a hundred years ago, I assume you're a reporter. One of the things you want to do is talk to people. You can look at Twitter all day if you want, but if it's on Twitter then someone else has already got it. Now you can do a good job at synthesizing what's on Twitter or what you're seeing on Facebook. But if you wanted to get right at the core of news, then you have to go find it yourself. You can't have it being given to you by another, I'll say quasi news producer like Twitter or Facebook. You still have to go to the city council meeting and meet the city council members and meet the people in the audience who are watching and ask them, "Why are you here?" to get their good stories.

Graham differentiated between getting digital records from a desk in the newsroom and going to get them in person.

You've got to go look at records if you cover the courthouse. We get them in a different way now. It's more electronic. So in some ways it's more convenient to look at those records than when I started and it was all in paper and you have to go there to get them.

But one of the great advantages of actually going to the courthouse to have to ask for records is you almost have to have a conversation with a few real people. You have to go up to the clerk and say "How you doing today? What's going on?" And sometimes she or he would tell you something and you didn't know . . . 'cause they're the ones who either will give you the good stories, the good tips, the things to look into or how to shape your stories. It's almost in some ways too convenient to get certain types of records [online] because you don't have to actually talk to anybody.

So this is one of the things I preach, especially to the younger reporters who are often very digitally savvy and can mine things out of social media.

Craig Pittman's reporting experience likewise gave him a sense of the importance of in-person contact to get valuable information and stories.

When I covered courts in the 1990s, I went to the courthouse every day, whether there was a trial to cover or not, just to chat with the clerks, the bailiffs, the judges' assistants, the court psychologist, prosecutors, judges, defense attorneys, even the blind guy who ran the cafeteria. They were all great sources about what was going on. If you work a beat, you have to cultivate those sources by becoming part of *their* daily routine.

"Hey, what's going on?" is a great opening comment, and then if you can exchange info with them about something happening elsewhere in the building, you become a trusted source for *them* and they are more likely to pass along info to *you*.

Graham's and Craig's perspectives speak to Carmines and Zeller's point about achieving validity. To know what to measure, to identify the red-circled bull's-eye, journalists need to invest their time exploring the social world, developing critical theories, thinking of specific stories to test, and then looking for data.

Graham said one of the great benefits of being a journalist is the chance to have experiences with people you would not otherwise come in contact with and to be surprised at what you didn't know. Graham and most every other editor I interviewed worried about young reporters not having enough of those experiences on a personal level. Graham summed up the value of that kind of in-person experience.

You're going to learn a lot, spending time at a news organization. You're not going to learn nearly as much about the world and the community you live in if you work at a different type of profession. This industry teaches you a lot about how things work in your community. So even if you decide after five years to go into something else, you've just had five valuable years.

It's like five years of someone paying you to educate yourself about the world, to learn about how your city council works, how your school board works, or how your state government works, that type of thing. And just talking to real people, to know how it feels to get you out of your own cocoon, your own sort of safe place where everyone sort of thinks the same way as you do.

One of the things I love about journalism, my own beliefs are constantly challenged and sometimes they're changed. I still believe in that core value. We surround ourselves too often by people who think too much like we do, and the years of social networking reinforce that to the point where it starts to be a problem. But as a journalist you go out and you meet that guy who came from an agricultural background.

Now I was a city kid. You go out and you have to interview the farmer whose crops are decimated by something and you're like, "Wow, he's seeing the world or she's seeing the world in a different way than I am."

To me, one of the great things about this industry is, you will find out how other people think and how they think differently than you do, and that to me, as a young reporter, was one of the richest things about the job. I'm not really sure young reporters are all having that same experience today.

And, unfortunately, people in the communities we serve are not having that experience with them, either.

10

Journalism, Period.

Maybe the fate of journalism comes down to a battle for thumbs. Imagine:

A local news consumer in Tampa, Florida, pulls out her mobile device. She is twenty-five years old. There are upcoming local and national elections. On the screen are icons. A blue "f" for Facebook. A green "T" for *Tampa Bay Times*.

Her thumb hovers over the icons. It is guided by neurological connections in her brain that have been shaped in powerful ways. A jumbled and mysterious network of nerves and neurons jump at light speed around master narratives hardwired by family, history, and heritage. Natural selection guides impulses that have been with humans for tens of thousands of years. There are also new mental adaptations to digital technology that are getting wired so quickly that no one could possibly know what they all mean. Out of that jumble, some nerves lead to her thumb.

Local journalism's business model hangs in the balance.

Here is a potential win for legacy journalism business models: when that consumer looks at those two icons, she remembers an ad campaign that broke down media in the digital age to simple humanizing versus dehumanizing social forces.

"f": Confusing news values, spreading distrust, and selling your data since 2004.

"T": Serving trusted news to your community with integrity since 1884. Journalism. Period.

The consumer's thumb wavers toward the "T." She imagines the faces of *Times* journalists. She knows them. She has met them on assignments. She has attended their sponsored events. She listens to their podcasts. She has seen their documentaries on public television. They work in partnership with local university professors and civic groups to produce smart, meaningful stories on multiple platforms about difficult community issues. The *Times* food critic recommended that great Thai restaurant where she and her partner went for their first date. She will feel smart, positive, and part of a local community when she pushes "T." She remembers a town hall forum sponsored by the *Times* that was a safe space for Republicans and Democrats to debate differences. She remembers the investigation about education inequalities when she was a senior in high school. "T" is a healthy digital social space to consume trusted local stories.

She moves her thumb to "f." She wonders what her friends are doing. She will hear gossip, maybe see a cute cat doing something awesome. But she has no expectation that anything under "f" will be professional news. She knows anything that claims to be news under "f" is probably just selling something. Maybe Russian propaganda, maybe right-wing propaganda, maybe left-wing. Maybe political clickbait produced by a sixteen-year-old in Kazakhstan for kicks and profit. Who knows?

Legitimate news producers stopped posting there years ago. Credible news organizations blocked links to and from social media sites, removing all pretense of professionally sourced information on social media platforms. Those historic legacy organizations clearly, honestly, and boldly communicated the change. They explained that professionally produced local news is a culturally unique experience. They intentionally branded themselves as not being on social media. Local news is a totally different button, a distinct space with unique rules and expectations. Everyone knows that.

The woman wonders how the latest local debates went. There is a feature story she has been meaning to read about a childhood friend, and she wonders if the rain will hold off long enough to get drinks on the beach at sunset.

"T" is her community. It embraces history, respect, truth, and sanity. She trusts "T."

Her thumb presses that "T." Our news consumer and the news she consumes are humanized. A *Homo dramaticus* enters a space that is well defined as trusted local storytelling. A basic human desire is fulfilled. She begins viewing content produced as a public good.

Democracy wins.

Or, her thumb presses "f." She does see a cat doing something awesome. She laughs. She also sees a link to a YouTube video espousing a conspiracy theory about high school students at a rally being paid to be "fake" protesters by gun control lobbyists. She knows it is not true. Social media are social media, and news media are news media. She asks herself, "Who still posts that kind of ridiculous, unbelievable crap on social media? Who has time for that?"

She does not press "f" expecting trusted storytelling. The "f" space is defined by gossip, entertainment, and social connections. She understands clearly that the content on "f" is not professionally produced with time-honored ethical standards. It is a purely social experience. It is not a space that is designed to serve the public good.

Democracy wins again.

* * *

Society and democracy suffer when social media and legacy news try to coexist in one culturally ambiguous space. The reasons boil down to the ancient and primal origins of why healthy human communities have long needed trusted storytellers.

Today's singular mediadome will continue to break trust, ensure that there will be more lost local journalists, and continue a trajectory into an information apocalypse.

It will take intentional cultural clarity to reclaim public belief that local journalists are trusted storytellers who produce news as a public good. Targeted changes in daily journalism practice can build that clarity. Emerging technology can rebuild local trust. Legacy media can disrupt social media's dominance over a perilous media landscape. Local newsrooms can find a way to be a clear alternative to national cable media overdramatics.

An anthropology of a newsroom suggests that journalists can be independent, local fish in clear local waters, trusted where we swim. I believe local news will thrive only after that culturally unambiguous media space is established, a place where local storytellers can be trusted. My hope is that this work may contribute to those efforts.

According to a poll in August 2018, of 1,193 voters nationwide conducted by Quinnipiac University, 51 percent of Republicans said the "news media" were the "enemy of the people." The master narrative that supports that point of view is not going away on its own.

When I began my career at the *Times* two decades ago, the news media and public trust in media existed in a different world. Today most people define "the media" through the lens of a frightening national master narrative. That narrative lumps traditional media together with social media platforms (that politically manipulate users, boldly lie, guide them with secret algorithms, and sell their data) and cable news networks (that report from obvious political silos, twenty-four hours a day whether there is news or not). Public belief in the professional standards of local legacy print organizations like the *Times* that have been around for more than a hundred years with well-established codes of ethics and practices is nearly dead.

Looking at perception of the media as a whole today, the skeptical people in that 2018 Quinnipiac poll weren't completely wrong. The media in the digital age do not uniformly serve democracy. Complicating the picture, politicians, multibillion-dollar media companies, and special interests blatantly leverage, capitalize on, and amplify that growing distrust.

I wrote this book with an urgent sense of purpose. There really is no more time to move slowly. I believe we need to confront and address the primal, cultural roots that have broken trust and sown deep discord in *Homo dramaticus* society today. The stakes are getting higher and time is getting shorter.

Drawing from media anthropologists and practice theory, I examined one newsroom and asked deceptively simple but sneakily powerful questions: How do we practice daily journalism today? What practices strengthen local storytelling and help reclaim broken trust in *Homo dramaticus* communities? What practices weaken trust? I sincerely want to know how local news organizations like the *Tampa Bay Times* can disrupt today's powerful national narrative of hate and distrust in our own local communities. I want to open conversations about practices that might earn back trust and help build a better digital business model. I sincerely want discussions that may help restore our historical public service narrative. I want to convince people that time-honored news values still define working journalists in their hometown.

Ideas

Here are some ideas for those kinds of discussions. They are anthropological in nature and look for specific cultural solutions to vexing problems. The ideas are intended to help work toward rebuilding trust in local storytelling as a public service in the digital age.

Be a Disrupter

(Act boldly and remove professional news content from social media platforms. Create unique digital media spaces.)

Social media platforms have made token efforts to support journalism, but they are not getting into the business of producing journalism as a public good or truly reinforcing other business models that do.

Local newsrooms should consider cutting them off—cold turkey—and then boldly marketing legacy journalism as a unique digital space. Yes, there would be significant short-term drops in traffic, but as a Danish broadcaster has shown, that traffic can rebound, and the new traffic will likely be higher quality in terms of time on site and brand recognition.[1] In the long term, unique visitors to legacy news platforms are a path to success. Building social media followings for revenue is far less viable to local media business models than building unique audiences and creating their own sustainable markets. More importantly, a crucial cultural distinction between news media and social media can be made. Today's unclear and toxic media environment can be made clear again.

Social media are often used to divide the public for political gain, and the damage to society that results has only become clearer in recent years. From Russian ads to Cambridge Analytica to YouTube algorithms that perpetuate conspiracy theories to young audiences, to Donald Trump being banned from social media sites, any debate on the subject continues to narrow. Social media are being leveraged as powerful political tools to create dangerous master narratives in increasingly perilous times. To be on the right side of history, legacy journalism organizations should seriously consider a bold, unambiguous, and public stand against dehumanizing social media spaces in the digital age.

Be Defiantly Human

(Humanize a dehumanized media ecosystem. Publicly recognize the imminent danger of today's political master narratives. Be a clear alternative.)

To better humanize local media spaces, we can take important lessons from well-known humanists in history. Primo Levi, an Auschwitz survivor and profound literary witness of the Holocaust, warns,

> Every age has its own fascism and we see the warning signs wherever the concentration of power denies citizens the possibility and the means

of expressing and acting on their own free will. There are many ways of reaching this point, and not just through the terror of police intimidation, but by denying and distorting information, by undermining systems of justice, by paralyzing the education system, and by spreading in a myriad subtle ways nostalgia for a world where order reigned, and where the security of a privileged few depends on the forced labour and the forced silence of the many.[2]

Levi connects the rise of those dangerous master narratives to human suffering:

When this happens, when the unspoken dogma becomes the major premise in a syllogism, then, at the end of the chain, stands the Lager [Auschwitz]. It is a product of a conception of the world carried to its logical consequences with rigorous consistency; as long as the conception exists, the consequences remain to threaten us.[3]

Today's media environment feeds into that same kind of frightening chain: rising populism, social polarization, a nostalgic call to a better era, and villainization of media institutions writ large, in an era of economic inequality and public distrust of institutions. We should be concerned about what lies at the end of that chain. The history Primo Levi endured warns us not to normalize social instability. Our trust crisis and the dangerous master narratives driving media feel historically perilous.

It is possible that the most fervent humanists are people who have personally experienced extreme dehumanization. Maybe their lessons learned would be better applied preventively. That was the life purpose Levi took from surviving Auschwitz: "It must be a warning dedicated by humanity to itself, which can bear witness and repeat a message not new to history, but all too often forgotten: that man is, and must be, sacred to man, everywhere and forever."[4]

That is all to say local journalism can, and I argue should, recognize real dangers and embrace Levi's bold, defiant, decisive humanism, not as a purely moral or spiritual exercise but as a means to explore practical, applied solutions to a broken business model for a news industry that has lost control of its own narrative in the public eye.

Journalists already humanize others as a matter of course in our work, but today we should also humanize the supposed enemies of the state— ourselves and the way we deliver news. We should seek out new story forms and adopt practices that allow us to rehumanize ourselves in our communities.

Like podcasts.

Siobhan McHugh explores a mix of technology and humanization that explains the recent explosion of podcasts: "As is well documented . . . the confluence of two events in October 2014 had a significant impact in media circles: the launch by Apple of a native podcast app that made it much easier to download a podcast direct to an iOS mobile device and the publication of a spin-off of American storytelling show *This American Life*, [and] a serialized, podcast-first true-crime investigation called *Serial*. . . . *The New Yorker* claimed that podcasting was 'humanizing the news.'"[5] For tens of thousands of years human storytelling was an oral tradition. Maybe podcasts just feel natural.

Possibly as a reaction to a dehumanizing media landscape, digital audiences are gravitating toward those humanized story forms. A 2018 podcast consumer study by Edison Research shows that podcast listenership had grown year over year. More significantly, the study found that podcast listeners stayed engaged.[6]

During my career, many legacy journalists have shied away from using the word "I" in stories. There has been a sentiment that we should not draw attention to ourselves. There was often a feeling that writing in the first person might make us less objective. Today it may be important that we embrace the idea of coming out of the byline shadows and make an effort to become better known in our communities as individuals. Legacy brand digital platforms may benefit from the kind of direct traffic that results when readers connect with familiar, individual, trusted faces. Technology can be our friend there. The world is exploding with new story forms that are good at humanizing news, in audio, video, and in print.

When looking to those emerging story forms, we could also embrace lessons from other humanists. Kurt Vonnegut claimed he never wrote a story with a villain. Maya Angelou reportedly said people will forget what you say, forget what you do, but will never forget how you made them feel. Primo Levi proposed waging war on undeserved privilege but acknowledged it is a war without end.[7]

Local journalism business models could be well served by intentionally embracing new storytelling technologies that embody humanitarian perspectives and rejecting technologies and platforms that dehumanize.

Disinvest and Reinvest

(Disinvest in technology that harms local storytelling. Invest in technology that supports local storytelling.)

Social media producers at the *Times* are routinely stretched thin. They are often asked to both produce daily stories and promote staff content. One producer described using half their time promoting content (20 hours a week) and half their time producing daily stories (5 stories a week), that gives those journalists just four hours per story.

A better option would be giving them back the full forty hours to be a digital content producer for the *Times*'s own local media platforms. The company could also give the full-time employees currently dedicated to Instagram their forty hours a week back. The video editors spending most of their time editing for algorithms and building followers for a YouTube channel can have her hours back too. Beat reporters can have chunks of their weeks back, as can the photo staff.

Harvard scholar Jeffrey Schnapp describes data as the raw material of our age: "Data is the defining cultural material of the twenty-first century: it is our marble and clay, our coal and petroleum; but raw data alone doesn't do anything; they have to be collected, processed, curated, and shaped."[8]

Past industrial giants created monopolies that controlled the coal and petroleum that moved machines. Today's information and tech giants control the data and stories that move culture, shape human behavior, and steer politics. Data are the coal and petroleum of the digital age.

Independent, demonopolized, ethical, local data collection, processing, and curating should be the job of local journalists. We are uniquely positioned to do that work. We can build a business model doing it. If we disinvest staff hours spent working on social media platforms and reinvest the skills in shaping local data for our own digital spaces, we can create a product that defines local news distinctly, fosters unique local engagement, and builds community trust. We can do more local GIS mapping projects, community engagement events, and interactive local data visualization presentations. Human resources in a newsroom are shrinking, and they are unfortunately zero-sum. Disinvestment from creating data for social media platforms translates to reinvestment in ourselves and our communities.

Fill Black Holes

(Recognize and address newsroom black holes. Partner up to get the help we need.)

Here are ideas on how to fill the Get Off Your Butts Black Hole.

We can host community events. Just before Covid hit, my boss at the *Times* and I partnered with the Dr. Carter G. Woodson African American Museum, African American Heritage Trail, University of South Florida St. Petersburg journalism department, and *Weekly Challenger* newspaper on a Black history drive. It was held on a Saturday at the museum. We set up video interview stations, portrait stations, and a photocopy station and had journalists recording audio informally of people who attended. There were tangible results: multiple daily news stories, a magazine portrait piece, and a long-term project revolving around residents of a neighborhood displaced by the city using eminent domain to make way for a baseball stadium in the 1980s.

We also plan to put a map of that neighborhood online and start filling it with stories, pictures, audio, and video. The idea is to create an online digital communal space where former residents are invited to post their stories, pictures, and memories on the map.

More importantly, locals met journalists. We listened to them and they listened to us. Maybe the people who came out will remember what we said and the journalism we did. But the real goal was to be sure they remembered how we made them feel.

*   *   *

We can do small surveys that measure specific local questions. Those survey efforts can help fill both Metric Black Holes, and the Bull's-Eye Black Hole.

The small surveys method developed by Rachel Kaplan in the 1990s at the University of Michigan addresses specific local questions in a way that is low in cost, manageable, and methodologically rigorous. They can be done with programs like SurveyMonkey, but the best results for local journalism will come by administering them in person. They can contain targeted multiple-choice questions as well as open-ended questions about potential local investigations.

*   *   *

Rescuing local journalism will take a village. Because so many local journalists have been laid off, news deserts and ghost papers need human resources. Universities, community groups, fellow media companies, and new local journalism start-up companies are full of them.

Local universities in particular have resources, longitudinal research commitment, and expertise. There is a desire at universities to make research efforts public. Simple partnerships offer unlimited potential for new perspectives, cross-training to improve disciplines, branding advantages, and real, tangible benefit to local communities. A University of North Carolina Center of Innovation and Sustainability in Local Media study makes this recommendation: "Newspaper owners—especially those in rural and low-income communities—need university faculty and students to produce applied research that assists them in developing and implementing new and *sustainable* business strategies, as well as tools for measuring progress against goals."[9]

My own decision to become involved in an anthropology graduate program boiled down to an adventure in new resources and new possibilities. Honestly, I needed to feel that sense of hope, even if just for my own mental well-being. I found that academics, researchers, and local journalists share a sincere desire to produce media as a public good, with the long-term goal of bettering communities. They commonly strive toward Arendt's definition of good storytelling and knowledge production. There are differences in goals, methods, and expected outcomes. But we also share another common denominator; legacy media and institutions of knowledge are both under attack by politicized and dangerous master media narratives.

Those partnerships also can fill Metric Black Holes. Academic partnerships mix methods in ways that improve on how journalists measure and report on the social world. Openness to those new methods invites a more critical exploration of blind spots and Metric Black Holes that aggregated-data news stories very often miss.

Partnerships with other news agencies offer opportunities to combine resources in a landscape defined by scarcity. A 2016 UNC report describes one such collaboration.

Two recent journalistic endeavors by investment-owned newspapers illustrate that civic-minded editors—at both large and small papers—can rise to the challenge when they have the backing of corporate headquarters. Reporters at the *Sarasota Herald-Tribune*, owned by New

Media/GateHouse, worked collaboratively for a year with journalists at the independently owned *Tampa Bay Times*, detailing the increase in violence and abuse at state-run mental facilities after major cuts in funding. The two papers shared the 2016 Pulitzer Prize for Investigative Reporting. At the same time, Community News Holdings (CNHI), the oldest of the large newspaper investment groups, founded almost 20 years ago, has been upgrading its coverage of state and regional issues in seven states where it has the largest number of papers, most with circulation under 10,000. CNHI has designated one journalist in each of those states to produce both regional enterprise stories and cover statehouse news about policy issues that affect the communities where its papers are located.[10]

I was a member of the reporting team on that partnership between the *Sarasota Herald-Tribune* and the *Tampa Bay Times*. I know it is true that partnerships come with friction, old-school territorial instincts, and complications. However, there is no denying both the potential and necessity of a future that embraces a legacy journalism team mindset.

Commit to Unique Digital Spaces for Professional Work

Our most talented sports photographers were asked to start an @tampa baytimeslightning Instagram account for coverage of the Tampa Bay Lightning hockey team. They posted amazing pictures every game. They were so very good at what they did. Dirk Shadd, the lead photographer, had been shooting the Lightning for about twenty years.

And Instagram was not paying them, or the *Times*, a penny.

In fact, their hard work and talent were training people to not go to our own local digital space. The theory was viewers could go to the Instagram bio page, find our link, and click to go to our own platform. But they won't. They've already seen the photos, and research shows they were unlikely to remember the *Tampa Bay Times* brand at all.[11]

That Instagram account was a lost opportunity for the *Times* to develop an audience for ourselves. As we grew and nurtured a Lightning Instagram following, we were just giving away an opportunity to develop a unique audience for our own brand. Worse, we were forfeiting staff treasures, people who have spent decades becoming the absolute best at what they do, to Instagram. For free. And Instagram gets rights to use the photos.

The argument is that people will click through to our site. They most likely will not.

The argument is that we could eventually monetize traffic from the account when we got enough followers. Historically, that has not worked, but even if it did, we would likely make pennies on the dollar compared to building direct traffic on a business model we own.

The argument was that there is brand-recognition value, but there was only brand confusion and loss of control over our own narrative.[12]

Slow Down to Speed Up

(Provide on-demand news, when there is news. Don't when there isn't.)

Before long, news printed on dead trees will not hit doorsteps. In 2020 the *Times* decreased print circulation from every day to twice a week. But our daily meetings were still geared around what will appear on the front page of an electronic edition that mirrors the former print paper and is not our main digital product. To me, those meetings feel like an outdated habit. It might be time to stop acting like we have newspaper sections to fill.

On the last day of my 2017–2018 Knight-Wallace Fellowship at the University of Michigan I was eating barbecue sandwiches with another fellow, John Shields, who worked for the BBC. He also spent much of his fellowship time exploring how to improve the journalism mess. So we were doing what we nearly always did, bantering about "the information apocalypse."

He threw out an idea he heard at the Online News Association conference.

"What if on a day when there wasn't news, we just said, 'There was no news today?'" he asked. "We've all been there, trying to fill a huge news hole on a slow news day. Since news is now on-demand, what if we just covered news when there is news and concentrate on the big picture when there isn't?"

There is always a twenty-four-hour news cycle, always X number of pages of newsprint to fill. At the same time, there is too much useless, confusing information in people's lives. A trusted news organization could better respect news consumers' time. It might actually help a news organization's credibility to know when to shut up?

There is a model. Shields was remembering an ONA conference lecture at which New York University media scholar Jay Rosen spoke about *De Correspondent*, a Dutch news website which had built into its business model "freedom from the twenty-four-hour news cycle" and was billed an "antidote from the daily grind." Rosen explains in a Knight Foundation article, "When you're not straining to find a unique angle into a story that the entire press pack is chewing on, it's easier to avoid clickbait headlines, which undo trust." He acknowledges there is risk.

> If you're not covering the stories that everyone is hearing about ad nauseam, will you begin to sound inessential and out-of-touch? The Correspondent has an answer to that: "not the weather but the climate." It's a phrase the editors use to keep themselves on track. It means: ignore the daily blips, focus on the underlying patterns. "Not the weather but the climate" is just a slogan. You have to execute on it, and that is always hard. But it is the right slogan when you're trying to optimize for trust. And if you *can* execute on it, you won't seem out of touch at all. You will feel more essential.[13]

Shields and I sipped beer and bantered simplified slogans back and forth. We settled on "News when there's news."

Ask People to Pay

So how can establishing a clearer cultural experience for legacy print organizations translate into money to pay journalists?

Marty Baron, former executive editor of the *Washington Post*, explained the company's advertising paradox in a Knight Foundation interview:

> Basic economics say that if you sell an item in scarce supply, the price will go up, and the scarcer the supply, the higher the price. If the supply is infinite, the price will go down. There are a certain number of page views worldwide, it's a very large number, which is the advertising inventory. What's our answer to the need to make more money? Generate more page views. As we generate more page views, the supply of available inventory goes up and rates go down. The results are you aren't making any more money and may make less. I liken this to being on a treadmill and you're going, but you're not going anywhere.

Then someone speeds it up and you're going faster, but you're still not going anywhere. Then someone speeds it up more and more until you collapse because you can't sustain it anymore. In many ways, we are on that treadmill, and no one knows how to get off. If you were to step off the treadmill, you would collapse and hit your head against the next treadmill and you'd be done. So how do you get off in a safe way and not know that in fact what you are going to do is tumble down because you can't sustain yourself. We don't know about that.[14]

People will ultimately be asked to pay for content. I believe *Homo dramaticus* will pay money to be in a trusted local storytelling environment. Humans are wired for those cultural spaces. We crave stories that speak to us where we live and that serve long-term, communal goals. To build a better business model, legacy newsrooms need to reestablish cultural clarity in trusted news brands, especially in the generation that has grown up without that clarity. When professional news is posted on untrusted platforms, it muddies journalism's time-honored identity, one post at a time.

Legacy media have lost much of the public's cultural understanding of what they are being asked to pay for. Many local newsrooms are allowing faith in a century or more of local credibility and trust, journalistic rigor, and a commitment to fair and balanced reporting to disappear into digital landscapes that do not share their vision. No one in that vast and morally uncertain landscape is going to recover their vision for them.

Breathe and Talk to Ghosts and Children

Local storytelling is always going to be here. Good journalism will find a way. Legacy media will rebuild trust.

It has been nearly three years since I read my dead uncle's book and began questioning my moral purpose as a journalist. I spent a full academic year as a Knight-Wallace Fellow at the University of Michigan reflecting. I returned to the *Times* and spent two more years back in a newsroom in deepening crisis. I have put considerable effort into this book wondering almost daily with journalism friends what is next for journalism and for us.

I have wondered what my target audience would say, what my two ghosts and my little girl would say.

The ghost of my Uncle John encourages me to be bold, fight to break the destructive narratives recycled from history that saturate media today, and oppose people who take advantage of those narratives.

I believe the ghost of Nelson Poynter would remove legacy media from social media ecosystems. I think he would strive for a more diverse local newsroom. I believe he would boldly take journalism out of social media networks and pioneer a new business model. The logo and slogan of the Poynter Institute for Media Studies is "Poynter." It's pronounced "Poynter, period." The message is that nothing should supersede Poynter journalism ethical standards. We need well-defined digital spaces that are "Journalism." Journalism, period. Not Journalism, question mark.

But for me, the real questions boil down to bedtime.

After arguing with my daughter to brush her teeth and put on her pajamas and after negotiating extra chapters of *Magic Tree House* that took us past official bedtime, I feel sleepy listening to her whisper make-believe games to her stuffed animals. I watch her through half-opened eyes (because fully open Daddy eyes are a bedtime kiss of death). Watching her through my eyelashes I wonder at what age she might look at my work, like the day I looked at my uncle's. I wonder what I would want her to see.

Answers vary wildly night to night.

After a day talking to really intelligent grad students who do not have any understanding of the journalism I dedicate my life to, I am discouraged. When a class of those really smart students lumps me into "the media," and not in a good way, I feel like maybe I am done with my old career. How could I imagine my daughter looking at me the way those students do?

Reading emails from parents the day after the publication of our story on special-needs children being taken to mental health facilities in the back of police cars, I am ready for battle. How could I quit local journalism when the stakes are highest? That person would not be my daughter's father.

As I wrote what I believed was this concluding chapter, I hoped this book might benefit local journalism and raise awareness of the importance of our mission in dangerous times. I hoped it might comfort confused journalists like myself, my wife, my *Times* colleagues, and my former Knight-Wallace Fellows—because I am so very proud to count myself among them. I hoped my daughter, when grown, will understand why I stuck with local journalism and fought for it, regardless of the outcome. And I sincerely hoped the effort put into these pages would help you in some small way, in dark media times.

I finished a draft of this manuscript at the end of February 2020.

Then, in a blink, everything changed.

11

2020–2021

There were faint clues on Wednesday, February 26, 2020, to predict how badly the rest of the year was going to suck.

Josh Solomon, the city hall reporter, and I were sitting in a cramped cubicle on the seventh floor of the Real Estate and Property Management Department of the City of St. Petersburg. Pillared stacks of weathered-brown public records boxes formed a forest-like perimeter between us journalists and an office bustling with city workers.

Josh kept the crown of his round head shaved smooth. A thin beard began where Buddy Holly–style glass frames met his ears. His thinly trimmed beard made three peaks along his chin—one at each corner of his mouth and one directly in the middle. Normally, it looked like a pedestal holding up an impish smile that, when it flashed, gave the impression of a child up to mischief.

But today the boyish pedestal-smile sat glumly flat and unfamiliar. Word was out in the newsroom that we would be hearing about more layoffs soon. As we waited for that shoe to drop, his unlined eyes scraped through municipal records that documented how the city valued the mostly Black-owned properties taken through eminent domain in the early 1980s to clear land for Tropicana Field.

One legal folder at a time, we put details in a spreadsheet, then photographed appraiser reports and contracts. An employee in the department occasionally popped his head over a stack of boxes. He told us how we reminded him of the crappiest job he ever had, photocopying legal records in college. He told us it was mind-numbing. It sucked his soul. It was why he got an education. He joked he would never do a crappy job like that again. You know, like our job, that day.

I made the mistake of telling him a 2019 CareerCast report rated newspaper reporter as the third-worst job in the world, just behind taxi driver and logger. And today we're logging records, slowly whittling down the treelike stacks of brown boxes around us.

"How's it going loggers!" he chirped.

It was going slowly. Sandpaper on eyeballs slowly. Animal in a tar pit slowly.

"Check your email," Josh said, cryptically.

There was a staff memo from our communications director. Starting in a week, staff pay would be reduced 10 percent. The cuts would last thirteen weeks. The *Times* lost some big ad accounts. We missed the profit targets to meet financial obligations. Additional staff reductions were likely in the coming weeks.

I excused myself to call my spouse. When I returned, Josh was alone and exasperated. He had absolutely no idea how to cut 10 percent from his budget and still make ends meet. He said the five top *Times* executives were taking 15 percent pay cuts. He started to vent:

> Fifteen percent to them is still totally different than 10 percent to me. I put up a relatively high percentage in my 401(k), and it means that I don't have a lot of room afterward. I mean, I already felt underpaid. I look around the room and all of us just work so hard. And this isn't exactly the industry you're in if you don't like what you do because we put up with too much crap and we get paid too little to do this if we didn't love it. And my pay just went from roughly $41,000 annually, to I guess, roughly $37,000 annually.

He looked down and thought for a moment.

> Now, I'll probably do it for thirty-seven grand a year, but it's just deflating. This wasn't the direction I anticipated my pay going, right?

Financial ground truth at the *Times* was sobering. The company lost big ad accounts and was suddenly in a tough position. There would be layoffs in the next two weeks. They would not drag them out. They would cut staff to a level they think would prevent more layoffs in the coming year.

On the bright side, Josh was just a few hours from vacation. He was headed to New York for a buddy's engagement party, and it's no secret that New York is Josh's happy place.

We fell silent and went back to logging. He stumbled onto a document indicating that the city may never have found the owners of the land where the pitcher's mound of Tropicana Field now stands. Hot on a mystery and digging through the folder for answers, Josh's smile broke free again. So, what, no one was ever paid for the pitcher's mound of a Major League Baseball team?

I pointed out that we still have really cool jobs. He agreed. "I think we all lean on news," he said. "I think we're all trained to lean on news. News provides us purpose, right? Which I really do think is the best thing we can do for our own mental health. There's news to cover. There are issues to wrestle with. That's what we do. And what a cool job, you know?"

The Next Monday

The following week, Josh was back from vacation, and we were back to logging. He was feeling rough. Maybe he was having a hard time bouncing back from his New York weekend? Weirdest thing, though, he couldn't taste or smell anything at all. The doctor had no idea why. She gave him some steroids and said it would likely just pass.

We were back at the city building making our way through records of the homes and businesses on Third Avenue South, a street that ran right through the heart of what is now Tropicana Field. The neighborhood in the footprint of the stadium was taking shape in our minds and on our Excel spreadsheet.

We took a lunch break and grabbed some tacos.

"Really, you can't even taste hot salsa?" I asked, dipping my chip in the shared bowl between us.

Josh dipped a chip. "Absolutely nothing. It's a total waste of money and Mexican food," he joked.

"That is a shame."

Double dip.

"It has chipotles in it. You gonna eat the rest of that taco?"

Under Water

I have a favorite recurring dream.

I am under water. Usually, I am at West Coronado Community Recreation Association, a small neighborhood pool down the street from my boyhood home in El Paso, Texas.

So many magic summers revolved around WCCRA. I became a lifeguard in high school just so I could be paid to spend my days there. I came back every college summer to work, coach the swim team, and give swim lessons.

My favorite time was sunrise, the front gate locked behind me, after swimming laps and before getting to the morning lifeguard chores. I swam a warm-down under water, watching light patterns and feeling currents rush over my face and body for as long as I could before having to come up for a breath.

In my dream, I hit the point where my lungs begin to strain, and suddenly remember I can breathe under water. I pull in a deep breath, pull my arms to my side, and keep feeling the peaceful sunrise water flowing over my chest and legs.

One night in early March, I was dream-swimming in morning WCCRA waters. As usual, I suddenly remembered I could breathe. I inhaled, but this time, thick water filled my lungs. I bolted awake, pulled air through my mouth instead of my nose, and immediately started hacking. My chest filled with air, but my lungs were stiff. They felt lined with something thick and brittle.

I went to the kitchen, boiled water, and breathed steam. It felt really good. I breathed hot vapor until the kettle cooled, warmed it again, and breathed some more. Then I made hot chamomile tea with lemon and sat on the couch with the brim directly under my nose, eyes closed and able to breathe.

I didn't think for a moment I had Covid-19. The first suspected local transmission had only been documented, in California, not long before, in late February. Josh had just returned from a wedding in New York. He wouldn't know for several months, but a bunch of his friends tested positive for Covid antibodies. He was mostly asymptomatic except for the loss of taste and smell that baffled his doctor.

I was pretty lucky. I had a low-grade fever for a few days. For about a week, I felt mucky and sucked a lot of steam, but I never felt worried. My spouse barely caught a cough. My daughter didn't miss a beat.

But the 2020 slide had begun.

In early March, working remotely became mandatory for all *Times* staffers. On March 18, eleven staffers got laid off. By the end of March, advertising revenues were in a nosedive, and the print publishing world felt like it was crumbling.

March 18. Layoffs

An article about the March 18 layoffs described the loss of Craig Pittman as a "gut punch."[1]

It was. For all of us. Craig began working for the *Times* in 1989. He covered environmental issues for twenty-one years. He was a Scout leader. He was an early adapter to social media and garnered a huge following. He wrote books. One of them, *Oh, Florida! How America's Weirdest State Influences the Rest of the Country*, is a *New York Times* bestseller. His fifth book, *Cat Tale: The Wild, Weird Battle to Save the Florida Panther*, was published just a few months before he was let go. He had an amazing work ethic and was just always a fun person to be around. In fact, his pod was nicknamed "The Fun Pod."

The mess of books, files, and notes on Craig's desk was the stuff of legend. A few years back, an inspection by the fire marshal resulted in a companywide memo that desk clutter had reached hazardous levels. The memo might as well have had Craig's name on it. He managed to cut back enough of the growth to pass inspection, but it just grew back.

An internet search for "Tampa Bay Times journalists" will turn up Craig's name prominently, along with the *Times* CEO and just a few other journalists. All that is to say, when I heard he was laid off, I felt the gut punch. I remember my first thought clearly.

"If they let Craig go, how in the hell am *I* still here?"

To me, it felt like a turning point. I suspect a lot of my colleagues had similar thoughts.

Craig was sitting in an auto mechanic waiting room when he got the news. He recalls,

It was my third day of working from home, and I can't remember exactly what was going on with the car. I think I'd taken it in for a routine oil change, and something sort of went wrong afterward. But they said bring it back. So I brought it back.

And sitting in the waiting room, this is like around 10:30 in the morning, I got a text that said, "Can we talk?" I knew immediately what it was.

And so yeah, that was it. And then I was given until 5 p.m. to clear and clean up my desk, and you saw my desk. That was the labor of Hercules right there. But several of my coworkers happened to be there and help me with that. . . . So, I managed to get it all down into the van. Thank heavens, I was driving the van that day and not the Nissan.

The good news is they didn't charge me for the car repair.

In a story published in the *Times*, executive editor Mark Katches said that round of layoffs was not related to advertising losses from the growing pandemic. It was "too soon to tell" what that impact would look like.[2]

March 30. The Unthinkable

At 11:00 Monday morning, I opened a historic email from *Times* chairman and CEO Paul Tash explaining that advertising sales had plunged due to the pandemic. The newspaper had been publishing seven days a week since November 3, 1924, and had never missed a day. Beginning the next week, the *Times* would be printed and delivered two days a week, Wednesday and Sunday. There would be furloughs and reduced hours.

Layoffs would be coming.

I sat for a moment looking at my computer screen, dumbstruck.

Then I gathered up some lighting gear. I had an appointment to photograph a college professor who was using his home 3-D printer to make face shields for frontline workers.

In a question-and-answer session posted on the Poynter website that same day, Tash explained,

> Ad sales are running down about 50%. We expect this plan to make up roughly half of that gap. At that rate, we can tough things out for a few months. If things get worse, or if the crisis goes on indefinitely, we'll have to reconsider our approach. . . . This is the plan for today. A month ago, I would not have imagined what is now reality, so I am not especially confident about my ability to predict the future in another month, or two or three.[3]

That same morning Gannett, the largest newspaper company in America, announced mass layoffs, pay cuts, and furloughs as well.

*   *   *

When I got to my assignment, the professor had also heard the news about the *Times* abandoning daily publication. He said he was the kind of person who just loved the feeling of a morning paper in his hands and asked me how much time I thought the newspaper had left.

I leveled with him and told him I felt just emotionally bottomed out. Not missing a day of print publication is built into our DNA. Knowing there would not be a paper next Monday felt absolutely surreal.

"Did you ever hear about the 1921 hurricane, when the power went out at the *Times* building and everyone was working by lantern?" I asked him. He hadn't.

"They couldn't print the paper without electricity, so a plant operator connected a linotype machine to his two-cylinder motorcycle with a belt and kept the throttle open. I think that's the closest we've ever come to missing a day. But we didn't."

There was an awkward silence and a lump in my throat.

I asked him if I could set up lights for a portrait near the printer in his garage. He could wait inside in the air conditioning for a few minutes, and I'd let him know when it was all set. He said sure and left me alone.

I walked to the back of the stranger's garage, sat on an ice cooler, and put my hands on my face. Tears began to flow. Then sobs.

Payroll Protection: A Lifeline

In April, courtesy of a $2.2 trillion federal Coronavirus Aid, Relief, and Economic Security Act, the *Times* received an $8.5 million government loan that allowed it to restore the 10 percent pay cut and recall some furloughed employees.

The loans, designed to help small businesses make payroll in the opening days of the pandemic, were based on 2019 payroll numbers and covered eight weeks. The loan amounts would be forgiven by the federal government as long as the money was spent on payroll, with some allowances for rent, utilities, and mortgage interest.

"This loan gives us more time to ride out the crisis before we have to make even more changes," Tash said. "It makes a big difference, and we are grateful for it."[4]

Narrative Dissolution

Since Josh and I had had Covid, and we still had a bajillion boxes to go through, we got back together to continue logging municipal records

around properties taken though eminent domain in the footprint of Tropicana Field.

I was also working as picture editor that day. That meant, between records, I was organizing photo coverage, attending meetings on Microsoft
Teams, and scheduling photographers.

Since we were now only printing physical newspapers twice a week,
there was no print edition coming out the next day. Just an e-edition. As I
got off an online meeting held to plan the layout of that electronic edition,
I mumbled, half to Josh, half to nobody,

"Like it matters."

"Right?"

Readership of the e-edition was low. My sense of well-being that day
was pretty low, too.

We went back to the records. For a few minutes, there was only the quiet
white noise of an air conditioner and the turning of pages.

Josh broke the rhythm.

"Know what I was doing the day we got the news we were going to two
print days a week?" he asked.

Josh and I had spent so many hours together logging records that we
sometimes just started verbalizing thoughts out loud. So he continued before I responded. Because, of course I wanted to know. He said,

I was coming back from court. I had covered a hearing because hearings were still happening at the time, and my car—it felt like I was drag-
ging a tree limb. Like the whole car started to shake and make this awful
noise.

So at the 38th Avenue North exit of 275, I actually pulled off. As I
stepped on the clutch to approach the intersection, the engine just
turned off. So, I knew there was something majorly wrong. I pulled off
into the grass and called AAA and called Tara, who came to get me.
And that was the day they announced that we were going to reduce our
print days from seven to two days. And they were going to furlough a
good chunk of the plant staff. So, Tara and I took that call while waiting
for the tow truck on the exit ramp in her car.

So, that sucked. I'd had that car forever. And I loved that car.

Quiet. Page flip. Quiet. Page flip. Page flip.

He continued,

We all know the implications of missing a day. We're a daily newspaper, right? I mean, that's a point of pride. When was the last time we missed a day? People pay for 365 newspapers. We provide 365 newspapers, there's no ifs, ands, or buts about that. The news is the news. We staff every day of the week. We write news every day of the week. That's what we're in it for. So, I remember thinking that if we're going to give that up, that we must be on the brink of obliteration or disappearance.

That's what I remember, thinking, "Okay, I guess I'll be moving home with my parents soon."

Josh and I were both trying to figure out how our careers might be meaningful again, someday.

Protests and Narrative Dissolution

In the midst of pay cuts, layoffs, the quarantines, and the paper cutting back to two print days a week, George Floyd's murder by a Minneapolis police officer sparked months of daily civil rights marches in Tampa and St. Petersburg.

Those protests provided a sense of purpose in ways that boosted our morale. For us, days became defined simply and clearly. There was a job to do. Our job to do. The fast pace and constant breaking news kept us engaged in our careers.

After the pace of the protests died down, our sense of self collapsed again. Josh worried,

Now what do I want to write about? How am I going to fill my days, because now I'm not at the march at 1 p.m. or 4 p.m. or 7 p.m. every day? That's when the dark days of the pandemic hit me. It was just like, I have no purpose now. That is when it all kind of really set in.

There was less obvious pandemic news to cover in the city. I felt like, what am I doing? What value am I providing now? And by then, working from home was less fun because now I missed my colleagues. There's an energy exchange that happens in a newsroom that I wasn't having.

He spent a workday just watching basketball. Nobody noticed. He took long naps in the middle of the day. Nobody cared.

Josh could have been describing my own experience. I was having the exact same struggles.

"This is exactly what [anthropologist] Cheryl Mattingly meant by narrative dissolution," I thought. Mattingly wrote, "Locating ourselves within an intelligible story is essential to our own sense that life is meaningful."[5]

Social psychologists Mary Gergen and Kenneth Gergen similarly observe, "Narratives apply structure to events, ordering the chaos of 'one damned thing after another' into a meaningful trajectory."[6] A journalist identity and all the daily rituals that come with the job normally did exactly that. But all of that had been completely disrupted.

Truth is, we were not really that interested in logging records. We were killing time. We were getting out of the house. And we both knew it.

Drive

One Saturday, Josh got in his car and just started driving north. Destination: maybe New Jersey. He recalled,

> I think I felt like I had the weight of the world on my shoulders. You know, I cover this community, and it's a pretty big community. There's a lot going on, and I felt like I just didn't have the energy.
>
> Oftentimes, most of the time, I feel like I can rise to the occasion. We all have a job to do. We do it the best we can, and usually that's good enough. But I just felt like the best that I could give wouldn't be good enough.
>
> Stories that I know I should be writing were starting to pile up, and I just started feeling kind of paralyzed by all that. Which is I think a feeling we've all had. But it hit me starting in July [2020], and it got worse into August.
>
> I had a whole week where I did very little work. And it's not because I didn't want to do the work. I just kind of felt like I *can't* do the work. I felt literally paralyzed. I would wake up. I was on the calls I needed to be on. I watched the meetings I needed to watch. I was on Slack. I was responsive. I was present. But I felt immobile.
>
> And I decided I'm not doing anybody any good. This isn't good for me. I'm providing no value to the readers or the company. So, I very abruptly asked for a week off. I felt like those last few days probably

shouldn't count as work days anyway. I probably needed to just step out a little bit.

So very abruptly on a Thursday, I asked for the following week off, and thankfully, they gave it to me.

He chewed sunflower seeds on the drive. He scream-sang Billy Joel songs. He tried to keep the miles per gallon fuel meter at the optimal setting for as long as possible. He did get to New Jersey. Then he turned around.

Quiet. Page flip. Quiet. Page flip. Quiet.

Election Day

There were two sides of the fishbowl in the Pinellas County Supervisor of Elections Office on election day 2020—the vote-counter side and the counter-observer side. A thick pane of glass separated the two.

I sat with a handful of lawyers, volunteers, and other journalists on our side, watching election officials look over contested and overseas ballots.

When it was announced that the vote total reached 78 percent of all registered voters in the county, a new record, Supervisor of Elections Julie Marcus jumped up. She raised her thumbs high in the air and exclaimed "Boom!"

It made a cool picture.

About half an hour after I sent it, Marcus saw it on the *Times* website, printed it out, and proudly held it up on her side of the glass. That was rewarding for me. I was a community journalist contributing something on a historic day. I felt like I was in my happy place. In this crazy 2020 Covid year, it had been a while since I felt that sense of purpose.

A lawyer for the Biden campaign joked freely with the journalists in the observation room. He was dressed comfortably, and seemed at ease. He had a five o'clock shadow and uncombed hair. He dressed in faded jeans and worn-out boat shoes. His blue denim shirt was untucked.

A Republican lawyer two chairs down from him was dressed ready for court. He was shaved. His hair combed and gelled. Pressed slacks. Ironed shirt. Polished shoes. He kept to himself and did not join the banter.

In our professional-social gathering, he reminded me of Pierre Bourdieu's unmarriageable man at the Christmas dance.

I felt like there was a tangible, silent presumption of liberal bonds

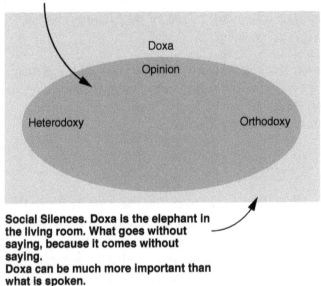

This circle represents what we report and talk about openly.

Doxa

Opinion

Heterodoxy

Orthodoxy

Social Silences. Doxa is the elephant in the living room. What goes without saying, because it comes without saying.
Doxa can be much more important than what is spoken.

Figure 11.1. Pierre Bourdieu's concept of doxa. Text and arrows added by the author, illustration by Steve Madden. © English-language edition, Cambridge University Press, 1977, Pierre Bourdieu, *Outline of a Theory of Practice*. Reproduced with permission of The Licensor through PLSclear.

between the Democrat lawyers, volunteers, and journalists. For many anthropologists, those silent assumptions scream for attention.

The scene made me remember a short editorial in 2013 by Gillian Tett, an anthropologist turned *Financial Times* editor. It is titled "What Pierre Bourdieu Taught Me: Journalists Should Take Nothing for Granted but Instead Look at All the Silences in the World and Ask: Why?" In the article she includes an illustration Bourdieu used to suggest that what people intentionally don't discuss in public can matter much more than what they do discuss (figure 11.1).

Bourdieu contends that those social silences can be what matter most in shaping political, economic, and social conditions. He asserts, "What is essential goes without saying because it comes without saying."[7]

To me, the scene on our side of the glass in the election observation room felt like living in that diagram.

Bite Me Twice, Shame on Me

Our side of the fishbowl was electric just after 8 p.m., as polls closed in the Florida Panhandle's Central time zone. A blogger and several volunteers refreshed the Florida Division of Elections webpage incessantly. Lawyers and poll watchers buzzed in anticipation.

Florida's sixty-seven county elections supervisors had counted early voting and mail-in ballots as they arrived throughout the weeks before the election. So a total of all the pre-election day votes was expected to be made available right after polls closed. Those numbers would be telling and possibly decisive. The crowd on our side of the fishbowl made commentaries like television pundits. Most of it had a pro-Democrat slant.

"If Florida goes, ding-dong the wicked witch is dead," the blogger sang, merrily.

Many of the reporters and observers in the room laughed or smiled at his theatric rendition of the Wizard of Oz song.

I looked over, and the Republican lawyer remained silent, glued to his smartphone.

Tett also wrote about laughter and social bonding, "Laughter, after all, is never neutral or irrelevant—or not to anthropologists. We tend to ignore it, since it seems just like an inevitable piece of social interaction or a psychological safety valve. But laughter inadvertently defines social groups since you have to have a shared cultural base to 'get' a joke. Insiders know when to laugh, even instinctually."[8]

By 8:15 p.m., the blogger began to suspect conspiracy. He alleged Republican interference. Why else weren't all the numbers up?

I checked the Associated Press website. It had collected counties' numbers individually and had a total. I checked the *New York Times,* and it had done the same. It was 47.9 percent Biden, 51.2 percent Trump. Both put the odds of a Trump victory in Florida at greater than 95 percent.

I told the blogger to check the news sites. I explained that news services had tallied individual Florida counties for a total more quickly than the supervisors of elections.

When I told him the probability of a Trump victory, the room got silent. I wondered if it was appropriate for me to be involved in the conversation. I told myself not to react either way, as people in the room began chiming in their disappointment. I looked for the Republican lawyer.

He had left the room. At this point, with Florida in his favor, it looked like a Trump victory in the national count was very possible.

Everyone seemed surprised. They asked how the polls and the media had gotten it so wrong. Again.

Maybe there were two possibilities. One, many Trump supporters were just too suspicious of a liberal conspiracy to talk to pollsters and reporters. Two, media organizations did not include or acknowledge the kind of social silences Bourdieu wrote about, in large swaths of American communities. Institutionally, journalists did not listen to those screaming social silences.

Or maybe reason 1 + reason 2 = reason 3. Swaths of America are gripped by conspiratorial thinking, *and* large sections of American communities are unacknowledged. Those ignored communities can become a vacuum to be filled by alternative and partisan media.

Either way, it seemed like a bad situation and a failure of journalism. Neither election result was likely to change that. Even at the time, having no idea who won the election, I worried about the direction currents in media and politics might be taking the nation.

It was the elephant in the election press room.

I wondered if who won might be less important than the information apocalypse that is defining society and the loss of professional storytellers in communities. Those worrisome tides are much stronger in 2021 than they were in 2016. America is more siloed. Conspiracy theories are more mainstream. "The media" are even less well-defined to the general public. People are even more distrustful of information they consume. More Americans on all sides feel like they are not being heard.

So it was another moment to ask an important question about the power of storytelling in media today. I wondered, regardless of who won, would the root causes of political unrest and media distrust in America change?

Wednesday, January 6, 2021

Just before 2 p.m. on January 6, I got an email that the *Tampa Bay Times* would outsource printing of its newspapers starting in March, would be closing its printing plant and laying off 150 press workers. The company was also cutting pay for newsroom staffers by 10 percent.

I had a 2 p.m. business phone call.

Unbeknownst to the people on the call, a violent mob was swarming into the US Capitol, incited by tweets and rhetoric from a sitting president, with the intention of disrupting Congress from certifying the presidential election.

I saw the news footage a few minutes after we hung up.

At 3:15 p.m. I thought, "I couldn't make this day up if I tried."

I decided that it was five o'clock somewhere, poured a drink, and watched to see if there would be bloodshed in the halls of the Capitol.

Twitter and Facebook locked Trump's account during the coup attempt. Facebook, YouTube, and Twitter removed a Trump video addressing the rioters.

I flipped between Fox News and CNN, soaking in spin-wrapped coverage.

I thought about the warning from the Holocaust survivor, chemist, and writer Primo Levi that every age has its own fascism. Staring at television coverage of the assault on the US Capitol, I remembered how he cautioned future societies that people will always try to deny and distort information, undermine systems of justice, and leverage nostalgia for a past age. Levi warned that such a chain of events leads to dangerous, violent, and dehumanizing consequences with logical consistency.[9]

I thought about friends at the plant who would be among the 150 people laid off. I marveled that the *Times* only delivers a print product twice a week, and soon would not have the ability to print its own newspaper.

Many fundamentals of the media landscape that got the *Times* to this point remained unchanged and largely unchallenged.

Two Pickup Trucks

The following Friday, we were making plans to cover local Trump rallies on Saturday morning. *Times* editors were combing their already thin staffs to cover the events. I was working as weekend picture editor. We were asking people to work on the weekend, two days after pay cuts.

Editors were worried about safety. So were staffers.

A young staff photographer asked me, "Did you see what they wrote on the Capitol walls? 'Murder the media.' Did you see the video of the crowd assaulting the Associated Press photographer?"

The day of the Capitol violence, President Trump told those supporters, "The media is the biggest problem we have, as far as I'm concerned."

He continued, "All of us here today do not want to see our election victory stolen by emboldened radical-left Democrats, which is what they're doing. And stolen by the fake news media." On January 6, media crews were targeted and harassed. Equipment was smashed. A camera cord was tied into a noose.

On the following Saturday, January 9, 2021, I headed to a rally at DeSoto Square Mall in Bradenton, about an hour to the south. Two months earlier, on the Saturday after election day, thousands of Trump supporters had gathered there in support of the president. I wasn't sure what to expect. I left early so I could introduce myself to some of the organizers before the rally began.

When I arrived at 10 a.m., there were just two pickup trucks sitting in an otherwise empty parking lot. They were flying flags: "Don't Tread on Me," "Trump 2020," a skull above assault-rifle crossbones.

The organizers were pleasant as they informed me that my employer was part of a deep state conspiracy that was comprised of the media, Democrats, and most Republicans. They said Donald Trump was the only one who wasn't part of it.

The tone of the conversation was completely normal. We could have been talking about the weather. There was no doubt, no irony, no hint that the claims were unconfirmable conspiracies. The assumption was that all the judges who dismissed dozens of lawsuits in state and federal courts, scores of citizen poll workers in multiple states, Trump's own attorney general, the Republican Senate majority leader, the Pentagon, the National Guard, and the media establishment were coordinating against Trump—without leaving a single piece of hard evidence pointing to wrongdoing.

I considered joking that, if news organizations were sophisticated enough to be part of a conspiracy like that, we would be able to figure out a way to pay journalists and keep the presses running.

We shot the breeze for about ten minutes. They told me the rally was canceled because of a credible threat against their group that they would not disclose. There would likely be another rally somewhere that day, but they would not post any information about it on Facebook or Twitter. It would be word of mouth only, for everyone's safety.

I told them I appreciated that they have differences with the media and thanked them for taking time to talk with me.

I thought about the role of stories in the human brain, why conspiracy theories work for us, and how this group's beliefs in many ways were not that different from what Jonathan Gottschall describes in calling people *Homo fictus*. On some level, we all live in our own story-based Neverland. Maybe, in the end, even the wildest conspiracy theory is not so different from the diverse Neverlands that live in each of our heads.

I thought about how this group's human drive to believe was an act of faith not so very different from my own.

It may not be so different from the human process that transpired when an ancient Egyptian priest explained to throngs of believers how Ra, the Sole Creator, was tricked into whispering his Secret Name, the source of all his power, to Isis, a devious goddess on the rise.

The group's faith might make as much sense as the pre-Columbian Aztec belief that Quetzalcoatl, the Feathered Serpent, descended into an underground hell with his dog-headed god companion, Xolotl, to anoint the bones of long-dead ancestors with his own blood to create the humans who walk the earth today. I thought about the real human-blood sacrifices that happened on the top of a temple dedicated to Quetzalcoatl in Tenochtitlan.

This group's political beliefs were a story brain-hack we all experience on some level, a series of story-induced cognitive shortcuts to help make sense of a confusing world in turmoil. Their beliefs explained the unexplainable and created a shared culture that might help them belong, survive, and thrive. There were tricksters, heroes, villains, drama, morality, and a call to action. Yes, much of it sounded crazy to me, but the stories that play in human brains have been full of crazy for a long, long time.

Were we really all that different?

One big difference is how the human need for stories gets weaponized for purposes of power and control.

That weaponization, and the social media platforms that made it possible, has been a theme in this book from the beginning. My laid-off co-worker Donna Richter and I talked at the YMCA under a television screen that featured a tweet from Trump calling journalists "enemies of the people." Way back then, presidential tweets inciting hatred and violence were still shocking. Eventually, the message became normalized.

The doggedly consistent and repetitive messaging is no accident. Social psychologist Jan-Willem van Prooijen's research highlights how "the brain mistakes familiarity for truth."[10]

In her book *When God Talks Back*, Tanya M. Luhrmann explores "how sensible, reasonable people, living in more or less the same evidential world as the skeptic, are able to experience themselves as having good evidence for the presence of a powerful invisible being who has a demonstrable effect on their lives and are able to sustain a belief in that presence despite their inevitable doubts."[11]

Luhrmann's answer to how people are able to have that experience? Practice, devotion, and repetition. She explains, "What enables them to sustain their commitment is a learning process that changes their experience of mind. . . . [T]his new use of the mind allows God to come alive for people."[12]

Training the mind in a benevolent quest for spirituality is not the same as training a mind to create conspirators for reasons that boil down to selfish, greedy lust for power. Those are two very different, equally powerful ways humans use stories. But either way, the repetition of a narrative is key to that mind training.

I did not judge the group's political beliefs or the human act of believing. I do judge the playwrights of those narratives. I do think US politics have been intentionally and meticulously weaponized by dangerous new media tools that have been invented since I started my career at the *Times* in 1997.

I do think professionally produced journalism should not coexist on those platforms.

I regret the deep impact on our democracy, trust in professional journalism, and villainization of academia. More emotionally, I grieve for all the lost journalists and the loss of career identity and livelihoods of many members of my own journalism family.

On January 8, 2021, Twitter banned Trump from posting on the platform, stating, "After close review of recent Tweets from the @realDonaldTrump account and the context around them . . . we have permanently suspended the account due to the risk of further incitement of violence."

In the Graveyard

Claire McNeill, a fellow *Times* journalist, and I stood at the edge of an open grave with a group of University of South Florida students who were about to exhume a body. We were doing a feature story on unsolved cold cases. We planned to follow this unidentified body and two others from the graves to the lab, to facial reconstruction, to (hopefully) resolution.

One of the students wore a faded-green USF anthropology shirt. I recognized it before she turned around. I knew what was written on the back. The shirts were given out by the department during orientation a few years earlier. When she did turn, I nudged Claire and pointed to the quote:

"The purpose of anthropology is to make the world safe for human differences."

Ruth Benedict

That is the same quote I saw, way back when I was an undergraduate, that made me believe anthropology and journalism occupy common ground.

"These are my peeps," I told Claire, with more than a touch of pride. They were. They were from the USF Anthropology Department. My department. They were archaeology students, and I was on the cultural anthropology track, but a bunch of us had classes together. It felt good to be participating in my two favorite worlds, journalism and anthropology, at the same time.

"I saw that quote way back when I was an undergrad, and it made me want to be a journalist," I told her.

"We sure do need those spaces now," she replied.

There was a long pause.

"Have you talked to your dad about the election?" she asked.

On previous assignments, Claire and I discovered we both come from families that have become deeply divided. We both have conservative parents who question our role as journalists.

"The Covid spike is bad in El Paso, so my parents are really taking quarantine seriously," I said. "My mom asked me to call my dad more often, so I'm trying to talk to him without going to politics. But it's hard. He just has to go there."

"Yeah, it's getting harder and harder."

Looking into an open grave, thinking about how polarized storytelling, and families, have become felt gloomy.

I looked at Benedict's quote on the shirt. Then I looked around at the students and at Claire. I was surrounded by good and decent people who were sincerely called to public service, working together and hoping to bring closure for three unknown and forgotten deceased people and their families.

I began to feel a slow, warming certainty. My own personal sense of purpose, my real job, is simple. It hasn't changed at all: to help make the world safe for human differences. Despite all the damage to local journalism, the chaos of the past few years, the persistent fear of being unemployed, and all the uncertainty, I still feel a sincere call to public service.

I just lost my connection to it in all the confusion.

I looked up out of the grave and around at a crowd of people with hearts dedicated to making their communities better places.

I thought again about Hannah Arendt's ideas on how to measure whether a story is good or bad for society. She asks about the intention of the storyteller and the long-term effects of the story itself. Was the goal public service? Would the story help put a community in conversation with itself in ways that are larger than the storyteller's interests? Or was it told as an act of individual empowerment? Was the storyteller power-hungry, manipulative, self-centered, or greedy?

Those questions are as old as stories themselves. They live inside our human nature in ways that run deeper than today's media crisis.

Yes, the digital age is challenging democracy. But even if legacy media institutions no longer produce storytelling as a public service, there is something even deeper in the hearts of good people that will carry on.

Story Endings

On September 14, 2021, my dad was hospitalized with kidney failure. On the day he was to be released back home, October 23, my mother, who had few health issues, died suddenly. Her aortic artery ruptured as she lifted a television. I was with Claire again when I got the phone call. We were driving in the Florida Keys to an assignment. I will never forget her kindness on that day.

My brother and I flew to El Paso, Texas, to help my dad transition. He failed to thrive and passed away from multiple complications two months later, on December 22.

On February 4, 2022, I provided the *Times* with a prepublication copy of this book for their review. A week later, I was called to a morning meeting and fired, with no severance. It was the week of my 25th employment anniversary.

I was told statements in the book violated *Times* policy on working journalists and political speech. I was reminded of facts I knew well. *Times* journalists are prohibited from supporting candidates publicly. We don't contribute to political campaigns or causes. We don't post our political opinions on social media.

The news felt surreal. The meeting was brief. I emphasized that I really wanted any and all feedback on the contents of this book, in terms of fairness, representation, and accuracy. I followed up with an email to *Times* editor Mark Katches reinforcing my desire for feedback. I received no response. I turned in the final manuscript mid-May.

Under different circumstances, joining the ranks of lost local storytellers would have been a singularly defining event. In the wake of losing my parents, it wasn't. It all mixed into one grieving process, and a range of emotions, that will probably never be distinguishable.

This book describes how stories order the chaos of life events into narratives that make sense of it all. They serve important social functions. They make private events public. They create culture. They help form identity and well-being. They are political. They can be manipulative. They can be told to help a person get what they want, survive, and thrive.

Kurt Vonnegut said there are six types of stories. Journalist and author Christopher Booker spent 34 years writing a book that claimed there are seven basic plots. Legendary Marvel Comics producer Stan Lee said there is only one story: "Who am I?"

I did not have a clear answer to that question anymore. As I tried to make sense of who I was without parents or a clear career identity, I did what any self-respecting *Homo dramaticus* would do. I imagined all kinds of narratives to make sense of events, for all the reasons discussed in this book. But all those stories felt like kitsch, lies, and brain candy.

When I was told I was fired, my head started spinning. Words just popped out of my mouth:

"I love you, and I love the *Times*."

There was an uncomfortable and awkward silence. I felt my face flush. In that moment, professing my love to the guy firing me felt like an exceptionally stupid choice.

But it was absolutely true.

It took some time, but one day I realized the simple feelings that first came out of my mouth during that meeting made my world feel safe for human differences. I'm good with that.

I do love the *Tampa Bay Times*. I especially love the many journalist friends who have become like family in the past two and a half decades. They continue to light up their communities in dark times despite all the challenges and obstacles being thrown at them. Many of them brought light to my life in difficult times, in ways that will always be cherished. I am so proud, and lucky, to have been among them. I love the thousands of people I met on assignments over the years, and all the life lessons they shared. I love local journalism.

Balance

Here is something I haven't lost: a conviction that when we feed our ancient storytelling brains a better diet, we will have healthier communities. By better diet I mean more narratives that make the world safe for human differences in an increasingly complex world. Stories that acknowledge the unspoken and intentionally listen to today's screaming social silences (especially when they make us uneasy), embrace contradictions, and strive to navigate our differences. Humans still crave stories told as public service, stories that help address the long-term interests of our communities, trust-building stories and well-defined spaces where they are told.

Homo sapiens use stories to structure power. For us, controlling a public narrative means controlling the social world, whether in the name of personal gain or public service.

Trump was ultimately removed from social media platforms because his self-serving narratives were deemed by those platforms to be too dangerous for democracy. But that didn't solve the problems we will continue to face in this media age. Every ingredient of the digital media environment he took advantage of is still in place. There will always be stories pushed on society that make dangerous villains out of decent people, from the left and the right. They will be told for the short-term and selfish interests of people seeking power and wealth. Today's, and tomorrow's, technology will keep amplifying selfish and greedy storytelling in unprecedented ways. In 40,000 years of communal storytelling, the social purpose of stories hasn't changed much, but the technological power to leverage those stories certainly has. More people can reach out and lie to you today than at any point in human history. So, the impact of the information apocalypse on society will continue to be frightening.

Yes, local journalism teeters on the brink of collapse, but more and more people seem ready for a healthier media diet. I believe there is a real cultural desire for well-defined media spaces that get filled with people who could be called good storytellers, people who are called (however imperfectly) to journalism as a public trust. I have spent three decades (however imperfectly) surrounded by such people.

I have faith in homeostasis. Much like nature and living organisms are remarkable in their ability to seek a stable equilibrium when systems get out of whack, human societies may intuitively seek a better balance in the culture-building stories we consume.

My life, in the five years covered in this book, was defined by a steadily constricting circle. When I began my journalism career, the space to create stories to help make the world safe for human differences seemed limitless. The general public understood and believed in time-honored journalism standards. Most people I approached in my daily work life believed we had honorable intentions. But the circle kept getting smaller. More journalist friends lost jobs, less quality local journalism was produced, public trust was decimated, and my own career identity slowly eroded.

But at some point, even in the worst storm, high tide comes, and there is nothing left but for the waters to change course. Historic media institutions may or may not endure. Complicated legacies, outdated newsroom habits, financial realities, and an inability to innovate may be too much to overcome. But media intuitions and politics-as-usual can be reimagined. Vacant media spaces create opportunity, and the human need for healthier systems of communally beneficial storytelling feels inevitable.

Because it feels inevitable, it also feels exciting.

Ultimately, it is in everyone's long-term interests to create media spaces that can be trusted. For tens of thousands of years, humans have needed well-intentioned storytellers to help navigate inevitable contradictions, complexities, and dangers in the human social world.

Certainly, the future will not deliver perfect or infallible storytellers. Just people called to journalism as public service and a secure place for them to work. People who tell stories framed in ethical standards to serve long-term societal goals rather than as means to selfish, short-term rewards.

That trusted storyteller role was baked into the recipe for building heathy human societies at the dawn of culture.

So, really, in the end, what other choice do we have?

Acknowledgments

To each journalist who shared their story: thank you. You gave me so much more than I could ever fit in a book—or even in words.

I grew up at the *Tampa Bay Times*. Over two and a half decades, peer friendships became like family. A big, crazy, amazing, creative, inspirational, often patient, and amazingly dedicated family. We have all been through so many stories and so much change together. There is a long and heartfelt list, full of memories, all-so-human highs and lows and life lessons. For that, I am so very blessed and lucky.

Some have left us: Bruce Moyer, you taught me to trust my first instincts, and I miss you all the time. Karen Pryslopski, I will always remember: "It's all in pencil." Terry Tomalin, for wonderful adventures and the mantra: "Terry would go." Paul de la Garza, you are always in my spirit: "Atácale!" Mike Konrad, thank you for showing so many of us the ropes.

Boyzell Hosey has been a rock, and an inspiration, for more than twenty years. Lara Cerri, Ted McLaren, Josh Solomon, Dirk Shadd, Doug Clifford, Sue Moyer, Will Vragovic, Martha Asencio-Rhine, Jennifer Glenfield, James Borchuck, Joe Walles, Sonya Doctorian, Patty Yablonski, Fred Victorin, David Adams, Susan Taylor Martin, Sue Morrow, Skip O'Rourke, Tara McCarty, Don Morris, Carrie Pratt, Connie Humburg, Kelley Benham French, Terry Chapman, Tom Tobin, Jim Damaske, Stefanie Fletcher, Jamal Thalji, Sherman Zent, Kenny Irby, Monica Herndon, Luis Santana, Edmund Fountain, Cherie Diez, Ric Ferro, Fraser Hale, Jamie Francis, Danese Kenon, John Timpe, Krystal Kinnunen, Michael Kruse, Jack Rowland, Chris Urso, Kathleen Flynn, Chris Zuppa, Scott Keeler, Brian Baer, Joni James, Tom French, Stan Alost, Suzette Moyer, Brittany Volk, Lane DeGregory, Jeff Klinkenberg, Bill Duryea, Kat McGrory, Claire McNeill, Mike Wilson, Ben Montgomery, Bill Varian, Leonora LaPeter Anton, Maria Carrillo, Amy Hollyfield, Paul Alexander, Tom Scherberger, Maurice

Rivenbark, Sharon Kennedy Wynne, Graham Brink, Neil Brown, Stephen Buckley, Mark Katches, Paul Tash, Andy Barnes. There are far too many to name everyone. So, to the entire *Times* family, thank you.

Meredith Babb, who is now retired from University Press of Florida, believed in me. She dished out perfect doses of encouragement and tough love, gave brilliant feedback, and got the manuscript out to the best peer reviewers I could have imagined. Sian Hunter and Eleanor Deumens jumped in after her and shepherded the work, with patience and kindness, through the craziness of a pandemic and personal tragedy, in ways that will always be deeply appreciated. Brad Scriber fact checked sections and made everything he touched better. Tana Silva's attention to detail, perspectives, and suggestions were gifts. I will never forget the kindness and reassurance of media lawyer Lynn Oberlander.

Words cannot express my debt of gratitude to Rob Hooker. The scholarship, lived history, and meticulous attention he brought to this book are priceless and will always be cherished. My thanks to Donna Richter also transcends words. She not only shared her own story but fact-checked the book, and saved me from myself.

I simply could not be more fortunate than to have received feedback from *Tampa Bay Times* alumnus Craig Pittman, who has long been an inspiration to so many of us. My thanks to Steve Madden for illustrations and cover inspirations. William Schulte, associate professor of mass communications at Winthrop University, sent comments that elevated, clarified, and inspired without fail. Cynthia Barnett, Saundra Amrhein, and Danielle Dreilinger, thank you for all the fellow-book-writer therapy sessions.

This whole anthropology journey started with a cup of coffee in 2015 with Liz Bird, who eventually became my adviser at the University of South Florida. Thank you, Liz, for your tireless guidance. Daniel Lende showed me the magical ways social theory comes alive in fieldwork and that the way through the writing is through the writing. Antoinette Jackson forever changed how I define, and live in, the present. Tara Deubel deepened what is possible with a camera and limped with me through teaching visual anthropology in a crazy Covid year. Steven Jones helped me find humanity and hope in digital spaces when I needed it most. Christian Wells and Sarah Taylor made me love, and fear, statistics.

So much of this book came out of the time I spent as a Knight-Wallace Journalism Fellow at the University of Michigan. I am grateful that Wallace House director Lynette Clemetson believed in me—but far more grateful for her insistence that I believe in myself. During my year in Michigan, Ruth Behar taught me the craft of ethnographic writing. At the same time, Jim Burnstein taught me the structure, the "physics," of scriptwriting. Together they created a cocktail that informed much of this work and dramatically changed the direction of my academic journey. Avik Basu taught me that not everything that can be counted counts and not everything that counts can be counted. My Aunt Martha Rainbolt walked me through the past to help me be present.

The greatest gratitude lies with family. This book is dedicated to my parents, who passed away just before it published. My mother, Janet Pendygraft, left us in October 2021. My father, Joe Pendygraft, passed two months later. I thank them for so many years of the silent sacrifices loving parents make for unthankful children. Thank you. My older brother, Scott, for at some point deciding to stop beating me up and becoming my best friend. His wife, Rosie, and my nephews, Aidan and Austin.

My chosen brothers and sisters Traci "My Chief" Presley, Xavier Alvarez, Chas Powers, Gary Jensen, Warren Cottle, and Wendy "Widi" Wood live inside me and pick me up in dark times, even when no one is around. Because of my Aunt Nancy Jensen and Uncle Moon, I will always believe in the magic of fairy tales.

Dr. Edward Stein, my father-in-law, was insatiably curious about every step of my journey. He listened attentively, for so long, with such sincerity, to completely unformed ideas. Then he would wrap them up in just a few brilliant sentences and give them back as precious gifts. It was he who told me one afternoon, after hearing all I had to say, "The fish is in the water and the water is in the fish." He passed away in 2020, and I miss his wisdom. The wisdom of my mother-in-law, Sherry Stein, was more brass tacks. Don't doubt it—Bubbie knows best.

My spouse, Letitia Stein Pendygraft, whose innumerable sacrifices, inspiration, perspective, brilliant mind, and love make everything possible.

My daughter, who is simply my whole heart.

Notes

Chapter 1. Dangerous Times and Safe Spaces

1. Sonya Doctorian, the director of photography in 2000, told me in 2020, "In January 1995, the SPT photo department had 39 FTEs. When I departed in Sept. 2000, we had 49. We'd also increased our internships to two to include a Tampa summer paid internship. [*St. Pete Times* CEO] Paul Tash was willing to invest in a department that worked, that got results—and in those days, he could afford to. It's certainly different now."

2. Quoted in William Haviland and Harald Prins, *Cultural Anthropology*, 402.

3. Penelope Muse Abernathy, *Rise of a New Media Baron*, PDF pp. 11–16. Abernathy, *News Deserts and Ghost Newspapers: Will Local News Survive?*, pp. 5–14. Abernathy notes in another report, "Half of the 3,143 counties in the country now have only one newspaper, usually a small weekly, attempting to cover its various communities. Almost 200 counties in the country have no newspaper at all. The people with the least access to local news are often the most vulnerable—the poorest, least educated and most isolated" (*Loss of Local News*, n.p.). Also see Margaret Sullivan, "When Local News Goes Away, Citizens Suffer: Gannett's Megamerger Will Probably Just Inflict More Pain," *Washington Post*, August 16, 2019.

4. "U.S. Newspapers Have Shed Half of Their Newsroom Employees since 2008," Pew Research, April 20, 2020, https://www.pewresearch.org/fact-tank/2020/04/20/u-s-newsroom-employment-has-dropped-by-a-quarter-since-2008/. "U.S. newsroom employment has fallen 26% since 2008," Pew Research, July 13, 2021, https://www.pewresearch.org/fact-tank/2021/07/13/u-s-newsroom-employment-has-fallen-26-since-2008/

5. Joseph Campbell, *Hero with a Thousand Faces*; Jonathan Gottschall, *Storytelling Animal*; Bruce Hood, *Domesticated Brain*; Richard G. Klein and Blake Edgar, *Dawn of Human Culture*; John D. Niles, *Homo Narrans*.

6. Charles Darwin, *Descent of Man*, 166. See also David S. Wilson, *Darwin's Cathedral*, 5.

7. Tracy Miller, *US Religious Landscape Survey*. See also Tanya M. Luhrmann, *When God Talks Back*, xi.

8. Hannah Arendt, *The Human Condition*, 50. Michael Jackson also cites this Arendt passage in *Politics of Storytelling*, 16.

9. Jerome Barkow, "Beneath New Culture Is Old Psychology," 630.

10. Quoted in Thomas Meany, "Bild, Merkel, and the Culture Wars: Inside Story of Germany's Biggest Tabloid," *The Guardian*, June 16, 2020, https://www.theguardian.com/world/2020/jul/16/bild-zeitung-tabloid-julian-reichelt-angela-merkel-germany.

11. Knight Commission on Trust, Media, and Democracy, *Crisis in Democracy*, n.p. In the report Alberto Ibargüen, Knight Foundation president and CEO, contextualizes today's explosion of communication technology: "For a hundred years after the invention of the printing press, people had trouble figuring out what was true and how to handle so much more information. Today, we're living just that kind of 'Gutenberg moment.' The Internet has transformed what we know and how we know it and, therefore, how we think about the world. . . . Because we're just at the beginning of the tech revolution, it's not too late. We can still examine the effects of technology on our democracy and actually decide what we—individuals, press, platform, and philanthropy—can, and have the will to do, to shape the future we want."

12. David Foster Wallace, "This Is Water," commencement address to Kenyon College graduating class of 2005, Gambier, OH, May 21, 2005.

13. Arthur Miller, "Shadows of the Gods," 35.

14. Clifford Geertz, *Interpretation of Cultures*, 5.

15. William Gibson, "Google's Earth," opinion, *New York Times*, August 31, 2010, http://www.nytimes.com/2010/09/01/opinion/01gibson.html. The concepts discussed here come from discussions, readings, and participation in a class taught by Steven E. Jones, a digital humanities professor at the University of South Florida; a specifically pertinent source is Steven E. Jones, "Turning Practice Inside Out," 267.

16. Gillian Tett, presentation in "More Than Models: The Media and the Economy at a Time of COVID-19," American Anthropological Association webinar, April 10, 2020, https://www.youtube.com/watch?v=FDaehx6iBTk.

17. Kirin Narayan, *Alive in the Writing*, 2.

18. In a first review of this manuscript, Winthrop University associate professor of mass communications William Schulte observed how the *Tampa Bay Times* can be viewed as a canary in a coal mine.

Chapter 2. 2016

1. Warren Breed, Newspaperman, News, and Society.

2. The ethnographic use of "symbolic capital" here is taken from Pierre Bourdieu's Theory of Practice. Practice theory frames much of the work in this book. The approach examines how the individual human drive to be successful interplays with a person's specific structural ecology. Sherry Ortner notes that practice theory "seeks to explain the relationship(s) that obtain between human action, on the one hand, and some global entity which we call 'the system' on the other" ("Theory in Anthropology since the Sixties," 148). A practice approach has been refined and adapted as a useful tool for media studies by my own academic adviser, Elizabeth Bird, as well as Nick Couldry, John Postill, and other authors of media ethnographies.

3. Warren Breed, "Social Control in the Newsroom," 335.

4. Lyndsey's and Jennifer's approaches are very different in terms of practice theory,

which considers how individuals' diverse motives and intentions make and transform the world in which they live. Nick Couldry boils media practice theory down to the deceptively simple question "What are people doing that is related to media?" (Media, Society, World, 35).

5. Pierre Bourdieu, "The Peasant and His Body."

6. Gillian Tett, Silo Effect, 28.

7. Jennifer Orsi spent three years working in marketing and communications for a financial company. In 2021 she joined the USA Today Network as executive editor of the Sarasota Herald-Tribune and the network's Florida regional editor.

8. Pierre Bourdieu, Outline of a Theory of Practice, 72

9. This framing of a newsroom ethnography was helped by a manuscript review and personal communication with William Schulte.

10. In the newsroom there are moments best described by Anna Lowenhaupt Tsing's concept of "the grip of encounter," that is, the friction caused at the intersection of large-scale changes in social structures and individual ethnographic moments. Tsing's concept of ethnographic friction points emerged during moments of conflict throughout my time documenting the newsroom. Tsing observes, "As a metaphorical image, friction reminds us that heterogeneous and unequal encounters can lead to new arrangements of culture and power" (Friction, 5).

Chapter 3. Storytelling Animals

1. Richard G. Klein and Blake Edgar, *Dawn of Human Culture*, 8. The scholars write, "Arguably, the 'dawn' was the most significant prehistoric event that archeologists will ever detect. Before it, human anatomical and behavioral change proceeded very slowly, more or less hand-in-hand. Afterwards, the human form remained remarkably stable, while behavioral change accelerated dramatically. In the space of less than 40,000 years, ever more closely packed cultural 'revolutions' have taken humanity from the status of a relatively rare large mammal to something more like a geologic force."

2. Klein and Edgar, *Dawn of Human Culture*, 261.

3. Klein and Edgar, *Dawn of Human Culture*, 271.

4. The Sungir site is about 29,000 years old, but one can argue that older examples (the Chauvet Cave, Lascaux, Les Trois-Frères, Altamira, and others) push traces of human culture back to 32,000 to 40,000 years ago. The burial is discussed in Randall White, "Integrating Social and Operational Complexity: The Material Construction of Social Identity at Sungir," 120–137. See also Randall White, *Prehistoric Art: The Symbolic Journey of Humankind*; Klein and Edgar, *Dawn of Human Culture*, 258–260.

5. Klein and Edgar, *Dawn of Human Culture*, 272.

6. Richard Streckfuss, "Objectivity in Journalism," 973.

7. Streckfuss, "Objectivity in Journalism," 974.

8. Streckfuss, "Objectivity in Journalism," 978.

9. Walter Lippmann, *Liberty and the News*, 56.

10. Lippman, *Liberty and the News*, 82.

11. Streckfuss, "Objectivity in Journalism," 983.

12. Quoted in Hood, *Domesticated Brain*, 14.

13. Psalms 8:2.

14. Fulford, *Triumph of Narrative*, 123.

15. Hood, *Domesticated Brain*, 6–7.

16. Hood, *Domesticated Brain*, 4.

17. Antonio Damasio, *Self Comes to Mind*, 293. Quoted also in Lisa Cron, *Wired for Story*, 8.

18. Jonathan Gottschall, *Storytelling Animal*, 118.

19. David S. Wilson, *Darwin's Cathedral*, 26.

20. John D. Niles, *Homo Narrans*, 2. Niles makes the argument for his book in asserting, "My claim here is a more ambitious one: namely that oral narrative is and for a long time has been the chief basis of culture itself."

21. Jonathan Gottschall, "The Storytelling Animal: Jonathan Gottschall at TEDx FurmanU," May 4, 2014. https://www.youtube.com/watch?v=VhdoXdedLpY.

22. "Carl Linnaeus (1707–1778)," University of California Museum of Paleontology, Berkeley, https://ucmp.berkeley.edu/history/linnaeus.html.

23. Blake Snyder, *Save the Cat*, 22.

24. Snyder, *Save the Cat*, 56.

25. Friedrich Nietzsche, "The Wanderer and His Shadow," in his *Human, All Too Human*, 383.

26. Penelope Muse Abernathy, *Rise of a New Media Baron*, 20.

27. Daniel Smith et al., "Cooperation and the Evolution of Hunter-Gatherer Storytelling," 3.

28. Gottschall, *Storytelling Animal*, 119.

29. Michelle Scalise Sugiyama, "Literary Prehistory," 11.

30. Maureen Dowd, "The Ego Maniac in the Oval Is 'Exonerated,'" *New York Times*, April 20, 2019, https://www.nytimes.com/.

31. Donald Trump, Twitter post, August 18, 2018.

32. Arthur G. Sulzberger, "The Growing Threat to Journalism around the World," opinion, *New York Times*, September 23, 2019, https://www.nytimes.com/.

33. The relation between individual people and larger social forces is described by Anna Lowenhaupt Tsing's concept of "the grip of encounter," the friction caused between changing social structures and individual ethnographic moments (*Friction*).

34. Hannah Arendt, *Human Condition*, 50.

35. Adam Greenfield, *Radical Technologies*, 28–29.

36. Michael Jackson, *Politics of Storytelling*, 14.

37. Jackson, *Politics of Storytelling*, 259.

38. Hannah Arendt, *Men in Dark Times*, 21.

39. Arendt, *Men in Dark Times*, 3–31. Michael Jackson observes, "[Arendt's] judgment of whether a story is good or bad, right or wrong . . . is based on a story's aftereffects, particularly whether it fosters the democratic ideal of a community of equals who are in constant conversation with one another, adjusting the interests of each other to the interests of all" (*Politics of Storytelling*, 16). Ultimately, he says, Arendt found that socially benevolent storytelling focuses on "people acting together rather than any individual act of empowerment."

40. Arendt, *Men in Dark Times*, 22.

41. Gottschall, *Storytelling Animal*, xiv.

42. "Second star to the right and straight on 'til morning" are directions the children followed from Wendy's bedroom to Neverland in J. M. Barrie's *Peter Pan*.

Chapter 4. The Ghost of the Sacred Trust

1. Drawing on the work of *St. Petersburg Times* stalwarts Tom C. Harris and Dick Bothwell, Rob Hooker produced an 80-page history of the newspaper to commemorate the 100th anniversary of the news organization, *100 Years, St. Petersburg Times, July 25, 1884 to July 25, 1984: The Times and Its Times*. This book's account of that history comes directly from Hooker's scholarship.

2. Hooker, *100 Years*, 25.

3. Robert Pierce, *Sacred Trust*, xii–xiii.

4. Darwin Payne, "Robert N. Pierce, *A Sacred Trust*," 378.

5. Quoted in Bill Mitchell, "Who Owns the St. Petersburg Times? Why It Matters to Readers," Poynter Institute, October 10, 2002, https://www.poynter.org/archive/2002/who-owns-the-st-petersburg-times-why-it-matters-to-readers/.

6. Mitchell, "Who Owns the St. Petersburg Times?"

7. Margaret Sullivan, "When Local News Goes Away, Citizens Suffer: Gannett's Megamerger Will Probably Just Inflict More Pain," *Washington Post*, August 16, 2019, https://www.washingtonpost.com/.

8. Mark Katches, "Gannett and GateHouse Merger Changes the Media Landscape in Florida," *Tampa Bay Times*, August 6, 2019, https://www.tampabay.com/.

9. Rouson no longer has the original letter. He recited the last paragraph again in a second interview. It matched word for word.

10. Rosalie Peck and Jon Wilson, *St. Petersburg's Historic African American Neighborhoods*, 75. Goliath J. Davis in the foreword to *Urban Buffalo Soldiers: The Story of St. Petersburg's Courageous Twelve*, ii

11. Gene Roberts and Hank Klibanoff, *The Race Beat*, 365

12. Arsenault, *Freedom Riders*, 323

13. Hooker, *100 Years, St. Petersburg Times*, 64

14. Bourdieu, *Outline of a Theory of Practice*, 167

15. Jackson, *Urban Buffalo Soldiers*, 6.

16. Hooker, *100 Years*, 47.

17. Don Heider, *White News*, 83–84.

18. James Lull, *Media, Communication, Culture*, 33.

19. Schulte, *Social Construction and News Work*, 1.

20. Bruce Springsteen, "Complete Text of Bruce Springsteen's SXSW Keynote Address."

21. In Walter Fisher's concept of narrative paradigm versus the rational world paradigm, the latter assumes that people make decisions based on reason and logic ("Narration as a Human Communication Paradigm"). Fisher's narrative paradigm assumes that meaningful human communication is based on storytelling and reporting of events. Behavior and decisions are best explained through the narrative process.

22. Kyra Miller, "Context is Key: How journalists and historians can work together

to help audiences understand the news," *The Lenfest Institute*, August 26, 2019, https://www.lenfestinstitute.org/local-journalism/context-is-key-how-journalists-and-historians-can-work-together-to-help-audiences-understand-the-news/

23. Kelly McBride and Tom Rosensteil, introduction to *New Ethics of Journalism*, 3–4.

24. Sabrina Tavernise, Amy Harmon, and Maya Salam, "5 People Dead at Maryland's Capital Gazette Newsroom," *New York Times*, June 28, 2018, https://www.nytimes.com/2018/06/28/us/capital-gazette-annapolis-shooting.html.

Chapter 5. Brittany's Bowl

1. Answer: yes. A Bloomberg investigation concludes, "Facebook Inc. has been paying hundreds of outside contractors to transcribe clips of audio from users of its services, according to people with knowledge of the work" (Sarah Frier, "Facebook Paid Contractors to Transcribe Users' Audio Chats," *Bloomberg*, August 13, 2019, https://www.bloomberg.com/).

2. Mark Zuckerberg, "Facebook Can Help the News Business," *New York Times*, October 25, 2019, https://www.nytimes.com/.

3. Frier, "Facebook Paid Contractors."

4. The class was offered by Will Potter, the Howard R. Marsh Visiting Professor of Journalism, and assistant professors Josh Pasek and Brian Weeks.

5. Knight Foundation, "News Organizations, Technology Companies, Citizens Must Take Responsibility for Restoring Trust in Democracy," press release, February 4, 2019, https://knightfoundation.org/press/releases/news-organizations-technology-companies-citizens-must-take-responsibility-for-restoring-trust-in-democracy/.

6. Jill Lepore, "The Last Time Democracy Almost Died," *New Yorker*, January 27, 2020, https://www.newyorker.com/magazine/2020/02/03/the-last-time-democracy-almost-died.

7. Examples of newsroom studies employing applied practice and social capital theory are in research by S. Elizabeth Bird, "The Future of Journalism in the Digital Environment"; Breed, "Social Control in the Newsroom"; Pierre Bourdieu, *On Television*; Birgit Bräuchler and John Postill, *Theorising Media and Practice*.

8. Antonis Kalogeropoulos, Richard Fletcher, and Rasmus Kleis Nielsen, "News Brand Attribution," 592.

9. Amy Mitchell et al., "How Americans Encounter, Recall, and Act upon Digital News."

10. Antonis Kalogeropoulos, Richard Fletcher, and Rasmus Kleis Nielsen, "News Brand Attribution in Distributed Environments," 594.

11. Kalogeropoulos, Fletcher, and Nielsen, "News Brand Attribution," 594.

12. Elizabeth Shearer, "Social Media Outpaces Print Newspapers."

13. "2018 Edelman Trust Barometer," Edelman, January 21, 2018, https://www.edelman.com/trust/2018-trust-barometer. The barometer is a survey of more than 33,000 people in twenty-eight countries. The 2018 barometer was conducted October 28–November 20, 2017.

14. "2018 Edelman Trust Barometer," n.p.

15. Jessica Davis, "After It Stopped Posting to Facebook, a Danish Broadcaster Saw Its Traffic Stability Improve," *Digiday*, February 7, 2018, https://digiday.com/media/cutting-ties-facebook-danish-broadcaster-saw-traffic-stability-improve/.

16. Quoted in Davis, "After It Stopped Posting to Facebook."

17. The quote is from Virgil: "Audaces fortuna iuvat."

18. "Introducing Facebook News," Facebook, October 25, 2019, https://about.fb.com/news/2019/10/introducing-facebook-news/.

19. "Introducing Facebook News," Facebook.

20. Mike Isaac and Marc Tracy, "Facebook Calls Truce with Publishers as It Unveils Facebook News," *New York Times*, October 25, 2019, https://www.nytimes.com/.

21. Isaac and Tracy, "Facebook Calls Truce."

22. Claire Atkinson, "Facebook Announces Effort to Partner with Media to Promote Journalism," NBC News, October 27, 2019, https://www.nbcnews.com/news/all/facebook-announces-effort-partner-media-promote-journalism-n1072511.

23. Angel Au-Yeung, "Mark Zuckerberg's Net Worth Tumbles $18.8 Billion, More in One Day Than Ever Before," *Forbes*, July 25, 2018, https://www.forbes.com/.

24. Hayley Cuccinello, "Who Got Rich This Week: Zuckerberg, Bezos, and Three Other Billionaires Gain $13 Billion Combined," *Forbes*, April 27, 2019, https://www.forbes.com/.

25. Mike Isaac and Cecilia Kang, "Facebook Says It Won't Back Down from Allowing Lies in Political Ads," *New York Times*, January 9, 2020, https://www.nytimes.com/.

26. Quoted in Bill Chappell, "FEC Commissioner Rips Facebook over Political Ad Policy: 'This Will Not Do,'" NPR, January 9, 2020, https://www.npr.org/.

27. Jeremy Barr, "Mark Zuckerberg Celebrates the Launch of Facebook News with a Longtime Critic," *Hollywood Reporter*, October 25, 2019, https://www.hollywoodreporter.com/business/digital/mark-zuckerberg-celebrates-facebook-news-launch-longtime-critic-1250017/.

28. Stephen R. Barnard, "Tweet or Be Sacked," 191.

29. Barnard, "Tweet or Be Sacked," 201.

30. Abernathy, *Rise of a New Media Baron*; Kalogeropoulos et al., "News Media Trust and News Consumption," 22.

31. Berger, "Ways of Seeing," at 0:20.

32. Berger, "Ways of Seeing," at 11:10.

33. Berger, "Ways of Seeing," at 5:08.

34. David Fahrenthold, lecture, University of Michigan lecture, October 4, 2017.

35. Pierre Bourdieu, *Bourdieu and the Journalistic Field*, 30.

36. Bourdieu, *Bourdieu and the Journalistic Field*, 29–38. Bourdieu's use of field theory is most often applied as a research tool to enable the scientific construction of social objects between fields such as journalism, sociology, and politics. In this example I am using that tool to construct social objects between the legacy media field and the social media field, which did not exist fully at the time of Bourdieu's writing. Also, in the film *La Sociologie est un sport du combat* (2001, Pierre Carles, CP Productions and VF Films), Bourdieu compares his own field, sociology, to a combat sport: "I

often say sociology is a combat sport, a means of self-defense. Basically, you use it to defend yourself, without having the right to use it for unfair attacks." Bourdieu applies the analogy to his field and all professional fields in *The Field of Cultural Production* and *Outline of a Theory of Practice* as well as to journalism in particular in *On Television* and essays in *Bourdieu and the Journalistic Field*.

37. Bourdieu, *Bourdieu and the Journalistic Field*, 29.

38. Charles Blow, personal conversation, University of Michigan, September 7, 2017.

39. Bourdieu, *Bourdieu and the Journalistic Field*, 3.

40. Bourdieu, *Bourdieu and the Journalistic Field*, 43.

41. Bari Weiss, "Resignation Letter," BariWeiss.com, July 14, 2020, https://www.bariweiss.com/resignation-letter.

42. Ovadya is chief technologist at the Center for Social Media Responsibility at the University of Michigan, a Knight News Innovation Fellow at the Tow Center for Digital Journalism at Columbia University, and founder of the Thoughtful Technology Project.

43. Aviv Ovadya, "What's Worse Than Fake News? The Distortion of Reality Itself," *Washington Post*, February 22, 2018, https://www.washingtonpost.com/news/theworldpost/wp/2018/02/22/digital-reality/.

44. Ovadya, "What's Worse Than Fake News?"

45. Ovadya, "What's Worse Than Fake News?"

Chapter 6. Master Narratives

1. Robert Fulford, *Triumph of Narrative*, 32.

2. Fulford, *Triumph of Narrative*, 9.

3. Jean Zimmerman, "The Agonizing Collision of Love and Slavery in 'Thomas Jefferson,'" NPR, Michigan Radio, April 6, 2016, https://www.npr.org/2016/04/06/471619275/the-agonizing-collision-of-love-and-slavery-in-thomas-jefferson.

4. Michael Coard, "President Jefferson: A Pedophile Rapist," opinion, *Philadelphia Tribune*, March 3, 2018. https://www.phillytrib.com/commentary/coard-president-thomas-jefferson-a-pedophile-rapist/article_f841b673-50ac-5510-8330-20d3bac6f974.html.

5. Fulford, *Triumph of Narrative*, 7.

6. Tamim Ansary, *Invention of Yesterday*, 2.

7. Vonnegut, *Palm Sunday*, 286.

8. Vonnegut, *Palm Sunday*, 286–287.

9. Vonnegut, *Palm Sunday*, 288.

10. Vonnegut, *Palm Sunday*, 288.

11. Snyder, *Save the Cat*.

12. Tim Stout, "Blake Snyder's Beat Sheet," blog post, https://timstout.wordpress.com/story-structure/blake-snyders-beat-sheet/.

13. Sarah Klein and Tom Mason, "Ken Burns: On Story," YouTube video, 5:21, December 18, 2015, https://www.youtube.com/watch?v=VlZYgPllKNU. The quote is at 1:34.

14. Gretchen Busl, "Whoever Controls the Narrative Has the Power," TEDxTWU, June 6, 2016, https://www.youtube.com/watch?v=rNuzkAosEDw&t=260s.

15. Rachel Janik, "'Writing History with Lightning': The Birth of a Nation at 100," *Time Magazine*, January 8, 2012, 2.

16. Janik, "Writing History with Lightning," 2.

17. Executive Order 9586—The Medal Of Freedom, National Archives, https://www.archives.gov/federal-register/codification/executive-order/09586.html.

18. Amy Chozick, "Why Trump Will Win a Second Term," *New York Times Sunday Review*, September 9, 2018. https://www.nytimes.com/2018/09/29/sunday-review/trump-2020-reality-tv.html.

19. Craig Silverman, "This Analysis Shows How Viral Fake Election News Outperformed Real News on Facebook," BuzzFeed News, November 16, 2016, https://www.buzzfeednews.com/article/craigsilverman/viral-fake-election-news-outperformed-real-news-on-facebook.

20. Peter Warren Singer and Emerson T. Brooking, *Like War*, 120.

21. Singer and Brooking, *Like War*, 120.

22. Quoted in Desmond Ang, "The Birth of a Nation: Media and Racial Hate," 2020, 2. Ang took the Griffith quote from William G. Shepherd's article "How I Put Over the Klan" in *Collier's* of July 14, 1928.

23. Vonnegut, *Slaughterhouse-Five*, 9–10.

24. Kurt Vonnegut, "Kurt Vonnegut, Shape of Stories," YouTube video, 17:36, 2004, posted July 14, 2018, https://www.youtube.com/watch?v=GOGru_4z1Vc.

25. Vonnegut, "Kurt Vonnegut, Shape of Stories."

Chapter 7. Unicorn-Killing Broken Trust

1. Amy Mitchell and Jess Holcolmb, "State of the News Media," 4.

2. Elizabeth Grieco, "U.S. Newspapers Have Shed Half of Their Newsroom Employees since 2008," Fact Tank, April 20, 2020, Pew Research Center, https://www.pewresearch.org/fact-tank/2020/04/20/u-s-newsroom-employment-has-dropped-by-a-quarter-since-2008/.

3. "Employment Trends in Newspaper Publishing and Other Media, 1990–2016," US Bureau of Labor Statistics, June 2, 2016, https://www.bls.gov/opub/ted/2016/employment-trends-in-newspaper-publishing-and-other-media-1990–2016.htm.

4. Michael Barthel, "5 Key Takeaways about the State of the News Media in 2018."

5. Levin, *Unfreedom of the Press*, 2.

6. Jeffrey M. Jones, "U.S. Media Trust Continues to Recover from 2016 Low," Gallup, October 12, 2018, https://news.gallup.com/poll/243665/media-trust-continues-recover-2016-low.aspx.

7. Pablo J. Boczkowski and Eugenia Mitchelstein, *News Gap*, 22.

8. Boczkowski and Mitchelstein, *News Gap*, 24.

9. Quoted in "'Pendulum' Will Swing Back, Says Supreme Court Judge," *BBC Newsnight*, February 23, 2017, https://www.bbc.com/news/av/world-us-canada-39065541

10. Bob Woodward, "Bob Woodward Teaches Investigative Journalism,"

master-class promotional trailer, YouTube video, posted October 19, 2017, https://www.youtube.com/watch?v=mYC_ckXyizA.

11. Woodward, "Bob Woodward Teaches Investigative Journalism."

12. "Hatred of Journalism Threatens Democracies," 2018 Press Freedom Index, Reporters Without Borders, https://rsf.org/en/ranking/2018.

13. New York Times editorial board, "A Free Press Needs You," *New York Times*, August 15, 2018, https://www.nytimes.com/.

14. Scott Maxwell, "Once Again, Tribune Wants Veteran Journalists to Leave. Here's Why We Haven't . . . Yet," opinion, *Orlando Sentinel*, January 1, 2020, https://www.orlandosentinel.com/.

15. "The Worst Jobs of 2019," CareerCast, 2019, https://www.careercast.com/jobs-rated/worst-jobs-of-2019?page=2.

16. Maurice Maeterlinck, *The Life of the Bee*, 145–147.

Chapter 8. The Damned-Dirty-Trick Story: An American Master Narrative

1. Kendi, Stamped from the Beginning, 53.

2. John C. Rainbolt, The Alteration in the Relationship between Leadership and Constituents in Virginia 1660 to 1720, 429.

3. Curtis Milam, "How I Learned to Relax and Love Donald Trump," opinion, Philadelphia Inquirer, June 23, 2020, https://www.inquirer.com/.

4. Isabel Wilkerson, Caste, 18–19.

5. Wilkerson, Caste, 52, 53.

6. Rainbolt, The Alteration in the Relationship between Leadership and Constituents in Virginia 1660 to 1720, 428–429.

7. Carol Anderson, White Rage, 3.

8. John C. Calhoun, "Speech on the Oregon Bill," 420. The Oregon Bill proposed making Oregon an official US territory. In his speech of June 27, 1848, Calhoun argues against the equality principle of the Declaration of Independence.

9. Martin Luther King, "'Our God Is Marching On!' Reverend Martin Luther King, Jr. Speech, March 25, 1965," Montgomery, AL, posted at American Radio Works, http://americanradioworks.publicradio.org/features/prestapes/mlk_speech.html.

10. Quoted in "Reimagining the James Baldwin and William F. Buckley Debate," NPR, September 20, 2020, https://www.npr.org/transcripts/914548619.

11. Robert Kuttner, "Steve Bannon, Unrepentant," American Prospect, August 16, 2017, https://prospect.org/power/steve-bannon-unrepentant/.

12. David S. Wilson, Darwin's Cathedral, 228–229.

13. Gottschall, Storytelling Animal, 113.

14. Gottschall, Storytelling Animal, 116.

15. Gottschall, Storytelling Animal, 116.

16. Quoted in Phil McCausland and Anna Schecter, "Cambridge Analytica Harvested Data from Millions of Unsuspecting Facebook Users," NBC News, March 17, 2018, https://www.nbcnews.com/.

17. Cecilia Kang, Nicholas Fandos, and Mike Isaac, "Russia-Financed Ad Linked Clinton and Satan," New York Times, November 1, 2017, https://www.nytimes.com/.

18. "Exposing Russia's Effort to Sow Discord Online: The Internet Research Agency and Advertisements," report, US House of Representatives Permanent Select Committee on Intelligence, https://intelligence.house.gov/social-media-content/.

19. "Exposing Russia's Effort to Sow Discord Online."

20. Paul Farhi, "Trump predicted news ratings would 'tank if I'm not there.' He wasn't wrong," The Washington Post March 22, 2021, www.washingtonpost.com

21. Quoted from an interview in The Observer (London), November 26, 1961, in Sigurd Allern, "Fatal News Media Strategies: Cutting Cost to Save Profits," conference paper, Nopa 5 (2014): 11.

22. Ben Smith, "Inside the Revolts Erupting in America's Big Newsrooms," New York Times, June 7, 2020, https://nytimes.com/.

23. Michael Powell, in a Twitter post on June 6, 2020, contends, "A strong paper and strong democracy does not shy from many voices. And this one had clear news value." He also calls the New York Times editor's note an "embarrassing retreat from principle."

24. Tom Jones, "The Controversy at the New York Times Is over More Than Just One Op-Ed; The Future of the Times Could Be at Stake," Poynter, June 8, 2020, https://www.poynter.org/newsletters/2020/the-controversy-at-the-new-york-times-is-over-more-than-just-one-op-ed-the-future-of-the-times-could-be-at-stake/.

25. Quoted in James Vincent, "Former Facebook Exec Says Social Media Is Ripping Apart Society," The Verge, December 11, 2017, https://www.theverge.com/2017/12/11/16761016/former-facebook-exec-ripping-apart-society.

26. Nic Newman et al., Reuters Institute Digital News Report, 9.

27. Amanda Ripley, "Complicating the Narratives."

28. Ripley, "Complicating the Narratives."

Chapter 9. Four Black Holes

1. Craig's observations were provided during a 2020 peer review of this book.

2. Dominic Boyer, The Life Informatic, 130.

3. Thorsten Quandt, "News Turning and Content Management," 77.

4. Boyer, The Life Informatic, 130.

5. Gi Lee and David Cohen, "How Many People Are Subjected to Involuntary Psychiatric Detention in the US?," In a 2016 phone interview with Cohen, he expressed frustration, dismay, and suspicion as to why accurate data were not being collected on the United States' most-used legal deprivation of liberty.

6. Vincanne Adams, "Evidence-Based Global Public Health," 84. Adams and the editors of When People Come First, João Biehl and Adriana Petryna, draw on their experiences with evidence-based global health policy and politics in that volume. In their introduction, Biehl and Petryna make a strong case that when methods driven by big data, such as randomized controlled tests and large-scale data aggregation, are accepted as the gold standard for usable truth in research, "ethnographic evidence is readily seen as anecdotal and exceptional, unreliable on account of its granularity or the wiliness of its subjects. Yet, to make the case, we need a human story" (17).

7. Jim Rutenberg, "A 'Dewey Defeats Truman' Lesson for the Digital Age," *New York Times*, November 9, 2016, https://www.nytimes.com/.

8. Rachel Kaplan, "The Small Experiment," 170. Kaplan explains, "Small experiments provide ways to try things out. They are unabashedly imperfect. They are 'small' in cost, in number of participants involved, and especially in their intention. A manageable study, however, need not be conceptually sloppy. To be useful, even small experiments need to be thoughtful and disciplined."

9. Jonathan Shedler, "Selling Bad Therapy to Trauma Victims," blog post, *Psychology Today*, December 17, 2017, https://publicseminar.org/2017/12/selling-bad-therapy-to-trauma-victims/.

Chapter 10. Journalism, Period.

1. Jessica Davies, "After It Stopped Posting to Facebook, a Danish Broadcaster Saw Its Traffic Stability Improve," *Digiday*, February 7, 2018, https://digiday.com/media/cutting-ties-facebook-danish-broadcaster-saw-traffic-stability-improve.

2. Levi, *Black Hole of Auschwitz*, 34.

3. Levi, *Black Hole of Auschwitz*, 34.

4. Quoted in Stanislao Pugliese, *The Legacy of Primo Levi*, 7.

5. Siobhan McHugh, "How Podcasting Is Changing the Audio Storytelling Genre," 2.

6. "The Podcast Consumer 2018," Edison Research, April 19, 2018, http://www.edisonresearch.com/podcast-consumer-2018/.

7. Primo Levi observes, "The ascent of the privileged, not only in the Lager but in all human coexistence, is an anguishing but unfailing phenomenon: only in utopias is it absent. It is the duty of righteous men to make war on all undeserved privilege, but one must not forget that this is a war without end. Where power is exercised by few or only one against the many, privilege is born and proliferates, even against the will of the power itself" (*The Drowned and the Saved*, 42).

8. Quoted in Stephen E. Jones, "Turning Practice Inside Out," 272.

9. Abernathy, *Rise of a New Media Baron*, 68; emphasis in original.

10. Abernathy, *Rise of a New Media Baron*, 70.

11. Kalogeropoulos, Fletcher, and Nielsen, "News Brand Attribution."

12. Kalogeropoulos, Fletcher, and Nielsen discuss brand attribution, trust, and narrative in "News Brand Attribution."

13. Jay Rosen, "This Is What a News Organization Built on Reader Trust Looks Like," Nieman Lab, March 28, 2017, https://www.niemanlab.org/2017/03/jay-rosen-this-is-what-a-news-organization-built-on-reader-trust-looks-like/.

14. Quoted in Diane Lynch, *Above and Beyond*, 6.

Chapter 11. 2020–2021

1. Janelle Irwin Taylor, "Craig Pittman, Popular Environmental Reporter and Author, among 11 Cut from the Tampa Bay Times," *Florida Politics*, March 19, 2020, https://floridapolitics.com/archives/323799-tampa-bay-times-lays-off-at-least-one-reporter/.

2. "Tampa Bay Times Lays Off 11 Journalists," *Tampa Bay Times,* March 18, 2020, https://www.tampabay.com/news/business/2020/03/18/tampa-bay-times-lays-off-11-journalists/.

3. Rick Edmonds, "A Q&A with Tampa Bay Times Chairman and CEO Paul Tash about the Times' print reduction," updated March 30, 2020, https://www.poynter.org/business-work/2020/a-qa-with-tampa-bay-times-chairman-and-ceo-paul-tash-about-the-times-print-reduction/.

4. "Tampa Bay Times Gets Federal Loan to Help with Revenue Losses Caused by Pandemic," April 17, 2020, https://www.tampabay.com/news/business/2020/04/17/tampa-bay-times-gets-federal-loan-to-help-with-revenue-losses-caused-by-pandemic/.

5. Cheryl Mattingly, "Concept of Therapeutic 'Emplotment,'" 812.

6. Mary Gergen and Kenneth Gergen, *Social Construction of Narrative Accounts,* 174. The idea of narrative emplotment here builds on Paul Ricoeur, *Hermeneutics and the Human Sciences.*

7. Bourdieu, *Outline of a Theory of Practice,* 167.

8. Gillian Tett, *Anthro-Vision,* 147

9. Levi, *Black Hole of Auschwitz,* 34; Levi, *The Drowned and the Saved,* 7.

10. Kramer, "Why People Latch on to Conspiracy Theories."

11. Tanya M. Luhrmann, *When God Talks Back,* xvi.

12. Luhrmann, *When God Talks Back,* xvi.

Works Cited

Abernathy, Penelope Muse. *The Loss of Local News: What It Means for Communities*. Report. Chapel Hill: Center for Innovation and Sustainability in Local Media, University of North Carolina, 2018. https://www.usnewsdeserts.com/reports/expanding-news-desert/loss-of-local-news/.

———. *News Deserts and Ghost Newspapers: Will Local News Survive?* University of North Carolina Press, 2020.

———. *The Rise of a New Media Baron and the Emerging Threat of News Deserts*. Report. Chapel Hill: Center for Innovation and Sustainability in Local Media, University of North Carolina, 2016. https://www.usnewsdeserts.com/reports/rise-new-media-baron/new-media-barons/.

Adams, Vincanne. "Evidence-Based Global Public Health." In *When People Come First: Critical Studies in Global Health*, edited by João Biehl and Adriana Petryna, 54–90. Princeton, NJ: Princeton University Press, 2013.

Addams, Jane, Theodor Adorno, Gordon Allport, Sherwood Anderson, Raymond Bauer, Daniel Bell, Bernard Berelson, et al. *Mass Communication and American Social Thought: Key Texts, 1919–1968*. Lanham, MD: Rowman and Littlefield, 2004.

Anderson, Carol. *White Rage: The Unspoken Truth of Our Racial Divide*. New York: Bloomsbury, 2016.

Ansary, Tamim. *The Invention of Yesterday: A 50,000-Year History of Human Culture, Conflict, and Connection*. New York: Public Affairs, 2019.

Arendt, Hannah. *The Human Condition*. Chicago: University of Chicago Press, 2013.

———. *Men in Dark Times*. Houghton Mifflin Harcourt, 1968.

Arsenault, Raymond. *Freedom riders: 1961 and the struggle for racial justice*. Oxford University Press, 2006.

Askew, Kelly Michelle, and Richard R. Wilk, eds. *The Anthropology of Media: A Reader*. Hoboken, NJ: Blackwell, 2002.

Balaji, Murali. "Racializing Pity: The Haiti Earthquake and the Plight of 'Others.'" *Critical Studies in Media Communication* 28, no. 1 (2011): 50–67.

Baldwin, James. "Unnameable Objects, Unspeakable Crimes." In *Black on Black: Commentaries by Negro Americans*, edited by Arnold Adorff, 94–101. New York: Macmillan, 1968.

———. "White Man's Guilt." In "The White Problem in America," special issue, *Ebony Magazine*, August 1965, 47–48.

Barkow, Jerome. "Beneath New Culture Is Old Psychology: Gossip and Social Strati-
fication." In *The Adapted Mind: Evolutionary Psychology and the Generation of
Culture*, edited by Jerome H. Barkow, Leda Cosmides, and John Tooby, 627–638.
New York: Oxford University Press, 1992.

Barnard, Stephen R. "'Tweet or Be Sacked': Twitter and the New Elements of Journalistic Practice." *Journalism* 17, no. 2 (2016): 190–207.

Barthel, Michael. "5 Key Takeaways about the State of the News Media in 2018." Fact
Tank, July 23, 2019. Pew Research Center. https://www.pewresearch.org/fact-
tank/2019/07/23/key-takeaways-state-of-the-news-media-2018/.

Berger, John. "John Berger: Ways of Seeing, Episode 1 (1972)." YouTube video, posted
October 8, 2012. https://www.youtube.com/watch?v=opDE4VX_9Kk.

Biehl, João, and Adriana Petryna. Introduction to *When People Come First: Critical
Studies in Global Health*, edited by Biehl and Petryna, 1–22. Princeton, NJ: Princeton University Press, 2013.

Bird, S. Elizabeth, ed. *The Anthropology of News and Journalism: Global Perspectives*.
Bloomington: Indiana University Press, 2010.

———. "The Future of Journalism in the Digital Environment." *Journalism* 10, no. 3
(2009): 293–295.

Bird, S. Elizabeth, and Robert Ward Dardenne. "Myth, Chronicle, and Story-Exploring:
The Narrative Qualities of News." In *Media Myths and Narratives*, edited by James
W. Carey, 48–67. Newbury Park, CA: Sage, 1988.

Boczkowski, Pablo J. *News at Work: Imitation in an Age of Information Abundance*.
Chicago, IL: University of Chicago Press, 2010.

Boczkowski, Pablo J., and Eugenia Mitchelstein. *The News Gap: When the Information
Preferences of the Media and the Public Diverge*. Cambridge, MA: MIT Press, 2013.

Bourdieu, Pierre. *Bourdieu and the Journalistic Field*. Edited by Rodney Benson and
Erik Neveu. Cambridge, England: Polity, 2005.

———. *The Field of Cultural Production: Essays on Art and Literature*. New York: Columbia University Press, 1993.

———. *On Television*. London: Pluto, 1998.

———. *Outline of a Theory of Practice*. Durham, NC: Duke University Press, 2007.

———. "The Peasant and His Body." Translation by Rochard Niece and Loïc Wacquant.
Ethnography 5, no. 4 (2004): 579–599.

Bourdieu, Pierre, and Loïc Wacquant. *An Invitation to Reflexive Sociology*. Chicago:
University of Chicago Press, 1992.

Boyer, Dominic. *The Life Informatic: Newsmaking in the Digital Era*. Ithaca, NY: Cor-
nell University Press, 2013.

Bräuchler, Birgit, and John Postill, eds. *Theorising Media and Practice*. Vol. 4. New
York: Berghahn, 2010.

Breed, Warren. *The Newspaperman, News, and Society*. New York: Columbia University, 1952.

———. "Social Control in the Newsroom: A Functional Analysis." *Social Forces* (1955):
326–335.

Calhoun, John C. Speech on the Oregon Bill, June 27, 1848. In *The U.S. Constitution: A Reader*. Hillsdale, MI: Hillsdale College Press, 2012.

Campbell, Joseph. *The Hero with a Thousand Faces*. Vol. 17. San Francisco, CA: New World Library, 2008.

Carmines, Edward G., and Richard A. Zeller. *Reliability and Validity Assessment*. Newbury Park, CA: Sage, 1979.

Case, Anne, and Angus Deaton. *Deaths of Despair and the Future of Capitalism*. Princeton, NJ: Princeton University Press, 2020.

Chapman, John Wight, and Pliny Earle Goddard. *Ten'a Texts and Tales from Anvik, Alaska*. Vol. 6. Leiden, Netherlands: E. J. Brill, 1914.

Couldry, Nick. *Media, Society, World: Social Theory and Digital Media Practice*. Cambridge, England: Polity, 2012.

Cron, Lisa. *Wired for Story: The Writer's Guide to Using Brain Science to Hook Readers from the Very First Sentence*. Berkeley, CA: Ten Speed, 2012.

Damasio, Antonio R. *Self Comes to Mind: Constructing the Conscious Brain*. New York: Vintage, 2010.

Darwin, Charles. *The Descent of Man, and Selection in Relation to Sex*. Princeton, NJ: Princeton University Press, 2008.

De Laguna, Frederica. *Travels among the Dena: Exploring Alaska's Yukon Valley*. Seattle: University of Washington Press, 2011.

Dearborn, Lynne M., and John C. Stallmeyer. *Inconvenient Heritage: Erasure and Global Tourism in Luang Prabang*. Vol. 3. Walnut Creek, CA: Left Coast, 2010.

Erdoes, Richard, and Alfonso Ortiz. *American Indian Trickster Tales*. New York: Penguin, 1998.

Fassin, Didier. "Children as Victims." In *When People Come First: Critical Studies in Global Health*, edited by João Biehl and Adriana Petryna, 109–130. Princeton, NJ: Princeton University Press, 2013.

Feldman, Jack. *The Plays of Arthur Miller: Theory and Practice*. Madison: University of Wisconsin, 1975.

Fisher, Walter R. "Narration as a Human Communication Paradigm: The Case of Public Moral Argument." *Communications Monographs* 51, no. 1 (1984): 1–22.

Foucault, Michel. *Power/Knowledge: Selected Interviews and Other Writings 1972–1977*. New York: Pantheon, 1980.

Fulford, Robert. *The Triumph of Narrative: Storytelling in the Age of Mass Culture*. Toronto: House of Anansi, 1999.

Geertz, Clifford. *The Interpretation of Cultures*. Vol. 5019. New York: Basic, 1973.

Gergen, Kenneth J., and Mary M. Gergen. "The Social Construction of Narrative Accounts." In *Historical Social Psychology*, edited by Gergen and Gergen, 173–190. Mahwah, NJ: Psychology, 2014.

Ginsburg, Faye D., Lila Abu-Lughod, and Brian Larkin, eds. *Media Worlds: Anthropology on New Terrain*. Oakland: University of California Press, 2002.

Gottschall, Jonathan. *The Storytelling Animal: How Stories Make Us Human*. New York: Houghton Mifflin Harcourt, 2012.

Greenfield, Adam. *Radical Technologies: The Design of Everyday Life*. New York: Verso, 2017.

Han, Clara. "Labor Instability and Community Mental Health." In *When People Come First: Critical Studies in Global Health*, edited by João Biehl and Adriana Petryna, 276–301. Princeton, NJ: Princeton University Press, 2013.

Harrison, David. "Contested Narratives in the Domain of World Heritage." In *The Politics of World Heritage: Negotiating Tourism and Conservation*, edited by David Harrison and Michael Hitchcock, 1–10. Cleveland, OH: Channel View, 2005.

Haviland, William A., and Harald E. L. Prins. *Cultural Anthropology: The Human Challenge*. Boston: Cengage Learning, 2016.

Heider, Don. *White News: Why Local News Programs Don't Cover People of Color*. New York: Routledge, 2014.

Hood, Bruce. *The Domesticated Brain: A Pelican Introduction*. London: Penguin, 2014.

Hooker, Robert W. *100 Years, St. Petersburg Times, July 25, 1884, to July 25, 1984: The Times and Its Times*. St. Petersburg, FL: *St. Petersburg Times*, 1984.

Jackson, Michael. *The Politics of Storytelling: Variations on a Theme by Hannah Arendt*. Vol. 4. Copenhagen: Museum Tusculanum, 2013.

Jackson, Leon. *Urban Buffalo Soldiers: The Story of St. Petersburg's Courageous Twelve*. Pinellas Park, FL. The Ragnarok Group, Inc., 2020.

Jones, Steven E. *The Emergence of the Digital Humanities*. Oxfordshire, England: Taylor and Francis, 2013.

———. "Turning Practice Inside Out: Digital Humanities and the Eversion." In *The Routledge Companion to Media Studies and Digital Humanities*, edited by Jentery Sayers, 267–273. New York: Routledge, 2018.

Kalogeropoulos, Antonis, Richard Fletcher, and Rasmus Kleis Nielsen. "News Brand Attribution in Distributed Environments: Do People Know Where They Get Their News?" *New Media and Society* 21, no. 3 (2019): 583–601.

Kalogeropoulos, Antonis, Jane Suiter, Linards Udris, and Mark Eisenegger. "News Media Trust and News Consumption: Factors Related to Trust in News in 35 Countries." *International Journal of Communication* 13 (2019): 3672–3693.

Kaplan, Rachel. "The Small Experiment: Achieving More with Less." In *Public and Private Places*, edited by J. L. Nasar and B. B. Brown, 170–174. Edmond, OK: Environmental Design Research Association, 1996.

Keats, John. *The Complete Poetical Works and Letters of John Keats*. Edited by Horace Elisha Scudde. Moscow: Ripol Klassik, 1899.

Kendi, Ibram X. *Stamped from the Beginning: The Definitive History of Racist Ideas in America*. Hachette UK, 2016.

Klein, Richard G., and Blake Edgar. *The Dawn of Human Culture*. New York: Wiley, 2002.

Knight Commission on Trust, Media, and Democracy. *Crisis in Democracy: Renewing Trust in America*. Report. Washington, DC: Aspen Institute, 2019. https://knight-foundation.org/reports/crisis-in-democracy-renewing-trust-in-america/.

Lee, Gi, and David Cohen. "How Many People Are Subjected to Involuntary Psychiatric Detention in the US? First Verifiable Population Estimates of Civil Commitment." In Society for Social Work and Research 23rd Annual Conference, 2019, San Francisco.

Levi, Primo. *The Black Hole of Auschwitz*. Translation by Sharon Wood. New York: Polity, 2005.

———. *The Drowned and the Saved*. New York: Simon and Schuster, 2017.

Levin, Mark R. *Unfreedom of the Press*. New York: Simon and Schuster, 2019.

Lewis, Justin, Sanna Inthorn, and Karin Wahl-Jorgensen. *Citizens or Consumers? What the Media Tell Us about Political Participation*. New York: McGraw-Hill Education, 2005.

Lippmann, Walter. *Liberty and the News*. Allentown, PA: Mediastudies, 2020.

Lowenthal, David. *The Heritage Crusade and the Spoils of History*. New York: Cambridge University Press, 1998.

Luhrmann, Tanya M. *When God Talks Back: Understanding the American Evangelical Relationship with God*. New York: Knopf, 2012.

Lull, James. *Media, Communication, Culture: A Global Approach*. New York: Columbia University Press, 2000.

Lynch, Diane. *Above and Beyond: Looking at the Future of Journalism Education; A Report in Six Parts*. Miami: Knight Foundation, 2015.

Maeterlinck, Maurice. *The Life of the Bee*. New York: Dodd, Mead, 1901.

Mattingly, Cheryl. "The Concept of Therapeutic 'Emplotment.'" *Social Science and Medicine* 38, no. 6 (1994): 811–822.

McBride, Kelly, and Tom Rosenstiel. Introduction to *The New Ethics of Journalism: Principles for the 21st Century*, edited by McBride and Rosenstiel, 1–6. Thousand Oaks, CA: CQ, 2013.

McHugh, Siobhan. "How Podcasting Is Changing the Audio Storytelling Genre." *Radio Journal: International Studies in Broadcast and Audio Media* 14, no. 1 (2016): 65–82.

Miller, Arthur. "The Shadows of the Gods: A Critical View of the American Theater." *Harper's*, August 1958, 35.

Miller, Tracy. *US Religious Landscape Survey Religious Beliefs and Practices: Diverse and Politically Relevant*. Pew Forum on Religion and Public Life, 2008.

Mitchell, Amy, Jeffrey Gottfried, Elisa Shearer, and Kristine Lu. "How Americans Encounter, Recall, and Act upon Digital News." Pew Research Center, February 9, 2017. https://www.journalism.org/wp-content/uploads/sites/8/2017/02/PJ_2017.02.09_Experiential_FINAL.pdf.

Mitchell, Amy, and Jess Holcolmb. "State of the News Media." Pew Research Center, July 15, 2016. https://assets.pewresearch.org/wp-content/uploads/sites/13/2016/06/30143308/state-of-the-news-media-report-2016-final.pdf.

Narayan, Kirin. *Alive in the Writing: Crafting Ethnography in the Company of Chekhov*. Chicago: University of Chicago Press, 2012.

Nelson, R. H. *Make Prayers to the Raven: A Koyukon View of the Northern Forest*. Chicago: University of Chicago Press, 1983.

Newman, Nic, Richard Fletcher, Antonis Kalogeropoulos, David Levy, and Rasmus Kleis Nielsen. *Reuters Institute Digital News Report*, June 2017. https://reutersinsti-

tute.politics.ox.ac.uk/sites/default/files/Digital%20News%20Report%202017%20
web_0.pdf.

Nietzsche, Friedrich. *Human, All Too Human: A Book for Free Spirits*, translation by R. J. Hollingdale. Cambridge, England: Cambridge University Press, 1986.

Niles, John D. *Homo Narrans: The Poetics and Anthropology of Oral Literature*. Philadelphia: University of Pennsylvania Press, 2010.

Opler, Edward Morris. *Myths and Tales of the Jicarilla Apache Indians*. North Chelmsford, MA: Courier, 2012.

Ortner, Sherry B. "Theory in Anthropology since the Sixties." *Comparative Studies in Society and History* 26, no. 1 (1984): 126–166.

Otero, Lydia R. *La Calle: Spatial Conflicts and Urban Renewal in a Southwest City*. Tucson: University of Arizona Press, 2010.

Payne, Darwin. "Book Review. Robert N. Pierce, *A Sacred Trust: Nelson Poynter and the St. Petersburg Times*." *American Journalism Book Reviews* 11, no 4 (1994): 378–379.

Phillips, Evelyn Newman, "An ethnohistorical analysis of the political economy of ethnicity among African-Americans in St. Petersburg, Florida." PhD diss., University of South Florida, 1994.

Pierce, Robert N. *A Sacred Trust: Nelson Poynter and the St. Petersburg Times*. Gainesville: University Press of Florida, 1993.

Pinto, Sarah. *Daughters of Parvati: Women and Madness in Contemporary India*. Philadelphia: University of Pennsylvania Press, 2014.

Pugliese, Stanislao. *Answering Auschwitz: Primo Levi's Science and Humanism after the Fall*. New York: Fordham University Press, 2011.

———, ed. *The Legacy of Primo Levi*. New York: Palgrave Macmillan, 2005.

Quandt, Thorsten. "News Turning and Content Management: An Observation Study of Old and New Routines in German Online Newsrooms." *Making Online News: The Ethnography of New Media Production* 1 (2008): 77–98.

Rainbolt, John C. *From Prescription to Persuasion: Manipulation of Seventeenth Century Virginia Economy.* Port Washington, NY: National University Publications, 1974.

Rainbolt, John C. *The Alteration in the Relationship between Leadership and Constituents in Virginia, 1660 to 1720*. The William and Mary Quarterly: A Magazine of Early American History and Culture: 411-434. 1970

Ricoeur, Paul. *Hermeneutics and the Human Sciences: Essays on Language, Action, and Interpretation*. New York: Cambridge University Press, 1981.

Ripley, Amanda. "Complicating the Narratives: What If Journalists Covered Controversial Issues Differently—Based on How Humans Actually Behave When They Are Polarized and Suspicious?" The Whole Story, Solutions Journalism Network, January 11, 2019. https://thewholestory.solutionsjournalism.org/complicating-the-narratives-b91ea06ddf63.

Roberts, Gene, and Hank Klibanoff. *The race beat: The press, the civil rights struggle, and the awakening of a nation.* vintage books, 2007.

Roberts, Gene, and Hank Klibanoff. *The race beat: The press, the civil rights struggle, and the awakening of a nation.* vintage books, 2007.

Schnapp, Jeffrey T. "Aphorisms on the 21st Century Museum." Jeffrey Schnapp, blog post, January 26, 2015. jeffreyschnapp.com/aphorisms-on-the-21st-century-muse-um/.

Schudson, Michael. *Discovering the News: A Social History of American Newspapers*. New York: Basic, 1981.

Schulte, William. *Social Construction and News Work*. Amherst, MA: Teno, 2014.

Shearer, Elizabeth. "Social Media Outpaces Print Newspapers in the U.S. as a News Source." Pew Research Center, December 10, 2018, https://www.pewresearch.org/fact-tank/2018/12/10/social-media-outpaces-print-newspapers-in-the-u-s-as-a-news-source/.

Simner, Marvin L. "Racial Segregation in the Rise and Fall of 22nd Street South: The Unfolding Story of the Historic Black Business Recreational District in St. Petersburg, Florida." (2017).

Singer, Peter Warren, and Emerson T. Brooking. *Like War: The Weaponization of Social Media*. New York: Eamon Dolan, 2018.

Smith, Adam. "An Inquiry into the Nature and Causes of the Wealth of Nations: Volume One." London: W. Strahan and T. Cadell, 1776.

Smith, Daniel, Philip Schlaepfer, Katie Major, Mark Dyble, Abigail E. Page, James Thompson, et al. "Cooperation and the Evolution of Hunter-Gatherer Storytelling." *Nature Communications* 8, no. 1 (2017): 1–9.

Snyder, Blake. *Save the Cat: The Last Book on Screenwriting You'll Ever Need*. Burbank, CA: Michael Wiese Productions, 2005.

Springsteen, Bruce. "The Complete Text of Bruce Springsteen's SXSW Keynote Address." *Rolling Stone*, March 28, 2012. https://www.rollingstone.com/music/music-news/exclusive-the-complete-text-of-bruce-springsteens-sxsw-keynote-address-86379/.

Stanley, Jason. *How Fascism Works: The Politics of Us and Them*. New York: Random House, 2020.

Stephenson, R. Bruce. *Visions of Eden: Environmentalism, Urban Planning, and City Building in St. Petersburg, Florida, 1900-1995*. The Ohio State University Press, 1997.

Streckfuss, Richard. "Objectivity in Journalism: A Search and a Reassessment." *Journalism Quarterly* 67, no. 4 (1990): 973–983.

Sugiyama, Michelle Scalise. "Literary Prehistory: The Origins and Psychology of Storytelling." *Critical Approaches to Literature: Psychological* (2017): 67–83.

Tett, Gillian. *The Silo Effect: The Peril of Expertise and the Promise of Breaking Down Barriers*. New York: Simon and Schuster, 2015

———.*Anthro-Vision: A New Way to See in Business and Life*. Simon and Schuster, 2021

———. "What Pierre Bourdieu Taught Me: Journalists Should Take Nothing for Granted but Instead Look at All the Silences in the World and Ask: Why?" *FT Magazine*, July 26, 2013. https://www.ft.com/content/69bbdb4e-f4be-11e2-a62e-00144feabdco.

Thompson, Stith. *Tales of the North American Indians*. North Chelmsford, MA: Courier, 2000.

Tsing, Anna Lowenhaupt. *Friction: An Ethnography of Global Connection*. Princeton, NJ: Princeton University Press, 2005.

Tuchman, Gaye. *Making News: A Study in the Construction of Reality.* New York: Free Press, 1978.

Vonnegut, Kurt. *Palm Sunday: An Autobiographical Collage.* New York: Dial, 1999.

———. *Slaughterhouse-Five: Or, the Children's Crusade, a Duty-Dance with Death.* New York: Modern Library, 1969.

White, Randall. "Integrating Social and Operational Complexity: The Material Construction of Social Identity at Sungir." In *L'Os: Festschrift for Henriette Camps-Fabrer,* 120–137. Marseille: Université de Marseille, 1999.

———. *Prehistoric Art: The Symbolic Journey of Humankind.* New York: Harry N. Abrams, 2003.

Wilkerson, Isabel. *Caste: The Origins of Our Discontents.* New York: Random House, 2020.

Wilson, Jon, and Rosalie Peck. *St. Petersburg's Historic African American Neighborhoods.* The History Press, 2008.

Wilson, David S. *Darwin's Cathedral: Evolution, Religion, and the Nature of Society.* Chicago: University of Chicago Press, 2002.

Wolf, Eric R. *Europe and the People without History.* Oakland: University of California Press, 2010.

Zelizer, Barbie. *Taking Journalism Seriously: News and the Academy.* Newbury Park, CA: Sage, 2004.

Index

Page numbers in *italics* indicate illustrations.

Abernathy, Penelope Muse, 52
Adam and Eve (biblical figures), 112–13
Adam Baker et al. v The City of St. Petersburg, 70
Adams, Sam, 69
Adams, Vincanne, 167, 229n6
Adaptation, rationality versus, 145
Ads, purchased by Russian organizations, *149*, *150*, 151–52
Advancement, Black, 142–43
Advent, of cameras, 101
African American history events, 68–69
African People's Socialist Party, 98–99
Age, of information, 12–13
Algorithms, 13–14
Alive in the Writing (Narayan), 16–17
Allegory, of cave, 108–9
Anatomical change, behavioral change and, 40, 221n1
Anderson, Carol, 141
Angelou, Maya, 155–56, 181, 183
Anger, at journalists, 5
Ansary, Tamim, 111
Anthropology, journalism and, 3, 6–7, 178–79, 184, 209
Anthropology theory, 12–13
Antifa, 154
Anxiety, white, 140
Apocalypse, information, 106
App decision, of young news consumer, 175–76
Apple Podcasts, 181
Arendt, Hannah, 57, 59, 118, 132, 210
Aristocracy, digital platforms and, 140

Art: context and, 101–2; emergence of, 40
Audio transcribing, Facebook and, 224n1
Automotive industry, in Flint, Michigan, 29–30
Avery, A. P., 63

The Bachelor (TV show), 121
Bacon, Nathaniel, 138–39
Bacon's Rebellion, 138–39
Bad storytelling, good storytelling versus, 58–59
Baggett, J. M. "Doc," 62
Balanced reporting, 10, 130–31
Baldwin, James, 69, 138, 143–44
Ban, of Trump, from social media, 179, 208, 212
Bannon, Steve, 96, 144–45, 147–48
Barkow, Jerome, 10
Barnard, Stephen, 98–99
Barnes, Andrew, 65–66, 72
Baron, Marty, 187–88
Basic structure, of story, 42–43
Basu, Avik, 169
Béarn, France, 25
Beats: in Hollywood structures, 115–17; of Synder, 117–18
Bees, flies and, 135–36
Begala, Paul, 54–55
Behavioral change, anatomical change and, 40, 221n1
Benedict, Ruth, 3, 4, 209
Bennet, James, 153–55
Berger, John, 100–101
Berkeley, William, 138–39
Biden campaign lawyer, 201
Biehl, João, 229n6
Biewen, John, 137–38

Bild (tabloid), 10–11
The Birth of a Nation (film), 119–21
Black advancement, 142–43
Blaster (fictional character, *Thunderdome*), 104–5
Blogger, at Elections Office, 203
Blow, Charles, 104
Boczkowski, Pablo, 132
Booker, Christopher, 211
Bourdieu, Pierre, 24–26, 36–37, 70, 103–4, 201–2, *202*; on notion of "field," 103, 225n36; on symbolic capital, 220n2
Boyer, Dominic, 164–65
Brain, human, 46–47
Branding, of news, 93, 100
Breed, Warren, 21–22
Breitbart News, 96
Brink, Graham, 82, 172
Brittany's Bowl, 85
Brooking, Emerson T., 122
Brown v Board of Education, 69
B Story, in Hollywood plot, 116
Buckley, William F., Jr., 143–44
Bull's-Eye Black Hole, 167–69, 183–84
Bureau of Labor Statistics, US, 128
Burns, Ken, 118
Business models, Journalism, 100
Busl, Gretchen, 119
BuzzFeed (news website), 122

Calhoun, John C., 141–42, 148
Cambridge Analytica scandal, 97, 147–48
Cameras, advent of, 101
Campaign lawyer, of Biden, 201
Capital, symbolic, 22, 220n2
Capital Gazette shooting, 81–82
CareerCast report, 193
Career planning, 34–35
Carmines, Edward, 167–69, 173
Case, Anne, 144
Caste (Wikerson), 140
Caste narrative, 139–45
Cataglyphis bicolor desert ant, 49
Catalyst, in story, 115
Cave allegory, 108–9
Centrist journalists, as unicorns, 130–31
Cerri, Lara, 27–30, 38, 98–100

Chicago City News Bureau, 124
Childhood storytelling, 40–41
Choice, of stories, 7–8
Chozick, Amy, 121–22
Christianity, primitive, 114
Cinderella (fictional character), 113
City candidate forums, 98–99
Civil commitment numbers, counting of, 166
Civil rights, *Times* coverage by, 69, 74
Clark, Jim, 143–44
Class in America, race as, 139
Clinton, Bill, 54
Clinton, Hillary, 54, 145, 146, *150*, 151
CNHI. *See* Community News Holdings
CNN, 105, 205
Coard, Michael, 110
Comet Ping Pong restaurant, 146
Communal knowledge, 47
Community events, 183
Community journalism, 5, 8, 148, 173–74
Community News Holdings (CNHI), 185
Complexity: human, 123–24; in journalism, 75–78
Complicated topics, media and, 75–76
Conflicting stories, 8
Conspiracy theories, 10, 145–47, 204, 207–8
Contact with public of journalists, decline of, 164–66, 171–74
Content, Engagement, Revenue, 30–31, 102, 163
Content creation, focus on, 181
Context: art and, 101–2; of news stories, 100–102
Contradictions: of Jefferson, T., 133–34; in journalism, 75–78; of Poynter, N., 73–75
"Cooperation and the Evolution of Hunter-Gatherer Storytelling" (Smith, D.), 53
Copy-editor, 55
Coronavirus Aid, Relief, and Economic Security Act, 197
Corporate desires, 9
Cotton, Tom, 153–54
Couple, in neighborhood, 16
Courageous Twelve, 68–71
Coverage: of civil rights by *Times*, 69, 74; of Courageous Twelve by *Times*, 69–71; of local communities, 75–77; of protests, 125

Covid-19, 5, 194
Covid experience, of Solomon, 193
Crawford, Freddie, 70–71
Crist, Charlie, 125
Cultural cooperative group, 37
Cultural symbols, change in, 25
Cyberspace, 13

Damasio, Antonio, 47
Damned-dirty-trick narrative, 143–47, 152
Dance, in Béarn, 25
Dark Night of the Soul, in Hollywood plot, 116
Darwin, Charles, 7
Darwin's Cathedral (Wilson, D.), 145–46
Data reporting, 166–69
Daughter, of Pendygraft, 41, 45–46, 188–89
Davies, Jessica, 95
The Dawn of Human Culture (Klein), 39
Death, of parents of Pendygraft, 210
Deaths of despair, 144
Deaton, Angus, 144
Debate of journey, in Hollywood plot, 116
Decline, in agricultural jobs, 25
Deep fakes, 106
Defiant humanism, 180–81
DeGregory, Lane, 163–64, 165–66, 171
Demers, David, 23
Deserts, news, 5, 132–33, 219n3
Desk, of Pittman, 195
Digiday (newspaper), 95
Digital: age, 11, 16, 31, 148, 153; content, 31–32; journalists legacy journalists versus, 31–33, 92, 131; media, 31–33, 92, 179; media spaces unique, 179, 185–86; platforms aristocracy and, 140; politics, 121–23; printed paper versus, 21
Disinvestment, from social media, 182
Disney, Walt, 120
Disparity, wealth, 140
Distrust: of journalists, 6, 17–18, 124, 126–27; of media, 86–87, 93, 106, 126–27, 131–32, 177–78
Diversity, of *Times* board, 72, 76
Divide, racial, 139
Divisive narratives, 147, 179
Domesticated Brain, The (Hood), 46
Domino story, 41
Dowd, Maureen, 54

Doxa, of Bourdieu, *202*
Drama, human need for, 51–52
Dunedin, Florida, 61
Dunlap, Karen Brown, 73

Echo chambers, 11–12, 128–30, *129*
Economic crash, of 2008, 26
Edelman Trust Barometer, 94–95
Edgar, Blake, 221n1
Edgar, J. L., 61–62
Einstein, Albert, 166
Election (2016), 168
Election (2020), 201–3
Elections, Russian influence in, 148, *149, 150,* 151
Elections Office, Blogger, at, 203
Employment, newsroom, 5, 128, *129,* 133
"Enemy of the People," 56
Ethical storytelling, 123
Ethnography, 16–17, 130
Evansville Courier (newspaper), 28
Experiment, of TV Midtvest, 95
External forces, 90

Facebook, 85–87, 95–97, 105, 147–48, 156; listening to users and, 224n1; news consumer and, 175–77
Facebook News, 96–98
Fahrenthold, David, 102–3
"Failure Factories" (*Tampa Bay Times*), 76
Fake news, 122
"Fake News, Facts, and Alternative Facts" (course), 88
Farhi, Paul, 152
Farming, 25
"Field," notion of, Bourdieu on, 103, 225n36
Firing, of Pendygraft, 210–11
"First rough drafts of history," journalism as, 79
The Fiscal Black Hole, 161–62
Fisher, Walter, 222n21
Fleiss, Mike, 121–22
Flies, bees and, 135–36
Flint, Michigan, 29–30
Florida Holocaust Museum, 161
Floyd, George, 153–54, 199–200
Football game, play at, 91–94

Football photography, 90–91

Formal classification systems, informal and, 26

Formula for success, in print newsroom, digital era versus, 22–23

Formulas, Hollywood, 115–19

Fox News, 205

From Prescription to Persuasion (Rainbolt), 137–40

Front page, of newspaper, 21

Fulford, Robert, 46, 108–11

Furgurson, E. B., III, 81–82

Future, of journalism industry, 34–35, 212–13

"The Future of Democracy." (Leopore), 90

Gallaty, Conan, 76

Gannett, 196

GateHouse Media, 66, 184–85

Geertz, Clifford, 13, 14

Gibson, William, 13, 14

Ginsburg, Ruth Bader, 132

Goddard, Jean-Luc, 118

Good storytelling, bad storytelling versus, 58–59

Gore, J. Ira, 62

Gottschall, Jonathan, 47, 50, 53, 60, 146–47

Graham, Philip, 79

Greenfield, Adam, 57–58

Griffith, D. W., 119–21, 122

Habitus, 36–37

Hamlet (Shakespeare), 123–24

Hard-wired instincts, 135–56

Hare, Kristen, 5

"Hatred of Journalism Threatens Democracies" (Reporters Without Borders), 133

The Heart Gallery, 27

Heider, Don, 75–77

Hemings, James, 110

Hemings, Sally, 109–10

Hemmings, Polly, 110

Hero twin story, 42

Higher power, belief in, 7–8

History events, African American, 68–69

Hollywood formulas, 115–19

Hollywood structures, beats in, 115–17

Homo dramaticus, idea of Pendygraft, 51–52,

61, 79, 119–20, 148; payment for stories of, 188; as storytelling animal, 161

Homo fictus, idea of Gottschall, 50, 60, 207

Homo Narrans (Niles), 49–50

Homo neanderthalensis, 48

Homo sapiens, rise to prominence of, 39–40, 48–49

Hood, Bruce, 46–47

Hooker, Rob, 61, 69, 73–74, 223n1

Hope, for local journalism, 212–13

Hosey, Boyzell, 27, 74, 76–77, 162–63

Human brain, shrinking of, 46–47

Human complexity, 123–24

The Human Condition (Arendt), 57, 132

Humanism, defiant, 180–81

Human need, for drama, 51–52

Human psychology, 157

Human storytelling, politicized, 144

Human trait, stories as, 51–53, 60, 132, 161

Hurricane, of 1921, 197

Ibargüen, Alberto, 88, 90, 220n11

Immune system of democracy, press as, 131

Impeachment, of Trump, 125–26

Impoverished whites, manipulation, of, 139

Incognizant racism, 75–76, 79–80

Information: age of, 12–13; apocalypse, 106; technology and, 106–7

Instability, social, 180

Instagram, 91–92, 185–86

Instincts, hard-wired, 135–36

Intern, DeGregory and, 171–72

The Invention of Yesterday (Ansary), 111

Isaac, Mike, 96, 97

Isis (Egyptian goddess), 207

Jackson, Leon, 68–70

Jackson, Michael, 58, 222n39

Janik, Rachel, 120

January 6, 2021, 131–32, 204–5

Jefferson, Martha Wayles Skelton, 110

Jefferson, Thomas, 109–10, 133

Jesuit High School, 90–94

Jesus (biblical figure), 114

Jim Crow laws, 141

Job security, 35, 161–62

Johnson, Joshua, 156
Jones, Alex, 145–46
Jones, Tom, 154–55
Journalism: anthropology and, 3, 6–7, 178–79, 184, 209; business models of, 100; community, 5, 8, 148, 173–74; complexity in, 75–78; contradictions in, 75–78; disinvestment from social media and, 182; objective, 44–45, 131–32, 154–55; as public service, 11, 52, 132, 157–58; storytelling and, 43; training for, 88; watchdog, 133–34; yellow, 44. See also Local journalism
Journalism industry, future, of, 34–35, 212–13
Journalistic: ethics, 80–81, 131–32, 174; ideals, 31
Journalists, distrust of, 6, 17–18, 124, 126–27

Kaepernick, Colin, 111
Kang, Cecilia, 97
Kaplan, Rachel, 169, 183, 230n8
Katches, Mark, 67, 76
Kendi, Ibram X., 138–39
K'iche' Maya, 42, 43
King, Martin Luther, Jr., 142
Klein, Richard, 39–40, 221n1
Knight Commission on Trust, Media, and Democracy, 11, 220n11
Knight-Wallace Fellow, 186–88
Knowledge of human psychology, of talk show hosts, 157
Kuttner, Robert, 144–45

Lakewood High School, 28–29
Large journalistic enterprises, 8–9
Laws of storytelling, of Burns, 118
Layoffs, Newsroom, 5–6, 20–21, 29, 67–68, 136
Lee, Stan, 211
Legacy journalists, digital journalists versus, 31–33, 92, 131
Legacy media, 15–16, 45, 61, 124, 128–30, 129; payment for, 188; purpose of, 154
Lenses, anthropological, 14–16
Lepore, Jill, 90
Levi, Primo, 179–80, 205, 230n7
Lieb, Joseph, 71
The Life Informatic (Boyer), 164–65
The Life of the Bee (Maeterlinck), 135–36

Like button, 57
Like War (Singer and Brooking), 122
Limbaugh, Rush, 121
Lindelie, A. H., 63
Linnaeus, Carl, 50–51
Lippmann, Walter, 44, 45
"Literary Prehistory" (Sugiyama), 54
Local communities, coverage of, 75–77
Local journalism, 9–10, 32, 53, 134–35, 175; disinvestment from social media and, 182; hope for, 212–13; Levi on, 180–81
Local universities, newspapers and, 184
Long-term interests, short-term interests versus, 8, 92, 157–58
Low point, of Hollywood story, 116
Luhrmann, Tanya M., 207–8
Lull, James, 77

Macedonian teens, 122
Mad Max (fictional character, Thunderdome), 104–5
Mad Max Beyond Thunderdome (film), 103–5
Maeterlinck, Maurice, 135–36
Management style, of Orsi, 33–34
Manipulation, by stories, 59, 118–19
Marcgravia envenia plant, 48–49
Marcus, Julie, 201
Master narratives, 108–20, 139–41, 180
The Matrix (film), 13
Mattingly, Cheryl, 200
Maxwell, Scott, 134–35
McHugh, Siobhan, 181
McKenna, Lyndsey, 22–24, 27, 30–33, 38, 163
McKerrow, Joshua, 81–82
McMullen, M. Joel, 62
McNeill, Claire, 208–9
"Me and Bobby McGee" (song), 164
Media, distrust of, 86–87, 93, 106, 126–27, 131–32; political bias and, 177–78
Media bias chart, 89
"The media," confusion with term, 11, 94–95, 127–31, 177–78, 204
Mediadome, 103–5
Media environment, modern, 45
Media technology, 79
Media turmoil, 133–34

Men in Dark Times (Arendt), 59
Merger, between GateHouse Media and Gannet, 66–67
Metric Black Holes, 169–70, 183–84
Midpoint, of Hollywood plot, 116
Milam, Curtis, 140
Miller, Arthur, 12–13, 153–54
Miller, Kyra, 79
Mind, training of, 208
Mitchelstein, Eugenia, 132
Modern media environment, 45
Modern tricksters, 54
Morgan, Richard James, 62
Morpheus (fictional character, *The Matrix*), 13
Mueller, Robert, 151–52
Multitasking, 33–34
My Little Pony (TV show), 138
Mythology, trickster in, 54

NAACP. *See* National Association for the Advancement of Colored People
Narayan, Kirin, 16–17
Narrative: caste, 139–45; damned-dirty-trick, 143–47, 152; dissolution, 200; divisive, 147, 179; master, 108–20, 139–41, 180; paradigm of Fisher, 222n21
National Association for the Advancement of Colored People (NAACP), 72–73
Nationalistic storytellers, 121
National news networks, 128
Natural selection, 48–49
Need, for stories, 134–36, 146, 212–13
Negro News page, 70
Neo (fictional character, *The Matrix*), 13
Neverland, 60
"New Deployment of Police Based on Zone Needs Faces Federal Injunction Hurdle" (*St. Petersburg Times*), 71
News: branding, 93, 100; consumer app decision of, 175–76; consumer Facebook and, 175–77; deserts, 5, 132–33, 219n3; dissemination on Twitter, 99–100; media and social media Zuckerberg on, 97–98; on-demand, 186; outlets partisanship of, 127–28; on social media, 86–87, 93–99, 162–63; and social media as frenemies, 95–98; on untrusted

platform, 101; vetting of, 85–86, 88, 90, 93–94, 100
Newseum Plaque, 127–28
Newspaper circulation, 128
Newspapers: local universities and, 184; partnerships between, 184–85
Newspaper subscriptions, Trump and, 152–53
Newsroom: employment, 5, 128, 129, 133; ethnography, 16–17; layoffs, 5–6, 20–21, 29, 67–68, 136, 192–93, 195; structure of, 37
News stories, new ways of perceiving of, 100–101
News when there's news, 186–87
New Testament, 114
New York Times (newspaper), 105–6, 133–34, 149, 150, 151–52; Bennet and, 153–55
Nietzsche, Friedrich, 52
Nikolajeva, Nadia, 95
Niles, John, 49–50
Nudity trial, 23
Number, of journalists remaining, 132–33

Objective journalism, 44–45, 131–32, 154–55
Objectivity, 43–45
Occam's razor, 42
O'Connor, Stephen, 109–10
Oh, Florida! (Pittman), 195
On-demand news, 186
1A (radio show), 156
100 Years, St. Petersburg Times (Hooker), 61, 69
Opinion pieces, purpose of, 154–55
Opinions, unacknowledged, 204
Oral storytelling, 8
Orlando Sentinel (newspaper), 134–35
Orsi, Jennifer, 21–22, 33–36, 38, 162
Ortner, Sherry, 220n2
Outline of a Theory of Practice (Bourdieu), 36
Outsourcing, of printing of *Tampa Bay Times*, 205
Ovadya, Aviv, 106–7, 226n42

Palihapitiya, Chamath, 156
Palm Sunday (Vonnegut), 112–14
Paralysis, feeling of, during early pandemic, 200–201
Partisanship, of news outlets, 127–28, 131–32

Partnerships, between newspapers, 184–85
Patterson, Eugene C., 65
Payment, for news service, 187–88
Payroll Protection, 197–98
Pendulum, Ginsberg on, 132
Perceptions, of professional news, 101
Personalization, of news stories, 181
Peterman, Peggy, 73
Petryna, Adriana, 229n6
Pew Research Center, 8, 128
Photography, football, 90–91
Photojournalism, 4
Photojournalism style, change in, 28
Pied Piper of social media, 31–32
Pierce, Robert, 64–65
Pittman, Craig, 173, 195–96
Pizzagate conspiracy theory, 146
Planets mnemonic, 47
Plaque, at Newseum, 127–28
Plato, 108–9
Play, at football game, 91–94
Podcasts, 181
Polarization, of politics, 157
Political campaigns, Facebook and, 97
Political gain, social media and, 179
Politicized human storytelling, 144
Politics: digital, 121–23; families and, 210; polarization of, 157
The Politics of Storytelling (Jackson, M.), 58, 222n39
Polls, of 2016 election, 168
Poor whites, Black people and, 141–44
Poynter, Nelson Paul, 63–67, 109, 158; contradictions of, 73–74; vision of, 74–75, 79–80
Poynter, Paul, 63
Poynter Institute, 64, 67, 80–81, 189
Prehistoric preferences, food marketing and, 10
"President Jefferson" (Coard), 110
Press: as "enemy of the people," 56, 177, 205, 207; as immune system of democracy, 131
Primitive Christianity, 114
Printed paper, digital versus, 21
Promise, of Premise of story, 116
van Prooijen, Jan-Willem, 207
Protests, coverage of, 125

Psychology, human, 157
Public service, journalism as, 11, 52, 132, 157–58

Quality journalism, struggles of, 34–35, 38, 74, 99, 130; digital media and, 156–58
Quandt, Thorsten, 165
Quetzalcoatl (Aztec god), 207
Quinnipiac University poll, 177–78

Ra (Egyptian god), 207
Race, as class in America, 139–41
Racial divide, 139
Racism, incognizant, 75–76, 79–80
Rainbolt, John C., 137–41, 158, 188–89
Rainbow Dash (fictional character, *My Little Pony*), 138
Rally, at DeSoto Square Mall, 206
Randomized control testing (RCT), 169–70
Rationality, adaptation versus, 145
RCT. *See* Randomized control testing
Realism, scientific, 45
Reality TV, 121–22
Real life, beats of Snyder and, 117–18
Record on civil rights, of *Times*, 69
Recurring dream, of Pendygraft, 193–94
Reduction, in print edition of *Tampa Bay Times*, 195–97
Referrals, from social media to news site, 100
Reichelt, Julian, 10–11
Reliability, validity and, *167*, 167–70, 173
Reliability and Validity Assessment (Carmines and Zeller), 167–69
Religious faith, 8, 53, 155
Renaming, of *Homo sapiens*, 49–52
Reporters Without Borders, 133
Reporting: balanced, 10, 130–31; on diverse communities, 75–77
"Report on the Investigation into Russian Interference in the 2016 Presidential Election" (Mueller), 151–52
Republican lawyer, 201, 203
Resources, lack of, 34
Reynolds, C. S., 62
Richter, Donna, 55–56, 207
Riddles, of Hood, 47–48
Ripley, Amanda, 157–58

Ritual moments, 38
Rosen, Jay, 187
Rouson, Darryl, 72–73
Russian influence, in elections, 148, *149*, *150*, 151
Russian organizations, ads purchased by, *149*, *150*, 151–52
Rutenberg, Jim, 168

A Sacred Trust (Pierce), 64–65, 109
Safe spaces, 4
Sampson, Zack, 87–88, 90, 100
Sanderlin, James, 71
The Sarasota Herald-Tribune (newspaper), 184–85
Save the Cat (Snyder), 51
Schnapp, Jeffrey, 182
Schulte, William, 77
Scientific realism, 45
Sedentary work, of journalists, 164–66
Seeing White (podcast), 137–38
Serial (podcast), 181
Shadd, Dirk, 185
Shakespeare, William, 123–24
Shapes, of stories, 112–15, *113*, *114*
Shared stories, 11
Sharing stories with audience, need for, 58
Shedler, Jonathan, 169–70
Shields, John, 186–87
Shooting, at *Capital Gazette*, 81–82
Short-term interests, long-term interests versus, 8, 92, 157–58
Shrinking, of human brain, 46–47, *46–48*
Singer, Peter Warren, 122
Sister, of Rouson, 73
Slaughterhouse-Five (Vonnegut), 112, 123
Slavery, 139–40
Small-survey method, 169, 183
Smith, Ben, 154–55
Smith, Daniel, 53
Smith, Harold C., 71
Snyder, Blake, 51, 115–17; applied to Vonnegut's "Shapes of Stories," *117*
Social Construction and News Work (Schulte), 77
Social control, stories and, 53–57
Social instability, 180
Social justice, 155

Social media, 31–33, 85–87, 91–93, 101–2, 132; disinvestment from, 182; editors, 92; lack of payoff from, 163; news on, 86–87, 93–99, 162–63, 175–77; removal of news sites from, 179
Social power, of stories, 59
Social silence, 70, 202, *202*, 204
Social structures, change in, 38
Society of Professional Journalists, Principles of, 80–81
Solomon, Josh, 192–93, 198–201
Spouse, of Pendygraft, 18
Springsteen, Bruce, 78
St. Petersburg, Florida, 62, 192–93
St. Petersburg Times (newspaper), 3, 15, 18–19, 20, 31; origin story of, 60, 61–66
Staff meeting, 20–21
Stamped from the Beginning (Kendi), 138–39
"State of the News Media 2016" (Pew Research Center), 128
Stone, Roger, 54–55
Stories: basic structure of, 42–43; as distinctly human trait, 51–53, 60, 132, 161; hero twin, 42; manipulation by, 59, 118–19; shapes of, 112–15, *113*, *114*; social power of, 59
Stories to cover, choice of, 77–78
Storytellers: nationalistic, 121; trust in, 53–54, 85–87, 132
Storytelling, 3–4; ethical, 123; origin of, 40–42; as survival instinct, 7, 42–43, 45–46, 48–49
The Storytelling Animal (Gottschall), 60, 146–47
Story world, set-up of, 115
Stout, Tim, 115
Straub, W. L., 63
Streckfuss, Richard, 43–44, 45
Structure, of newsroom, 37
Struggles, of quality journalism, 34–35, 38, 74, 99, 130; digital media and, 156–58
Study, of trust in news brands, 93
Subjective view, of world, 111–12
Sugiyama, Michelle Scalise, 43, 54
Sungir, 40
Superiority, white, 120
Surveys, 183
Survival instinct, Storytelling as, 7, 42–43, 45–46, 48–49

Symbolic capital, 22, 220n2
Systema Naturae (Linnaeus), 50

Talk-show hosts, 157
The Tampa Bay Times, 67–68, 94, 102, 128, 175–77; pay cuts at, 193. *See also* St. Petersburg Times
Tash, Paul, 76, 196
Teaching experience, of Cerri, 27, 28–29
Technical innovations, evolution of, 46
Technology: information and, 106–7; media, 79
Tett, Gillian, 14, 25–26, 202–3
This American Life (podcast/radio show), 181
Thomas Jefferson Dreams of Sally Hemings (O'Connor), 109–10
Times board of directors, diversity of, 72, 76
The Times Publishing Company, 161
Tomasello, Michael, 45–46
Tracy, Marc, 96
Training, of mind, 208
Transcribing audio, Facebook and, 224n1
Tribalism, 157
Tricksters: modern, 54; in mythology, 54
The Triumph of Narrative (Fulford), 108–11
Tropicana Field, 192, 193
Trump, Donald, 54–56, 102–3, 121–22, 133, *149–50*; ban from social media of, 179, 208, 212; impeachment of, 125–26; influence on campaign of, 151–52; January 6 and, 205–6; newspaper subscriptions and, 152–53; Twitter and, 152; victory in Florida in 2020, 203–4
Trump Bump, 152
Trump supporters: conversation with, 206–7; pollsters and, 204
Trump tweets, placement of in *New York Times*, 148, *149*, 151–53
Trump victory, in Florida in 2020, 203–4
Trust: in media, 94–95, 106–7, 131–32, 156–57; in storytellers, 53–54, 85–87, 132; storytelling and, 11, 18
Tsing, Anna Lowenhaupt, 221n10
Turner, A. C., 62
Turner, Tina, 104
TV Midtvest, 95
TV Midtvest experiment, 95

"Tweet or Be Sacked" (Barnard), 98–99
"Tweet or be sacked" policy, in newsrooms, 98–99
Twenty-four hour cable networks, 105
Twitter, 91–92, 98–100, 105–6, 148, *149–50*; Trump and, 152
2016 election, 168
2020 election, 201–3

Uhuru Party, 98–99
Unacknowledged opinions, 204
Unicorns, centrist journalists as, 130–31
Unique digital media spaces, 179, 185–86, 213
United Artists, 120
Universality, of storytelling, 42
University of Michigan, 137–38, 187–89
University of North Carolina Center of Innovation and Sustainability in Local Media, 184–85
University of South Florida, 208–9
Untrusted platform, news on, 101
Urban Buffalo Soldiers (Jackson, L.), 68

Validity, reliability and, *167*, 167–70, 173
Varian, Bill, 5–6
Venus and Mars (painting), 100, 101
Veteran journalists, young journalists versus, 172–73
Vetting, of news, 86, 88, 90, 93–94, 100; Twitter and, 153
Virginia, 137–40
Virginia House of Burgesses, 139
Virginia Slave Codes of 1705, 139, 155–56
Vision, of Poynter, N., 74, 79–80
Volk, Brittany, 85, 100, 103
Vonnegut, Kurt, 111–14, 123–24, 181, 211

Wallace, David Foster, 12
Warrior ants, 49
Washington Post (newspaper), 66–67, 102–3, 153
Watchdog journalism, 133–34
Wayles, John, 110
Ways of Seeing (documentary), 101
Wealth disparity, 140
Weaponization, of stories, 207
Webs, of culture, 13–14

Weintraub, Ellen, 97
Weiss, Bari, 105–6
Welch, Edgar Maddison, 146
West Coronado Community Recreation Association (WCCRA), 183–94
"What Pierre Bourdieu Taught Me" (Tett), 202
When God Talks Back (Luhrmann), 207–8
When People Come First (Biehl and Petryna), 229n6
White, Randall, 40, 221n4
White anxiety, 140
White News (Heider), 75–76
White Rage (Anderson), 141
White superiority, 120
Who Wants to Marry a Multi-Millionaire (TV show), 121
Wilkerson, Isabel, 140, 144
Wilson, David, 145–46
Wilson, David Sloan, 49

Wilson, Jon, 68, 70
Wilson, Woodrow, 120
Woodward, Bob, 133
World Press Freedom Index, 133
WWCRA. *See* West Coronado Community Recreation Association
Wylie, Christopher, 147–48

Xolotl (Aztec god), 207

Young journalists, veteran journalists versus, 172–73
Young news consumer, app decision, of, 175–76

Zeller, Richard, 167–69, 173
Zimmerman, Jean, 109–10
Zoning plan, for St. Petersburg police, 71
Zuckerberg, Mark, 86–87, 95–98

JOHN PENDYGRAFT was born and raised in El Paso, Texas, and worked at the *Tampa Bay Times* from 1997 to 2022. Pendygraft has received national awards for feature writing, video, and still photography from the American Society of News Editors, Society of Professional Journalists, Scripps Howard, National Headliner Awards, Pictures of the Year International, and the Emmys. His documentary film revealing escalating violence and neglect in Florida mental hospitals was included in the winning entry for the 2016 Pulitzer Prize for investigative reporting, won a regional Emmy, and was a finalist for a national Emmy. In 2017–2018, Pendygraft completed a Knight-Wallace Fellowship at the University of Michigan, and he is a PhD candidate in anthropology at the University of South Florida.